FOREGROUNDED DESCRIPTION IN PROSE FICTION:

FIVE CROSS-LITERARY STUDIES

THEORY/CULTURE

Editors:
Linda Hutcheon, Gary Leonard,
Janet Paterson, Paul Perron

JOSÉ MANUEL LOPES

Foregrounded Description in Prose Fiction: Five Cross-Literary Studies

UNIVERSITY OF TORONTO PRESS

Toronto Buffalo London

© University of Toronto Press Incorporated 1995
Toronto Buffalo London
Printed in Canada

ISBN 0-8020-0727-9

Printed on acid-free paper

PN
816
.L75
1995

Canadian Cataloguing in Publication

Lopes, José Manuel
    Foregrounded description in prose fiction

    Includes bibliographical references and index.
    ISBN 0-8020-0727-9

    1. Romance fiction – History and criticism.
    2. French fiction – 19th century – History and criticism.
    3. French fiction – 20th century – History and criticism.
    4. Spanish fiction – 19th century – History and criticism.
    5. Portuguese fiction – 20th century – History and criticism.
    6. Description (Rhetoric).   I. Title.

PN816.L66 1995   809.3'922   C95-931544-6

University of Toronto Press acknowledges the
financial assistance to its publishing program of the
Canada Council and the Ontario Arts Council.

This book has been published with the help of a grant
from the Canadian Federation for the Humanities,
using funds provided by the Social Sciences and
Humanities Research Council of Canada.

Contents

Foreword

The development of literary theory in the second half of our century is marked by the fact that numerous critics and theorists in the West have discovered critical movements promoted by Eastern and Central European scholars of literature. At the same time, while such theorists as Vladimir Propp, Victor Shklovsky, Juryi Tynianov, Roman Jakobson, and Jan Mukařovský have considerably influenced literary theory in the West, Western critics and theoreticians have inspired new developments in the East. By the same token, the scope of literary theory has expanded to such a degree that, nowadays, any specific literary phenomenon can be scrutinized from various, albeit concurrent points of view. The cognitive process of analysing forms of literary theory has given rise to a number of critical, sophisticated idioms. Measuring their capacity to understand and explain literary forms involves confronting a concrete text with a given idiom. One may assume that the more the idiom discovers and unveils in the text, the more it acquires the status of an objectively valid critical tool. The above-mentioned interactive cooperation of Western and Eastern scholars has also yielded various syncretic critical idioms. Their lexicon is not only structurally determined but it also borrows from philosophical, sociological, semiotic, and linguistic domains.

The book that the reader has in hand can also be considered a product of this interactive process resulting in the assimilation and enrichment of critical categories that have travelled from Eastern or Central Europe to the West. The notion of 'foregrounding' that governs José Manuel Lopes' critical project and analysis is precisely such a category. *Aktualisace*, the Czech name for 'foregrounding', is somewhat similar to the famous *ostranienie* ('estrangement,' or in French *singularisation*) of the

Russian formalists. It has been coined and discussed by the influential Czech aestheticians Bohuslav Havránek and Jan Mukařovský, both prominent representatives of the Czech structuralist movement. 'Foregrounding', says Mukařovský, 'is the opposite of automatization, that is, it is the deautomatization of an act; the more an act is automatized, the less it is consciously executed; the more it is foregrounded, the more completely conscious does it become.'

Based on analyses of five novels from the French, Spanish, Brazilian, and Portuguese traditions, this book deals with the problem of description from the new perspective of its specifically narrative function. The author enlarges and redefines the idea of foregrounding as an aesthetic signal and as a representation of the literary text's referential dimension that is discursively transformed. He grounds his critical scrutiny on the assumption that, while using everyday language, any literary discourse significantly transforms it inasmuch as it must be functional, and thereby creates new specific values in terms of structures and effects. Most remarkable is the author's demonstration that the notion of foregrounding, when precisely applied to his approach to the five chosen texts, provides us with a deeper knowledge of the novelistic form. In light of the evolutionary perspective of the novel, one has to admit that description is by no means an ornamental structure. On the contrary, as Lopes successfully points out, it is a functional and strategically important element of the novel's specific idiom. One measures its functional dimension by establishing its narrative finality, hence such paradoxical, apparently oxymoronic expressions as 'descriptive narrations' or 'narrative descriptions.'

The book's manifold purpose and accomplishment may be defined in the following terms: it reorganizes and rethinks the critical material pertinent to description as a problem of literary technique and theory; it also reassesses the semiotic function of description as a crucial category in various textual modes and genres of prose fiction.

On the basis of the chosen material, the critic shows how the process of the 'foregrounding description' occurs, and the means by which it acquires specific aesthetic, semiotic, and textual qualities. The author finally points out how the very diversity of descriptive modalities in the five novels chosen gives rise to different specific roles for description. He shows how this diversity is an important element of the narrative, discursive, and mimetic economy of the novel.

Thus summarized, the purpose of J.M. Lopes' critical enterprise gives only an approximate idea of the book's richness and relevance. In fact, what seems to be the most valuable characteristic of this ambitious work is its overall balance between the theoretical, critical, and comparative approaches. This even balance allows him to mediate between the new understanding of description that he proposes, and the historical and aesthetic dynamics of the modern novel (understood from both diachronic and synchronic perspectives). All in all, and *mutatis mutandis*, Lopes' ambition may be equated with Erich Auerbach's finely accomplished undertaking in *Mimesis*: to describe 'represented reality' in the principal literatures of the West. The author succeeds in demonstrating how the changing functions of description reflect on the novel's development. The novel, that is, evolves from the rhetorical descriptive topos to a variety of forms that magnify the specific functionality of description. In this sense, his analyses of Zola's *Une Page d'amour*, Claude Simon's *Histoire*, Pérez Galdós' *La de Bringas*, Cornélio Penna's *A Menina Morta*, and Carlos de Oliveira's *Finisterra* are quite paradigmatic. The close readings of these novels compose what he calls a 'complex text type.' The generating principles of the modern novel are therefore, according to the critic, its 'very stylistic and ideological structures.' By emphasizing 'three main levels of inquiry: stylistic, discursive, and functional,' he endows his critical and cognitive objects with a relevant analytical perspective.

What sheds a new and revealing light on the problem of description is the relationships that the critic establishes between the descriptive segments and *mise en abyme*, a device that pervades such novels as *Une Page d'amour* and *La de Bringas*. The distinction between 'literal' and 'ideological' *mise en abyme* is a productive one, which logically arises out of the analysed novels' structures. The critic's analyses corroborate the usefulness of his categories and, above all, that of foregrounding. This allows him to account for aesthetic features of the modern novel, such as those exemplified by the book's textual corpus. On the basis of a comparative analysis of a literary corpus belonging to four distinctive literary areas, it becomes evident that the language of the novel has been prominently determined by its organic and necessary structures. These structures may be described and understood as specific axiological and aesthetic postulates of novelistic language. They are: realism practised as a complex and multivalent superimposition of views and textual and metatextual structures; *mise en abyme* as a sign of aesthetic autonomy; the independent and creative position of the narrator; and the coalescence of narrative and poetic structures. Lopes' study captures the complexity of novelistic discourse by systematically revealing the dynamic and variable relationship between narration and description.

José Manuel Lopes' discourse is both dense and precise. No significant detail escapes his attention. Once he has established the critical tools and perspectives, he accomplishes his work of analysis and commentary with a sound intelligence, lucidity, and matter-of-factness. This critical book is a valuable contribution to the scrutiny of an important problem related to the developing discourse of the modern novel, to literary theory, and to the rhetoric of fiction.

Wladimir Krysinski

Acknowledgments

I wish to thank Maria de São Pedro, my wife, for her continuous support while I was writing this book; O.J. Miller, for challenging my first assumptions about literary description and for all his fine editorial suggestions; Brian T. Fitch, for the many hours we spent exchanging ideas about my project, for all the changes he inspired me to make to this work, and for all his friendly words of encouragement; Mario J. Valdés, for his sound advice and suggestions regarding my chapter on Pérez Galdós; Ricardo Sternberg, for introducing me to the fictional works of Cornélio Penna; Jim Cummins, for giving me a job after my research support ran out; Wladimir Krysinski, for his kind preface; Jamie and Andrea McMillan, and Bonnie Bruder, for helping me refine the English translation of the first chapter of Galdós' *La de Bringas*; and last but not least, Darlene Money for her excellent final editorial revision of my manuscript.

FOREGROUNDED DESCRIPTION IN PROSE FICTION: FIVE CROSS-LITERARY STUDIES

Introduction

Critical works on fictional description have, with very few exceptions, demonstrated a bias against it, and considered it to be purely ornamental, redundant, or even irrelevant. Description, however, can play a very significant role, not only in more recent texts of prose fiction (for example, the French *nouveau roman*, or the post-modern novel in general), but also in those nineteenth-century realistic/naturalistic works that give description a foregrounded prominence.

My aim is to present not only a framework that can better foster and facilitate the analysis and appreciation of description, but also to examine in detail a series of relevant fundamental topics related to the subject, especially in respect to 'descriptions of space.'

Based on the 'figure-ground opposition' of gestalt theory, discourse-linguists, such as Hopper (1979), Dry (1983), Reinhardt (1984), and Fleischman (1985), tend to associate 'foreground material' with the narrative sequence of events, as opposed to 'background material,' which they view as being formed by all segments (for example, descriptive or digressive blocks) that do not propel narrative time. Although their observations prove to be quite useful at a micro-level of analysis (especially at the *stylistic* and *discursive* level of the model that I shall present), they nevertheless perpetuate the notion of literary description as mere background. One should note that, even though these discourse-linguists often base their research on literary texts, they mainly have recourse to examples that exhibit a predominantly realistic mode of representation. Thus, it would be rather difficult to apply, in the same way, their notions of 'foreground/background' to novels such as, for example, Robbe-Grillet's *La Jalousie* (which foregrounds, to the exclusion of almost all else, a great amount of what they would designate as 'background material'), or Simon's *Leçon de choses* (a novel where sequenced action, very often, no longer constitutes what could be designated as 'foreground').

In the following analyses, I use concepts relating to grounding distinctions to refer almost exclusively to description in prose fiction. Thus, I designate as *backgrounded description* any descriptive material that does not seem to play a predominant narrative function; conversely, the term *foregrounded description* applies to all descriptive segments shown to have a more relevant narrative role. These two notions can to some extent be associated with what Genette (1966) designates respectively as descriptions with a mere 'ornamental' function, as opposed to those that have a more 'symbolic' relevance (157). It should be noted, however, that the grounding distinctions I propose in this work do not depend, necessarily, on a set of formal textual qualities but rather on the modes of reader perception and reception. Thus, I do not use the terms *background* and *foreground* in the same way as they are used by members of the Prague school, such as Havránek (1942) and Mukařovský (1948), since for these critics both terms refer, respectively, to the Russian formalist concept of *automatization* and *de-automatization* of language. As we shall see, if in the case of certain realistic/naturalistic novels foregrounded elements may directly correlate with specific textual properties, this is not always the case in more recent fictional texts.

Although backgrounded description (or description with a backgrounding function) has been extensively analysed since Barthes' 'Introduction à l'analyse structurale des récits' (1966), by a great variety of critics, especially by Philippe Hamon (1972, 1981, 1991), the present study is limited to a series of examples of foregrounded description, as they present themselves in the five novels that provide the foundation of this study.

Moreover, to avoid a series of generalizations being drawn from a specific period or from a particular literature – a problem I address when referring to Hamon's *Introduction à l'analyse du descriptif* – I have opted for the inclusion of prose fiction texts published in three Romance languages and belonging to four different literatures (French, Spanish, Brazilian, and Portuguese). In addition, I have chosen novels ranging from nineteenth-century realism/naturalism to post-modernism.

Given this range of periods and literatures, I have initially selected a synchronic rather than a diachronic approach, although in the conclusion of the present work the latter is briefly discussed. My intention is, basically, to test the validity of a proposed theoretical framework across a variety of nineteenth- and twentieth-century literary examples, while bracketing off any issues relating to possible different genres or historical trends pertaining to description.

Since it is my belief that significant conclusions on the available criticism concerning literary description can only be arrived at once filtered through a very detailed analysis of literary texts, I have limited my study to five novels. Trying to avoid 'impressionistic' generalizations, I have had to disregard many other texts that might have proved just as relevant; in particular, prose fiction works belonging to Anglo-American modernism, French surrealism, and Italian futurism. The latter would, no doubt, reveal some interesting results regarding the available criticism on the semantics of phonics and rhythm in description – aspects of the question that I have not particularly explored in the present study.

Description, nevertheless (in the same way as narration), is a general category that is relevant to a variety of problems related to literary analysis. Thus, while analysing the five novels in the present study – following the critical framework proposed in chapter 1 – I have taken into consideration the main critical problems arising from a detailed analysis of their descriptive passages.

Based on a set of descriptions (or using the latter as springboards for my inquiry), I was led to explore not only their relationship with narration in each particular work, but also to view them as: two different types of *mise en abyme* (chapters 2 and 4); an implied reading of fictional referents pertaining to the visual arts (chapter 3); an unstable form of representation (chapter 5); comical sarcasm and parody (chapter 4); and a metatextual/metadescriptive device pointing to its own limits and possibilities (chapter 6).

As will be demonstrated, descriptions of space, in particular, prove to be 'masters of disguise,' for they not only present themselves as static *tableaux*, but may also reveal a 'narrativized' form of internal arrangement, when not building actual narrative bridges across discrete segments. In fact, descriptions prove to be far more pliable and versatile than narrations, since, unlike the latter, they are free from the constraints of logic and narrative grammar. This quality may account for their abundant and predominant use, particularly in many innovative twentieth-century works.

1

Towards a framework for the analysis of description in prose fiction

Descriptions have traditionally been treated by critics and readers alike as if they were no more than icing on the narrative cake.

Michael Riffaterre[1]

With the emergence of nineteenth-century European realism in prose fiction, literary descriptions of characters and space cease to be mere rhetorical devices associated to the classic notions of 'portrait' and 'tableau,' to become, more than ever before, important elements in the overall construction of narratives.[2] Thus, beyond such topoi as the 'classical portrait' and the '*locus amoenus*' (which were aesthetic conventions not always pertinent to a narrative development), realistic/naturalistic descriptions become more intimately linked to the very process of fiction writing. This process no longer functions as mere aesthetic pauses inserted onto a narrative axis, but as fundamental building blocks constituting first, a given historically and culturally determined mode of representation, and second, a series of semantic components able to reiterate, determine, and, in some cases, propel narration.

It is, therefore, surprising that literary critics since the nineteenth century have continued to view descriptions as an 'extra' or as a dispensable ornament of narration, if not as a cumbersome set of textual segments that, standing in the way of storytelling, function as mere 'catalysts,' that is, as a series of devices to interrupt or delay the sequential unfolding of plots (Barthes 1966). Such tendencies and opinions do permeate, with few exceptions, even more recent critical trends, such as French structuralism and semiotics, and although theoreticians, such as Gérard Genette in 'Frontières du récit' (1966), have mentioned that no narration is possible without description, Roland Barthes (1966, 1968) and later Philippe Hamon (1972, 1981, 1991), continue to view it as an ornament or as a mode of creating a 'reality-effect.'

Such biases against description appear unfounded, given that: 1) even novels that seem to rely mainly on dialogue would, without description, be reduced to a series of plot summaries with no particular literary interest, and 2) literary descriptions do not always function as simple markers of realism. This can be observed not only in some nineteenth-century novels, generally labelled under the headings of realism or naturalism, but particularly, in the French New Novel and in many other works that are presently perceived as post-modern prose fiction.[3]

The lack of interest that many critics (from Anglo-American New Criticism and Russian formalism to present-day narratology) seem to reveal towards description is probably due to the fact that, unlike narration, description seems to elude any attempts at being defined in a systematic way. In fact, according to Hamon, 'la description serait peut-être cet endroit du texte où la puissance générative du langage se montrerait sous son aspect le plus évident et le plus incontrôlable' (1981, 40). More recent approaches that do not limit themselves to a strictly linguistic or semiotic orientation, such as those developed by Alexander Gelley (1979, 1987), Edward Casey (1981), and Mario Valdés (1982) in the area of phenomenological hermeneutics,[4] aim at interpreting description as an indispensable component in any work of prose fiction. Especially in Valdés' mode of inquiry presented in *Shadows in the Cave* (1982, 119–40), or even in some recent works by narratologists such as Mieke Bal (1981, 1982), the objective is no longer to determine what one could name as 'descriptive universals,' but to stress the possible *functions* description carries out in a particular overall context.

Since description in prose fiction has not always been well accepted by critics and by readers in general, the purpose of this initial chapter is twofold: to review and comment on attitudes and approaches towards description by twentieth-century critics of various tendencies;[5] and to present a mode of inquiry that, while integrating contributions by previous critics, could further both the analysis and a greater appreciation of prose fiction where description predominates, or where description can be seen as playing a meaningful role. In the following chapters, description in a series of novels belonging to different fictional genres, cultures, and literary periods, will be analysed as a means of facilitating and focalizing the discussion of issues related to description.

8 Foregrounded description in prose fiction

1. DESCRIPTION AND TWENTIETH-CENTURY CRITICISM

If we examine the series of articles and full-length studies by Russian formalists – at least those that have been translated into English and/or French – we realize that no particular emphasis is given to descriptive segments/blocks in prose fiction. A.A. Reformatsky was probably one of the few exceptions; in 'An Essay on the Analysis of the Composition of the Novella' (n.d.), while analysing a short story by Maupassant, he does consider description as an important part of the text. None the less, in the case of Reformatsky, description is identified with any 'static' textual components, which, by their very nature, contrast with narrative 'dynamics.' The notion of description as a set of 'static motives' can also be found in Tomachevsky's 'Thématique' (1925). This notion may today seem rather simplistic, since – as we shall later see – not all descriptions or 'descriptive motives' are static.

The lack of interest in description on the part of Russian formalists is due to the fact that they were searching for a grammar of 'narrative functions' in a Proppian sense. One exception, however, is Yury Tynianov, who in the essay 'On Literary Evolution' (1929) mentions description not only as static background material, but as a mode of narrative production that can propel narration:

In a work in which the so-called plot is effaced, the story carries out different functions than in a work in which it is not effaced. The story might be used merely to motivate style or as a strategy for developing the material. Crudely speaking, from our vantage point in a particular literary system, we would be inclined to reduce nature descriptions in old novels to an auxiliary role, to the role of making transitions or retardation; therefore we would almost ignore them, although from our vantage point of a different literary system we would be forced to consider nature descriptions as the main, dominant element. In other words, there are situations in which the story simply provides the motivation for the treatment of 'static descriptions.' (70)

Tynianov does not expand on the notions expressed in the above quotation, nor does he give any examples of novels where the primary function of narration would be to 'motivate' description. One can only speculate that Tynianov was probably thinking either about literary works that relate travelling experiences, or about fictional works such as Andrey Biely's *St. Petersburg* (published for the first time in Russian in

1911), a novel built almost entirely on a set of descriptions. However, Tynianov's observations could apply to a great majority of French New Novels. In fact, Claude Simon, in an essay entitled 'Roman, description et action' (1980, 79) quotes the same passage, then explains, in a discussion based on texts by Faulkner, that contrary to more traditional approaches and modes of fiction writing, narration – especially at a micro-level can function as the linking or introductory device conducive to the production of descriptive segments.

A lack of interest in description also characterizes the writings of Anglo-American New Critics. Thus, apart from a few paragraphs on 'setting,' Wellek and Warren in *Theory of Literature* (1942, 220–1) and Wayne Booth in *The Rhetoric of Fiction* (1961, 62–3, 154–5) do not expand on the subject of description. Nevertheless, it is among the Anglo-American New Critics that we can find the roots of a later debate concerning the function and the relevance of descriptive passages in prose fiction. In rather vague and simplistic terms, these critics either assign to description a symbolic function that is never carefully defined or applied to specific texts (see Wellek and Warren, 221, and D.S. Bland, 331), or consider it as a cumbersome device whose main role is to afford the writer an opportunity to display his/her own stylistic craft, while annoying the reader with a cluster of irrelevant details. The latter position can be found in chapter 6 of Robert Liddell's *A Treatise on the Novel* (1947). According to this critic, 'fiction is the delineation of character in action, and the landscape in the background is merely incidental' (111). He goes on to explain in the same chapter that 'the function of background is negative and limitative since it keeps the characters still' (112), and to conclude that 'the reader who likes concentrating on the people and the happenings is not refreshed, but annoyed, to have to focus on the herbaceous border in the background' (120). Although Liddell agrees that in some novels by Dickens and Jane Austen description might have a symbolic value, he holds to his general stand against description. A similar approach towards description can also be found in Lukács' 'Raconter ou décrire' (1936). For this critic, 'la méthode descriptive mène à la monotonie de la composition, tandis que la fable racontée non seulement permet mais favorise et encourage une diversification de la composition' (163).

On the other hand, the idea of descriptive passages as reservoirs of symbolic meaning is discussed mainly by critics interested in the symbolics of 'fictional space' (for example, Bourneuf, Frank [1963, 1981], Gullón [1975, 1980], Issacharoff, Klinkowitz, Mickelsen, Mitchell [1980,

1989], and Zoran [1984]). Besides stressing the symbolics of space, Joseph Frank, probably the best known of these critics, whose essay 'Spatial Form in Modern Literature' was first published in 1945, argues, founding his case on texts ranging from Flaubert to Mario Vargas Llosa, that one of the characteristics of modern fiction is that in many cases discursive segments are meant to be apprehended by the reader not just as elements along a continuum, but as a set of dispersed and juxtaposed segments, as in a cubist painting: 'Past and present are apprehended spatially, locked in timeless unity that, while it may accentuate surface differences, eliminates any feeling of sequence by the very act of juxtaposition' (589). While Frank discovers in fiction a type of evolution for which he finds some parallels in the visual arts, he fails to address not only the problem of description in the novel (a concept that is hardly discussed by him or by the critics concerned with 'fictional space'), but also a question that would seem quite pertinent in the context of his research: how do narrative mechanisms function in texts that are generated according to a spatial mode of organization? In fact, in novels that rely mainly on a type of spatial arrangement, one could argue that the illusion of narrative time is no longer created through an obvious sequenced set of events. However, this does not mean that temporal orientation is altogether abolished. In some cases, the illusion of time-movement can be created through a set of descriptions the reader can organize in terms of plot. This characterizes novels such as Robbe-Grillet's *La Jalousie* (1957) and Claude Simon's *Leçon de choses* (1975).

In the early works by Roland Barthes, Tzvetan Todorov, and Claude Bremond, to mention just a few, we can see that French structuralists viewed the narrative text almost exclusively in terms of a plot subjected to its own syntactic structures and transformations. Description, when mentioned, was generally considered to be an 'extra,' something that was not pertinent to narration but could, in certain cases, complement it, especially as it pertained to the construction of the various characters.

In 'Introduction à l'analyse des récits' Roland Barthes tries to formulate what could be defined as a grammar of narrative texts (*récits*). Besides the novel and the short story, Barthes mentions paintings, cinema, and stained-glass compositions as examples of *récits*, while admitting that 'le récit peut être supporté ... par l'image fixe ou mobile' (1). However, he never explains how narration can be accomplished through a set of motionless images (or descriptive segments in a text), since his emphasis is mainly on the most obvious narrative aspects of the *récit*. From Barthes' conceptual framework, we could easily infer a clear distinction between narration and description, if not a sharp contrast. Narration would be determined by a logical sequence of main events, 'suite logique de noyaux, unis entre eux par une relation de solidarité' (13), that is, as a syntagmatic structure; while description, being constituted by sets of 'indices' and 'informants' working at a paradigmatic level, could be conceived as an interruption or postponement of the main line of events (the syntagmatic structure upon which the story develops and is carried out in terms of a plot).

In this article Barthes does not assign an entirely meaningless role to the descriptive aspects of the *récit*. He states, for example, that the characters in a story could be constructed not only as 'actants' (in the Greimasian sense of the term), but also as physical and psychological elements. This is to say, by their descriptive characteristics as well as by their role in the story. However, in another article, 'L'Effet de réel,' description seems to take on a purely superfluous role. Referring to description, Barthes states that 'sa structure est purement sommatoire et ne contient pas ce trajet de choix et d'alternatives qui donne à la narration le dessin d'un vaste *dispatching* pourvue d'une temporalité référentielle' (85), and he adds: 'La description apparaît ainsi comme une sorte de "propre" des langages dits supérieurs, dans la mesure, apparemment paradoxale, où elle n'est justifiée par aucune finalité d'action ou de communication' (85). Barthes proceeds then to analyse the description of Rouen in Flaubert's *Madame Bovary*. Given the quasi-visual characteristics of this segment, similar to the written description of a painting, he defines it as an imitation of an imitation[6] and concludes by saying that, in the realistic novel, the function of description is to create a 'referential illusion' as it points to a referent outside the text as a means of conveying a type of realism. Although one could argue that Barthes in 'L'Effet de réel' is mainly referring to a set of descriptive details the reader cannot process as relevant (from a symbolic or structural point of view) to the overall economy of the novel, his attack on Flaubert's descriptive passage seems extreme. In fact, in the third part of *Narratologie* (1981), Mieke Bal takes up the same description of Rouen to demonstrate that, when placed in its immediate context, as well as in the context of the whole novel, that same description ceases to be, as Barthes had stated, the imitation of a painting, to become a *mise en abyme* of the whole novel (106–7).

From Barthes' articles on narrative analysis as well as other works by structuralist authors of the same period, one could conclude that structuralists (in the same way as the Russian formalists who shaped their method of analysis), tended to focus almost exclusively on aspects of narration, discarding the descriptive elements that seemed to get in the way of the storytelling. This reification of the story as plot, together with their quest for the internal logics of a corpus of fictional works that exhibited mainly a realistic mode of representation, could lead us to the notion that a novel need only be read as a chronological sequence of events, that is, through the logic of its main 'functions', and that the longer or minor descriptive details are, in fact, meaningless and there-fore unimportant.

Such a critical tendency to dismiss description is challenged, however, by Gérard Genette. In 'Frontières du récit,' he states that modern fiction, specifically Robbe-Grillet's novels, has long been questioning the traditional notions of narrative, and he goes on to mention that, even in realistic novels, the relation between description and narration is not one of opposition, but rather one of cause and effect. While making a distinc-tion between 'ornamental description' and 'significative description' – that is, between description as a classical aesthetic convention and description as performing a relevant role in the overall economy of a fic-tional work – Genette states that description is more indispensable than narration: 'On peut donc dire que la description est plus indispensable que la narration, puisqu'il est plus facile de décrire sans raconter que de raconter sans décrire ... la description pourrait se concevoir indépen-damment de la narration, mais en fait on ne la trouve jamais à l'état libre' (156–7).

Such assertions, nevertheless, can be seen today as slightly exagger-ated, given that Genette, using two short sentences as an example, assigns descriptive-like qualities not only to all nouns but also to some 'action verbs.' In fact, it could be argued that such micro-textual ele-ments only become descriptive in so far as they can conjure up images within the imagination. These descriptive qualities, however, would cease to be intimately linked to the specificities of a text to become the subjective series of mental images each reader is bound to experience when reading any type of message. Furthermore, at a micro-textual level the distinctions between narration and description can become blurred, if not irrelevant at times, since, as I later demonstrate, it is not possible to make a comprehensive distinction between descriptive and narrative statements solely at the level of the mere sentence.

Although claiming that description constitutes the 'internal frontier' of all narrative texts, Genette does not expand on his reflections on the subject, not even in *Figures III* (1972), where he analyses in great detail

Proust's *A la recherche du temps perdu*, a highly descriptive fictional work. Barthes, on the other hand, was not to hold to the structuralist frame of analysis or to the clear-cut distinctions between description and narration he made in the articles referred to above. After *S/Z* (1970) – a book that marks a definite change in his critical approach – he sees the literary text as a constellation of meanings determining specific codes, and in *Sade, Fourrier, Loyola* (1971) he becomes even more interested in the various processes of symbolization that occur in a text, thereby not mentioning any distinctions between description and narration.

Other French critics did, nevertheless, continue the debate on both the characteristics and the relevance of descriptive passages in prose fiction – a subject that, as Genette pointed out, had produced, since Plato and Aristotle, a major impact on Western critical traditions: 'L'opposition entre narration et description, d'ailleurs accentuée par la tradition scolaire, est un des traits majeurs de notre conscience littéraire' (1966, 156). Thus, Philippe Hamon in 'Qu'est-ce qu'une description?' and later in *Introduction à l'analyse du descriptif* begins a thorough evaluation of the subject of description, a notion that had been left on hold, when not altogether discarded, by previous critics. Hamon's interest in description, however, stems from his critical readings and analyses of Zola's fictional works, and is therefore shaped by a culturally homogeneous textual corpus that, with very few exceptions, alludes to texts that are shaped (or perceived as being shaped) by a realistic mode of representation.[7]

Trying to grasp this critic's concept of description, one notices that, although in 'Qu'est-ce qu'une description?' he views description as forming 'un tout autonome, une sorte de "bloc sémantique"' governed by the metonymic relations it generates, he also sees it, in the same way as Barthes (1966), as an interruption of the syntagmatic axis of narration: 'Qui dit description dit interruption de la syntagmatique du récit par un paradigme' (468). According to Hamon, description would imply the introduction of a set of paradigms constituted by the author's own file or 'dossier de travail' on specific subjects – a notion no doubt based on Zola's method of fiction writing. Consequently, the main function of description would be that of exhibiting the 'author's' knowledge or vocabulary range, a fact the 'author' has to disguise by delegating description to other characters in the story. Thus, description would look like a 'regard prolongé du personnage' and would be naturally introduced through the dynamics of narration.

Observing description in a number of Zola's novels, Philippe Hamon lists a whole range of possible ways of justifying its occurrence. To make it fit into the patterns of the story the author could use: 1) zero moments of narration, for example, '"temps morts" dans une activité, "répit," "pause" etc. D'où de multiples scènes d'attente à des rendez-vous, d'oisiveté forcée (maladie, convalescence, immobilité passagère), des personnages de badaux, d'oisifs, de promeneurs insouciants, de paresseux, etc.' (468); and 2) a number of devices such as open doors and windows, 'des halles, des serres, des vitrines, des cabinets vitrés, etc.' (467), offering themselves as means through which viewing gives way to description. Hamon shows that description occurring as the result of the character's psychological make-up (for example, curiosity or inquisitiveness concerning specific matters), as well as by its placement after carefully chosen devices, is made to look as the consequence of the things it causes.

The fact that Hamon sees narration paving the way for description – that is to say, for its justifiable occurrences – might lead us to infer that, if description is an 'autonomous semantic block' governed by its set of 'sous-thèmes,' 'prédicats qualificatifs ... ou verbaux,' as well as by its 'agencement interne' (467), narration, on the other hand, is not entirely autonomous in relation to description. In fact, in the case of Zola, one could speculate that narration functions very much as a form of linking, organizing, and shaping into fiction a series of descriptions, many of these resulting from: 1) the 'author's' reactions to a series of observed social referents, and 2) the fact that 'scientific descriptions' occur frequently in medical, ethnological, and socio-historical works upon which Zola built his naturalistic program. Hamon himself admits that 'la caractéristique fondamentale du discours réaliste est de nier, de rendre impossible le récit, tout récit' (485). This affirmation, however, seems to contradict the fact that description may be an interruption of the main axis of narration or a form of 'remplissage vraisemblabilisant' (472; emphasis mine).

In fact, as we shall notice when analysing Zola's Une Page d'amour (1878), description can, in some cases, function as a particular form of a 'narrative modality,' as the point where narration abandons its typical narrative processes to continue at a descriptive level. Such shifts tend to occur whenever we are confronted with descriptions that might function as a mise en abyme of narration; that is, whenever we start reading certain descriptions taking into consideration the general context of the work in which they occur – something narratologists such as Mieke Bal constantly emphasize.

It is known that, especially in works that depend on specific sociocultural referents to create a realistic mode of representation, not all descriptions are equally important, be it from a stylistic or semantic point of view. Many, in fact, could be considered as devices the function of which is solely to create a realistic illusion. These, then, could be viewed as less significant background descriptions, and, therefore, as interruptions of the main line of events. However, other narrative elements could be perceived in the same way: all the narrative devices discourse linguists generally designate as 'background material,'[8] such as certain dialogues, digressions, summaries, together with all narrative segments that do not contribute to plot development. Thus, one should note that if realistic/naturalistic novels strive for an effect of realism, such an effect is not arrived at exclusively through a set of descriptions, but also by many other narrative devices that, given a specific context, can be read as 'background material.'

As we shall see, a more comprehensive approach to description would have to take into consideration that, in certain prose fiction texts, descriptive segments can function as *foreground* material, especially in many twentieth-century novels that deliberately challenge both narrative conventions and conventional forms of reading (that is, readings exclusively concerned with the main sequence of events).

Hamon's contributions to the analysis of description seem, however, quite pertinent, especially in areas dealing with the internal organization of the descriptive segment, a subject that he develops in *Introduction à l'analyse du descriptif* and that is later pursued by critics such as Jean-Michel Adam and A. Petitjean (1982, 1989). But the fact that Hamon bases his research on a predominantly realistic/naturalistic textual corpus, together with his tendency not to contextualize the descriptive segments he analyses, limit the scope of his inquiry and tend to reduce descriptions to a mere set of stylistic and discursive characteristics. In fact, as Mieke Bal states in 'On Meaning and Descriptions,' 'it is not possible to characterize the description adequately without taking the context into consideration' (1982, 130).[9] Later, in *Le personnel du roman: Le système des personnages dans 'Les Rougon-Macquart' d'Émile Zola* (1983), Hamon recognizes the importance of certain descriptions in Zola's works, not as mere 'reality effects,' or 'interruptions,' but as important narrative devices. Referring to descriptions of space in Zola's novels he states: 'cet espace n'est pas uniquement un espace "vraisemblable" destiné à provoquer un simple "effet de réel"' (208); moreover, he adds: 'Le lieu, chez Zola, et principalement dans ses réalisations fortement anthropomorphisées (Voreux, Paradou, Paris ...) tend à se définir comme personnage' (230). However, in *La Description littéraire de l'Antiquité à Roland Barthes: Une Anthologie* (1991), he still sees description as an 'etc.' Commenting on the first chapter of Simon's *Leçon de choses* (1975), which finishes with the abbreviation 'etc.,' Hamon observes in a footnote: 'ETC., tel pourrait être l'emblème de la description' (195).

In the presence of such statements, one realizes that some of Hamon's biases against description should be interpreted in light of a critical background where the subject had generally met with an indifferent or antagonistic reception. His almost exclusive emphasis on nineteenth-century realistic/naturalistic fiction also echoes the textual corpus structuralists and semioticians alike were choosing in order to infer a set of general rules governing all fictional texts. One should note that many examples of twentieth-century fiction, specifically the *nouveau roman*, were still being considered as exceptions to a norm. Such a norm was the stereotypical nineteenth-century novel, an imaginary construct the function of which was merely to illustrate a complex critical apparatus, that – striving for a scientific method – had tried to adapt to an aesthetic and deliberately fabricated type of discourse, the concept of 'norm and deviation' used in traditional linguistic analyses of everyday spoken language.[10] Today we know that such a project, as far as description is concerned, was in many cases a disservice, not only to the canonized works of nineteenth-century fiction (see Barthes 1968 on Flaubert's *Madame Bovary*), but also to a set of twentieth-century texts perceived by critics as a series of slightly anomalous examples.

Description, however, while it remained a marginal area of critical concern, was being analysed by other critics, such as Jean Ricardou. At the same time as Hamon was exploring the issue in nineteenth-century works, Ricardou was trying to analyse and explain it from the point of view of a reader and writer of *nouveaux romans*. In the same way as Genette in 'Frontières du récit,' and as in the criticism of other French New Novelists, namely Robbe-Grillet (1963) and Simon (1980), Ricardou dismisses the classical concept of mimesis. In *Problèmes du nouveau roman* (1967) he states: 'Loin de se servir de l'écriture pour présenter une vision du monde, la fiction utilise le concept de monde avec ses rouages afin d'obtenir un univers obéissant aux spécifiques lois de l'écriture' (25). He adds: 'en la fiction, le réel et le virtuel ont même statut parce qu'ils sont l'un comme l'autre entièrement gérés par les lois de l'écriture qui les instaure' (29).

Given such an approach to the literary text, Ricardou sees description not as a mere copy of an extratextual referent, but as a language-made object: 'A mesure qu'elle multiplie les raffinements et se précise jusqu'au luxe, une description obtient un objet conforme, en ses détails, à la nature du langage' (19). Therefore, for this critic, descriptions should be analysed as textual segments where, through language, one manages to create characters and objects whose existence is not meant to be exclusively checked against an assumed socio-historical reality.

In *Le Nouveau roman* (1973), Ricardou stresses again the importance of description in the context of the French New Novel, but it is particularly in the first chapter of *Nouveaux problèmes du roman* (1978), 'Le Texte en conflit: Problèmes de la belligérance textuelle à partir de *Madame Bovary*,' that he further expands on the stylistic features and functions of descriptive segments. Deliberately choosing a nineteenth-century example – the description of Charles Bovary's cap in Flaubert's novel, – he points both to its modernistic characteristics and to its narrative-like qualities. He starts by stressing, as he had done before (1967, 1973), that descriptions interrupt narration: 'Si la description prodigue au récit le poids de divers détails, c'est en le faisant toujours payer du prix fort d'une interruption' (27). But he immediately questions if the interruption and/or absence of action cannot become in itself a different type of action. While analysing the description of 'Charles' cap,' he demonstrates how that textual segment can: 1) activate in the reader's mind a series of implied actions (28–9); 2) function as a prospective and retrospective *mise en abyme* of narration (that is, as a 'description emblématique,' [29]); and 3) use a series of narrative-like devices to disguise its static nature (for example, time adverbs organized so as to create a 'pseudo-chronological perspective,' [30]).

What initially seemed to echo a well-established structuralist and semiotic concept becomes now quite clear: Descriptions interrupt, or rather disturb narration, not by introducing extraneous or irrelevant information but, precisely, by mirroring, refracting, and thus bringing into focus a series of narrative mechanisms. This is to say that Ricardou views description as constantly challenging the narrative process, not just by framing its semantic reception, but even by disguising itself, at times, as narration. Recognizing description as having narrative possibilities, Ricardou mentions: 'En tant que procédure défiant la représentation (le récit inénarrable), en tant que procédure contestant la représentation (les syncopes infligées au récit), la description achronique appartient bien, selon nous, quoique pratiquée dans le passé, à l'une des procédures modernes dont il importe d'assurer une rénovation entière'

(44). Expanding on the stylistics of the descriptive segment and on the metadescriptive nature of descriptions by Flaubert and Proust, Ricardou demonstrates how certain descriptions in the French New Novel aim at a similar effect.

Flaubert's description of 'Charles' cap' has, nevertheless, triggered a series of other critical receptions: from Jean-Michel Adam, who in 'Approche linguistique de la séquence descriptive' (1987) analyses it from a strictly linguistic point of view, to Jonathan Culler, who in *Flaubert: The Uses of Uncertainty* (1974) sees it as a parody of realistic descriptions. According to Culler, 'to give a sense of "the real" one must offer details which have no meaning' (76). Therefore, the description of 'Charles' cap' is for this critic nothing but a deliberate means for misguiding the reader, who tends to read descriptions searching for their symbolic meaning(s): 'The cap, one might say, is, in its excessiveness, a parody of a symbolic object, in that by throwing down a challenge it calls into play interpretative operations that are inadequate to the task it appears to set' (92).

Culler's distinctly deconstructionist assertion is based on the fact that symbolic meanings tend to be rather elusive and too subjective. Thus, he mentions that if one tries to find a symbolic meaning for a descriptive passage one can always find one, because there are endless semantic correlations one can establish among segments and/or among segments and contexts. However, after reading this argument in 'Description and Meaning,' a section of his book, one feels his own statements are equally subjective; because he focuses on the internal coherence of descriptive segments, thus losing sight of their semantic implications, one can always conclude they do not mean anything in particular. In fact, although developing opposite approaches to the analysis of the description of 'Charles' cap' in *Madame Bovary*, both Culler and Ricardou demonstrate that Flaubert's descriptions do challenge realistic forms of representation.

Should one, however, opt for Ricardou's approach, since it opens up a series of relevant aspects concerning description, one is still left with a basic question: Are all nineteenth- and twentieth-century descriptions as relevant to the functioning of the fictional text as Ricardou leads us to believe?

Although the answer might seem evident – since literary descriptions and their relevance do vary according to the specificities of a given work – it is useful to note in this context that critical approaches to description (or to other textual characteristics) are shaped by the critic's biases, interests, and expectations rather than solely by his/her preoccupations concerning objectivity.

Perception of genre is also important. For example, no matter what the critical approach, descriptive passages have never been deemed irrelevant in a lyrical poem, while similar passages in a novel have been viewed as unnecessary 'extras' or as cumbersome details. As critical concerns related to prose fiction have shifted from plot to 'text' (in a late-Barthesian sense),[11] so have critics become more concerned not only with description but with other aspects of fiction that discourse-linguists generally designate as 'background material.'

Ricardou's opinions on description, as well as Hamon's research and semiotic analyses in *Introduction à l'analyse du descriptif*, have given rise to several articles and books. Several journals have dedicated specific issues to the subject.[12] However, the only critic who comes close to proposing a general model of analysis is Mieke Bal in 'On Meaning and Descriptions' (1982). She names three phases one should take into account when analysing description: 'First, the descriptive excerpt is itself described. Second, relations with the direct context are investigated. And finally, the excerpt is placed back within the text as a whole' (131).

Although the framework I propose bears the same heuristic approach (that is, from micro- to macro-contexts), I take into consideration not only three main levels of inquiry but also the possible problems that might arise at each level.

2. TOWARDS AN ANALYTICAL FRAMEWORK

Description and narration constitute the two most basic modes of structuring any prose fiction text. Even novels that are built exclusively through dialogue, such as Robert Pinget's *L'inquisitoire* (1962) or Manuel Puig's *Maldición eterna a quién lea estas páginas* (1980), rely on this mode of structuring, as does a dramatic text performed for an audience, although, in the latter case, description may be either present at a visual level or reported through speech. Given that both modes of structuring are generally interdependent, it is sometimes difficult to define one without taking the other into consideration – especially when one tries to analyse them at a sentence level. This is probably the reason why certain structuralists and semioticians posit description and narration as a pair of opposites. And yet, since narration has been thoroughly defined by both discourse-linguists and literary critics, description tends to be defined by the latter as an obvious component easily identifiable: 'Le lecteur reconnaît et identifie sans hésiter une description' (Hamon 1972, 465), and 'descriptions do exist. We recognize them intuitively' (Bal 1982, 105). This attitude probably stems from the fact that more than narration (which can always be approached in terms of a 'grammar'), description must be consistently and sometimes contradictorily defined as one proceeds from a sentential/stylistic level to larger textual segments/blocks, and later, to an examination of the functions of description in the overall context.

Thus the framework I propose has three main levels of inquiry: a *stylistic* level, where description is analysed at a micro-sentence level; a *discursive* level, where analysis focuses on the internal organization of larger descriptive segments/blocks; and a *functional* level, where, through the correlation of descriptive segments with other segments in the text, such as narration, we can focus on the functions description might fulfil in the context of a given work.

It should be noted, however, that the division into three levels is made for purely methodological reasons; in any text, as well as in the realm of practical criticism, such levels are bound to be closely interrelated. Furthermore, each text might reveal specific descriptive characteristics. Hence, the proposed framework should not be considered as an end in itself but rather as a heuristic device enabling a more detailed analysis of various sorts of descriptions.

The stylistic level

Many misconceptions stem from the tendency to perceive a sentence containing a 'dynamic verb' as narrative (especially if the verb implies a series of logically concatenated actions), and to consider a sentence containing a 'stative' verb as descriptive.[13] One cannot deny the difference between the following sentences: (a) 'She wore a yellow dress,' and (b) 'He killed him.' In (a) the reader is invited to store a particular piece of information, while in (b) he/she can conceive the series of logically concatenated possible actions the verb itself implies. Because of the verbs in both sentences – the 'stative' *to wear* and the 'performative' *to kill* – one would not hesitate to classify (a) as descriptive and (b) as narrative, and to conclude therefore that descriptive and narrative sentences use different types of verbs. Thus, while descriptive sentences tend to use verbs indicating a quality or state, narrative sentences are only possible if they contain an action verb capable of summing up as an *achieved* or *accomplished result*, a series of implied verbs.[14] This is why a statement such as 'she walked,' cannot *per se* be classified as narrative unless we contextualize it, that is, read it in relation to other sentences as one of the actions in a narrative program.

Such a distinction proves to be unreliable, however, since not all descriptions, be they of characters or space, are static: a character can be described while engaging in a series of actions; similarly, the description of a forest during a storm is bound to contain sentences with action verbs. Yet these verbs are seldom subjected to any sequential constraints, and in many cases their 'dynamism' is either toned down or altogether neutralized: 1) by the use of durative/iterative 'verbal aspects' (for example, the imperfect tense in Romance languages); 2) by the use of non-tensed verb forms (such as the gerund or the infinitive); and 3) by the use of typical narrative tenses relating 'punctual' or 'perfective' actions in a metaphorical sense, such as in 'he killed him with his gaze' or 'she walked over dreams.'[15]

If we apply Paul J. Hopper's notions in 'Aspects and Foregrounding in Discourse' (1979), descriptive sentences, in the same way as any sentences pertaining to 'background material,' can be defined as clauses that 'support, amplify and comment on the narration' (216) but that, unlike narration, are not subjected to the same constraints regarding either temporal sequentiality, verbal tense/'aspect,' or cross-sentential coherence. However, what might be descriptive at a sentence level might become narrative (or vice versa) if placed in a larger context – that is, whenever a descriptive sentence points to an implied series of actions or whenever in a narrative sentence a 'perfective' action is stated metaphorically.

Although accurate definition is impossible, a variety of aspects can nevertheless be analysed at a sentence level, such as the stylistic characteristics of a given description, or, more precisely, the semantics of its morpho-syntax. Among other traits, one can analyse the following: 1) the choice and range of lexicon and its relevance; 2) verbal tenses and 'aspects,' and their immediate functions; 3) the meaning of connectors (such as adverbs, prepositions, or prepositional locutions as they relate to representations of time and space); 4) predominant figures of speech that can, at times, point to forms of discursive organization (for example, metonymical, metaphoric, allegoric, and so on); and 5) sentence rhythm and sound patterns relevant to the construction of meaning(s) (such as possible uses of conventional metrics in prose, or figures of speech emphasizing such aspects of the 'signifier' as alliterations or onomatopoeias).

It should be noted that, given the average length of a novel, a detailed analysis of a description at a sentence level can only be of interest as it relates to overall recurrent patterns.

The discursive level

At this level we deal with description as a series of segments or blocks one might isolate to study their internal mode of organization, as well as 'cohesion' and 'coherence' across sentences.[16] Distinctions previously mentioned between narration and description are far more obvious at this level. Narration can be defined as a series of logically concatenated actions pertaining to a main plot and therefore following a syntagmatic sequencing, while description can be defined as a set of particulars or attributes not directly subjected to the constraints imposed on narrative organization (Barthes 1966; Hamon 1972). The textual segments or blocks may range from a short paragraph to one or more pages, and contribute primarily to the building of either fictional characters or fictional spaces.

One may consider first the mode of conveying descriptive information. For example, is description conveyed as well-defined, easily identifiable textual blocks, or is it disseminated throughout the text? In nineteenth-century novels, specifically in Balzac or Zola, descriptive segments are usually easily identifiable, while in modern novels this is not always the case.

As far as the internal organization of the descriptive block is concerned, one should note how a main theme (Ricardou's 'thème-titre' [1978, 25], or Hamon's 'pantonyme' [1981, 140]) relates to a set of sub-themes. Generally speaking, nineteenth-century descriptions are constructed as mono-perspective, cohesive, and coherent blocks that contribute, at times, to an effect of visualization. In this case, the discursive qualities of the descriptive block can be seen as if placing it within a single main frame, that is, a single main theme developed through a set of metonymically connected sub-themes. A study of more recent novels, however, will reveal sometimes deliberate effects of 'discohesion' and 'discoherence' (a literary text is never 'uncohesive' or 'incoherent' in a linguistic sense), through which a main descriptive frame is split into a series of minor frames.[17] This usually occurs whenever, in a descriptive block, the 'descriptive voice' opts for conveying a multiplicity of visual perspectives of the same object(s) – a characteristic of some descriptions by Robbe-Grillet. Effects of discohesion and discoherence can also occur whenever descriptive detail is expanded so as to create an effect similar to a filmic zoom, thereby undermining immediate attempts at an overall perception of totality. What takes place, in this case, from a discursive point of view, is that the sub-themes of a general main theme become themselves main themes with a set of sub-themes.[18] The reader's attention and comprehension is, therefore, constantly shifted and refocused. As we shall see, this process is not uncommon in some of the descriptions of postcards in Simon's *Histoire*, where a baroque-like proliferation of detail leads to an erasure of the limits/borders imposed by a main frame.

Sometimes effects of discohesion and discoherence render impossible any process of visualization. In fact, such a process is directly related to the mode in which descriptive segments are connected inside a given block, and not so much to the amount of descriptive detail or to the reader's familiarity with the material described. Thus, visualization is hindered each time the reader is faced, inside a descriptive block, with a variety of main themes (or for that matter, with multiple/fragmented perspectives) instead of a more conventional mode of organization. This is actually a set of sub-themes, expanding a main theme – a mode of conveying descriptive information that seems to be favoured by realistic forms of discursive presentation.

But not all descriptions are static. Some draw a dynamic effect by adopting a 'pseudo-chronological perspective' (Ricardou 1978, 30), or what Hamon designates as a 'pseudo-narrative programme' (1981, 244). This is to say, in some descriptions information is organized not in spatial terms (in front, on the left side, further back, and so on) but in temporal ones. This dynamic effect is created, first, each time we are faced with the description of an activity (such as the painting of a portrait, the repair of a piece of machinery), and second, each time the connectors binding the various segments are arranged so as to create an illusion of logical sequentiality (for example, *first* she saw/heard A, *then* B, *later on* C, and *finally* D). Attention to the function and nature of verbs and connectors inside a descriptive block enables us to define the dynamic aspects of certain descriptions as well as the differences between descriptive and narrative dynamism.

Other aspects that can be analysed at this level are the nature of the 'descriptive voice'; the immediate receptor of a descriptive segment; the nature of the descriptive block; the role of the reader as an implied narrator; and the 'tone' of the descriptive block.

The voice that describes is not always the voice that narrates. Here, we can note whether characters become 'descriptors'[19] as well as consider the focalization and point of view of each descriptive block. Even in novels where description is generated by a third-person omniscient narrator, descriptive information may be focalized according to specific points of view, sometimes the point of view of one of the characters (for example, the panoramic descriptions of Paris in Zola's *Une Page d'amour*). Such descriptions should be analysed accordingly and, if building the perceptions of a given character, they should be further correlated with other descriptions of character.

Similarly, the immediate receptor of a description (that is, the 'descriptee') is not always the reader. A character may communicate to another character some descriptive information with the intention of shaping or altering forms of behaviour (as when, character A entices character B to travel to a distant place by describing it to him/her). Therefore, who describes for whom can be just as important as the notions of narrator and narratee commonly used in a variety of literary analyses.

Concerning the nature of the descriptive block, one can take into consideration such questions as: 1) Does the description aim at conveying a 'referential,' or a totally imaginary reality (for example, a view of Paris as opposed to a view of an imaginary planet)? 2) Is description based on specific aesthetic objects (for example, literary descriptions of paintings, photographs, sculptures, etc.)? 3) Does the description imitate or draw on other media, such as trying to create a pictographic or filmic effect?

In considering the role of the reader as an implied narrator, one might note that certain descriptive blocks trigger an implied narration. Examples of this could be the description of the body of a murdered victim in a detective story, or of a town after an earthquake (as with the description of 'Vanadium' in Robbe-Grillet's *Topologie d'une cité phantôme* [1976]) or any single description able to convey the results of a series of actions brought about by human or natural forces.

The tone of the descriptive segment is also important since it tends to shift, form, or expand the reader's immediate perceptions. Here, one can consider, for example, the construction and function of irony, or how the reader is solicited to follow the point of view of certain characters, the narrator (or even the narrator/descriptor), for example, the sarcastic descriptions in Pérez Galdós' *La de Bringas* (1884).

The functional level

In literary prose fiction descriptive segments do not occur in isolation.

This may seem quite obvious. However, most of the structuralist and semiotic attempts at defining description (namely Barthes 1966; Hamon 1972, 1981), seem to ignore the semantic dimensions resulting from the confrontation of various descriptive segments in a fictional work, or from a confrontation between descriptions and other textual components such as narration.

When reading across descriptive segments in fiction, as well as when trying to contextualize them, one should focus on the role played by description in the work – that is, on the particular *functions* of descriptive segments. When emphasis is shifted from internal structure to function, the differences between description and narration are no longer as obvious as they were at a discourse level. In fact, we may be dealing with narrative segments that have functions similar to description, or with a type of narration constructed from a set of descriptions.

Having chosen one or more descriptive blocks as the focus for the analysis of a predominantly descriptive fictional work (or a work where description plays a major role, that is, where it is *foregrounded*), one does not have to stop at the level of their internal organization; what can be analysed at a stylistic or discursive level, may in fact be expanded (if not challenged) whenever we proceed to draw a series of correlations: 1) among descriptions of the same type (be these of characters or space); 2) between descriptions of characters and descriptions of space; and 3) between descriptive and narrative segments. In this case, previously mentioned differences seem to fade away, for characters do exist inside or throughout a specific fictional space, and space tends, to a lesser or greater extent, to be positively correlated with the construction or with the ways through which we perceive the characters. Having proceeded to a correlation among descriptive segments (for example, the five major descriptions of Paris in Zola's *Une Page d'amour*), one can then analyse how a description or set of descriptions correlates with the events narrated, thus expanding on its/their semantic dimensions.

One should note that never before have notions such as description and narration been as challenged as in the French New Novel and, after that, in post-modern fiction. While in the former we often come across descriptions that narrate or vice versa (especially in the cases of Alain Robbe-Grillet and Claude Simon), in post-modern texts or in 'historiographic metafiction' in general,[20] we are faced with an erasure of the distinctions between historical and fictional representation. In fact, as fictional genres rely more and more on the notion of a reader as a participating entity, as a 'reader-writer,' description may no longer function as a mere *background* of narration but as the *foreground* according to which narration has to be inferred. In many of Robbe-Grillet's novels, for example, we find a series of motionless instants presented as a set of descriptions, which function very much like a set of pictures or slides the reader is solicited to place into a sequence in order to infer a story. The reader becomes an implied narrator – in fact, the only narrator – and is thus led to reflect, by his/her participation, on the modes according to which he/she comes to tell a story whose events have never been directly stated, either by an 'implied author,' or by a 'descriptive voice.' Another interesting example can be found in Claude Simon's later works of fiction. In this case, the boundaries between description and narration are effaced by the specific use of a verbal form: the French past participle. As we shall see in a later chapter, this verbal form has an important function in Simon's fiction as it creates an almost oxymoronic effect: it gives to narration a descriptive-like quality while 'narrativizing' a set of descriptions, thereby erasing the traditional boundaries that have kept description and narration as distinct textual structures.

Another notion that can be comprehensively analysed only at a functional level – that is, given a general context – is the notion of description as a *mise en abyme* (Ricardou 1978, 29). Certain descriptions can, in fact, become 'narrating instances' whenever they function as prospective and/or retrospective *mises en abyme* of the events narrated. Rather than simply dismiss such types of descriptions as mere redundancies, we may consider through what specific mechanisms do descriptions mirror and seem to expand the 'significance' of the events narrated. In the first chapters of both Zola's *Thérèse Raquin* (1867) and Pérez Galdós' *La de Bringas* (1884) there are particular forms of describing that announce not only the symbolic aspects of the respective novels but the very stylistic and ideologic structures according to which the novels are generated.[21] It is interesting that, especially in nineteenth-century novels, instances of foregrounded description do generally function as *mises en abyme*. This is the case in specific descriptions by Flaubert, as analysed by Mieke Bal (1981, 106–7) and Jean Ricardou (1978, chapter 1).

Before concluding the presentation of this framework, I should state that certain stylistic, discursive, and functional aspects of description in a work may strike each critical reader in different ways. Unable to analyse in detail every one of the descriptive segments or blocks in a work of fiction (especially in a novel), the reader is bound, through his/her reading, to make specific choices or options so as to communicate a textual 'significance.'[22] While a descriptive block can be divided quite precisely into clauses/sentences, the division of a text into discursive units – in the same way as their semantic and functional dimensions – cannot be made with the same degree of precision. This fact serves to remind us that literary analysis stems not from standardized rules that must be followed but from the variety of responses a work provokes in the reader.

The framework outlined in this chapter is meant as a guide to a basic form of inquiry and therefore does not aim at excluding other approaches to description in specific works or contexts. In fact, as we shall see, the application of this framework triggers further questions related to the stylistic, discursive, and/or functional aspects of description. These tend, at times, to focus on a particular level.

2

Description and *mise en abyme* in Zola's *Une Page d'amour*

Toute oeuvre d'art est comme une fenêtre ouverte sur la création; il y a, enchâssé dans l'ambrasure de la fenêtre, une sorte d'Écran transparent, à travers lequel on aperçoit les objets plus ou moins déformés, souffrant des changements plus ou moins sensibles dans leurs lignes et dans leur couleur. Ces changements tiennent à la nature de l'Écran. On n'a plus la création exacte et réelle, mais la création modifiée par le milieu où passe son image ... La réalité exacte est donc impossible dans une oeuvre d'art.

Émile Zola[1]

Unlike some of the twenty volumes that constitute Zola's *Les Rougon-Macquart, Une Page d'amour* (1878)[2] has never received wide critical attention. In fact, apart from some brief references by Philippe Hamon (1981, 1983) and by Raymonde Debray-Genette (1982), the critical bibliography on this specific novel consists primarily of Joy Newton's 'Zola et l'expressionnisme: Le point de vue hallucinatoire' (1971), in which she addresses some problems pertinent to the concepts of literary impressionism and expressionism.[3]

One is led to speculate on why *Une Page d'amour* has been ignored both by historicist criticism and by even more recent critical trends, since this novel reflects, according to Zola, his deliberate attempt at working on the notion and textual potentialities of fictional description. In a brief section of *Le Roman expérimental* (1880) entitled 'De la description,'[4] Zola makes specific references to *Une Page d'amour*: 'j'avais rêvé d'écrire un roman, dont Paris, avec l'océan de ses toitures, serait un personnage' (235). However, the five long descriptions of Paris in the novel were not well received by nineteenth-century critics and readers in general; they were criticized by writers such as Flaubert, who, in a letter addressed to Zola following the publication of the novel, states: 'Le récit m'a entraîné, j'ai lu tout d'une seule haleine. Maintenant voici mes réserves: trop de descriptions de Paris.'[5] Lamenting a general lack of interest in the descriptive aspects of *Une Page d'amour*, Zola attempts a response in the same section of *Le Roman expérimental*: 'Ce qu'on me reproche surtout, même des esprits sympathiques, ce sont les cinq descriptions de Paris qui reviennent et terminent les cinq parties d'*Une Page d'amour*. On ne voit là qu'un caprice d'artiste d'une répétition fatigante, qu'une difficulté vaincue pour montrer la dextérité de la main. J'ai pu me tromper, et je me suis trompé certainement, puisque personne n'a compris ...' (234).

The above quotation was included, with very few modifications, in the preface to the first illustrated edition of *Une Page d'amour* (1884).[6] In it, and still referring to the notion of description, the author says, 'Je ne défends donc pas mes cinq descriptions: je tiens uniquement à faire remarquer que, dans ce qu'on nomme notre fureur de description, nous ne cédons presque jamais au seul besoin de décrire; cela se complique toujours en nous d'intentions symphoniques et humaines' (1219).

Zola's need to defend his use of descriptive elements in the novel, informs us of some biases against description, some of which still surface in more recent critical trends. Indeed, the fact that *Une Page d'amour* has not elicited a great deal of interest on the part of readers and critics alike may well stem from certain stereotypes – which one still encounters in school manuals and literary histories – concerning description in realistic/naturalistic fiction, specifically, the notion of description as a mere *ancilla narrationis* or as a mere background for the characters' actions. Another reason for the lack of interest in this novel may lie in the fact that, as the title itself indicates, it is basically a romance or love story, and thus not open – in the same way as *L'Assommoir* (1877) or *Germinal* (1885) – to historically and/or sociologically based forms of literary interpretation.

For several reasons, my inquiry concerning *Une Page d'amour* focuses mainly on the predominantly descriptive fifth chapters in each part of the five-part novel. Not only are all five chapters linked by a common main theme (the description of a panoramic view of Paris), but also, and principally, they present us with, first, a distinctive shift from backgrounding to foregrounding description, and second, a set of descriptions that function as five *mises en abyme* of chapters that are predominantly narrated (chapters 1 to 4 in each of the five parts).

Indeed, the geometric-like organization of each part of the novel (4 + 1; four narrative chapters followed by a mainly descriptive one) is also reflected in the fifth chapters. Thus, the same view of Paris, at different times of the day and of the year, is described four times from the same place, Hélène's apartment window, and once from the cemetery where her daughter, Jeanne, is buried. In this way, the pattern is realized. The same pattern can be observed in the descriptive focalization. Although, as we shall see later, one may argue in favour of a double focalization (both through a main character and an external narrator), four of the descriptive chapters are focalized mainly through Hélène, while one of the chapters (chapter 5 of part 4) is almost entirely focalized through Jeanne. Similarly, if all five descriptive chapters can be seen to constitute *mises en abyme* of a narration that builds up Hélène as the main character, chapter 5 of part 4 varies the pattern; by being focalized through Jeanne, it gives us a child's view of the same landscape.

Given that each of the five parts is centred around one of five distinct plot developments, my brief summaries of the plot in chapters 1 to 4 of each part will provide context for analysis of the descriptive chapters.

1. THE FIRST DESCRIPTION OF PARIS

In chapters 1 to 4 of part 1 Hélène Grandjean has arrived in Paris from Marseille with her eleven-year-old daughter, Jeanne, and her husband. Hélène's husband, who came to the capital to seek a cure for his illness, dies in a hotel room shortly after their arrival. Hélène decides then to rent an apartment in Passy for her and Jeanne, who is suffering from tuberculosis. One night, Jeanne has a violent attack and Hélène goes out into the street to find a doctor. By chance, she meets Dr Henri Deberle, who comes to her daughter's aid. Hélène then becomes a friend of the doctor and his wife. While doing some charitable work, Hélène more than once meets the doctor at the house of a very poor sick woman, 'la mère Fétu.' Hélène develops a passion for the doctor. Since she became a widow, she has lived almost exclusively for her demanding sick daughter, and has therefore been practically isolated from the outside world. Her only regular visitors are a priest, 'l'abbé Jouve,' and his brother, Mr Rambaud, who sees Hélène as a model of virtue. One afternoon, when Hélène is playing on a swing in the Deberles' garden, she jumps off in mid-air just as the doctor comes into the garden, and dislocates one of her knees. This trivial narrative episode provides the situation in chapter 5, where for two weeks Hélène is immobilized in a chair, her only contact with the outside world being through her apartment window. Narration thus gives way to a mainly descriptive chapter.

The previous chapters are predominantly narrative. Apart from some brief depictions of Hélène's apartment and of the Deberles' house and garden, descriptions relate mainly to the presentation of the characters. These are generally described by a third-person narrator unlike Hélène, whose several descriptions are not only focalized through the same 'enunciative voice,'[7] but also through other characters in the novel. These descriptions are also very similar in style and follow the conventions of a realistic mode of representation. The long depiction of Paris that opens chapter 5, however, is quite different. What was before an 'objective mode' of describing becomes a highly metaphorical text. Such a shift in the tone of the 'enunciative voice' not only triggers a corresponding shift in the way the reader has been processing similar types of information, but also draws our attention to the particular status of this chapter: 'Les deux fenêtres de la chambre étaient grandes ouvertes, et Paris, dans l'abîme qui se creusait au pied de la maison, bâtie à pic sur la hauteur, déroulait sa plaine immense. Dix heures sonnaient, la belle matinée de février avait une douceur et une odeur de printemps' (845).

The above paragraph sets in time the main theme that will generate the first long description of Paris. None the less, in this case Hélène, the character through whom the description will be focalized, is not simply an idle spectator facilitating the author's need to insert a descriptive segment, since she is reading a book in front of her window: 'Hélène, alongée sur sa chaise longue, le genou encore emmailloté de bandes, lisait devant une des fenêtres' (845).

A particular situation is thus created from the beginning of this chapter. Hélène is reading Walter Scott's *Ivanhoe*, a historical romance she borrowed from Mr Rambaud's small library of 'ouvrages honnêtes,' and it is only as she proceeds in an erratic reading that she becomes more and more aware of the presence of an urban landscape. As a result, her vision of Paris is filtered by fictional contexts, or particularly, by the mental images triggered by specific reading material. It is this dialectical interaction between the reading experience of a romantic novel and the reality of a specific view of Paris that leads Hélène to engage in a spontaneously presented form of self-reflection.

At this moment the reader of this novel is faced with a similar and yet different situation. As a reader of *Une Page d'amour* he/she is also in the presence of a romance or love story, but the conventional 'romantic code' has been replaced, so far, by a realistic/naturalistic one. Possible modes of fantasizing about the nature of romantic love stories are indeed cautioned against by the text in a set of metafictional references focalized through Hélène:

D'ordinaire les romans lui semblaient faux et puérils. Celui-là, l'*Ivanhoé* de Walter Scott, l'avait d'abord fort ennuyée. Puis, une curiosité singulière lui était venue. Elle l'achevait, attendrie parfois, prise d'une lassitude, et elle le laissait tomber de ses mains pendant de longues minutes, les regards fixés sur le vaste horizon ... Comme ces romans mentaient! Elle avait bien raison de ne jamais en lire. C'étaient des fables bonnes pour des têtes vides, qui n'ont point le sentiment exact de la vie. (846–7)

These comments, together with the fictional situation already mentioned, create a particular type of *mise en abyme*. In *Le Récit spéculaire: Essai sur la mise en abyme* (1977), Lucien Dällenbach defines *mise en abyme* as 'tout miroir interne réfléchissant l'ensemble du récit par réduplication simple, répétée ou spécieuse' (61), and mentions three major types that constitute a reflection of: 1) the content of the fictional utterances ('l'énoncé'), 2) the 'enunciation,' and 3) of the 'code.' In this case, we are dealing with a *mise en abyme* of the enunciation,[8] a process further emphasized in this particular chapter of *Une Page d'amour*. As the foggy landscape changes into a sunny view, Hélène focuses her attention on a specific passage or on a particular *page* of the novel she is reading: 'Cependant, Hélène reprit son livre. Elle en était à cet épisode de l'attaque du château, lorsque Rébecca soigne Ivanhoé blessé et le renseigne sur la bataille, qu'elle suit par une fenêtre' (847).

The *mise en abyme* becomes then quite clear. Hélène is also sitting near a window, following not a medieval battle, but the symbolic fight between the foggy clouds and the sun. This 'battle' is also thematized in terms of an interior debate as Hélène's feelings change from an emotional numbness to a desire to fall in love and be loved. This series of mirroring effects places both the main character and the reader in similar situations. In fact, the reader is solicited to process the long description of Paris against first, the references made to a specific intertext, which in this case becomes a 'metatext' (Scott's *Ivanhoe*); then Hélène's self-reflective statements; and finally, the predominantly narrative context(s) occurring in chapters 1 to 4 of part 1.

We might expect a panoramic view of Paris to be described as a motionless 'tableau.' In this case, however, the description is rendered dynamic and narrative-like by the strategy of describing and by various stylistic devices. Paris is depicted not as an instantaneously perceived landscape, but as a set of discrete discursive segments that account for the changes provoked by natural forces such as fog versus light. This mode of describing a landscape through a chronological series of moments contributes not only to the creation of a narrative-like effect (that is, 'the same' as it changes along a temporal axis), but also to the literary depiction of Paris as a character beyond the mere rhetorical personification that opens and closes the following paragraph:

Ce matin-là, Paris mettait une paresse souriante à s'éveiller. Une vapeur, qui suivait la vallée de la Seine, avait noyé les deux rives. C'était une buée légère, comme laiteuse, que le soleil peu à peu grandi éclairait. On ne distinguait rien de la ville, sous cette mousseline flottante, couleur du temps. Dans les creux, le nuage épaissi se fonçait d'une teinte bleuâtre, tandis que, sur de larges espaces, des transparences se faisaient d'une finesse extrême, poussière dorée où l'on devinait l'enfoncement des rues; et, plus haut, des dômes et des flèches déchiraient le brouillard, dressant leurs silhouettes grises, enveloppés encore des lambeaux de la brume qu'ils trouaient. Par instants, des pans de fumée jaune se détachaient avec le coup d'aile lourd d'un oiseau géant, puis se fondaient dans l'air qui semblait les boire. Et, au-dessus de cette immensité, de cette nuée descendue et endormie sur Paris, un ciel très pur, d'un bleu effacé, presque blanc, déployait sa voûte profonde. Le soleil montait dans un poudroiement adouci de rayons. Une clarté blonde, du blond vague de l'enfance, se brisait en pluie, emplissait l'espace de son frisson tiède. C'était une fête, une paix souveraine et une gaieté tendre de l'infini, pendant que la ville, criblée de flèches d'or, paresseuse et somnolente, ne se décidait point à se montrer sous ses dentelles. (846)

The first striking aspect in the above paragraph is its capacity to evoke an imaginary impressionistic painting. A shift from previous modes of describing becomes, at this moment, quite clear. 'Mimesis,' as a heading for realistic modes of representation, ceases in this case to be a written/read 'transposition' of a possible observed view of Paris, to become something more complex: the literary construction of an aesthetic object (such as an impressionistic painting), the existence of which is only possible as a set of after-images or visualizations triggered by the metaphorical nature of the written text.

A comprehensive analysis of the stylistic, discursive, and functional aspects of this description should not necessarily take into account the imaginary pictographic text triggered by the metaphors used in the previous descriptive segment. In this case, however, I shall proceed to estab-

lish a series of parallels between the written text and the pictorial images
it conjures up, in an attempt to bring into focus a variety of analogous
processes used in different media. I shall therefore, in this context, consider questions such as the following: 1) What gives the above description such an impressionistic quality? 2) What constitutes its narrative-
like dynamism? 3) To what extent can it introduce a shift from previous
modes of descriptive production-reception, and to what purpose?

Critics such as Joy Newton (1967, 1971) have already pointed out, in
relation to *Une Page d'amour*, the many notations of colour and gradations of light so characteristic of impressionist painting. In this description, however, one of the impressionistic effects results not so much from
mere references to colour but, more precisely, to a 'pigmentation' to be
apprehended in relation to other colours: 'se fonçait d'une teinte
bleuâtre,' 'bleu effacé, presque blanc,' and 'poudroiement adouci de rayons.' Besides the notations of colour and shape (referred to as being
inscribed on a specific space), other elements are also described as two-
dimensional objects on a surface, such as 'silhouettes grises,' 'lambeaux
de la brume,' and 'des pans de fumée.' This aspect is further stressed by
a form of spatial orientation that seems to refer to several areas on a surface, for example, 'plus haut' and 'au-dessus de' instead of 'near versus
far.' Indications of a particular type of brush stroke used in many
impressionist paintings can also be read in the metaphorical segment:
'Par instants, des pans de fumée jaune se détachaient avec le coup d'aile
lourd d'un oiseau géant.' This statement, which allows us to imagine the
marks a brush full of paint can leave on a surface, leads us to reflect on
the dynamic aspects common to this description and to impressionist
painting in general.

Given the treatment of their subject matter, many impressionist
paintings are non-narrative. In fact, many can be seen as forms of landscape description. Their dynamism, however, seems to result mainly
from the fact that the act of painting can be apprehended as a clearly
indicated series of dots or brush strokes, that is, as a form of 'pictographic rhythm.' Nevertheless, although such technical characteristics
do indicate a series of actions, these cannot be read in a chronological
sequence and are, therefore, non-narrative.

The description of Paris in *Une Page d'amour*, mimics, to a certain
extent, the dynamism or the 'pictographic rhythm' of impressionist
painting. Thus, in the paragraph quoted above, the notion of movement
is inscribed not only through the changes resulting from the constant
interplay of light and shadow (or transparency versus opacity), but also

by the use of specific devices functioning at a stylistic level. In fact, when we examine the tensed verb forms used in the passage, we realize that the majority of them are 'action verbs.' Curiously, only two verbs in the long excerpt refer to some form of visual perception: *distinguer* and *sembler*. In this context, however, the long series of action verbs (*mettre, suivre, faire, déchirer, trouer, briser*, etc.) can only evoke an idea of movement or action in the same way as the brush strokes in impressionistic painting. In fact, the action of these verbs has been somewhat 'suspended' and their relation to time converted to a relation to space, as the following effects cumulate: 1) they cannot be inscribed into a consequential narrative axis; 2) rather than indicating a series of perfective/punctual actions they occur in the imperfect, a tense with a durative/iterative 'aspect'; 3) their iterative qualities are further stressed by the use of reflexive conjugations (for example, 'se faisait,' 'se détachait,' 'se fondaient,' 'se brisait'); and 4) they are used mainly in a metaphoric sense, conveying therefore not a series of actions but a particular form of visual perception.

What has been noted concerning the aspectual quality of verbs can, to a certain extent, be applied to the temporal expressions used in this passage. In fact, adverbial locutions – 'peu à peu,' 'tandis que,' 'par instants,' and 'pendant que' – convey not a punctual but an iterative/durative 'aspect.' None the less, together with the use of 'action verbs' and with the fact that what is being described is a landscape that is changing or about to change, they also convey an illusion of dynamism. This can be observed, too, in the use of certain 'weaved metaphors,'[9] such as the one revealed by the semantic isotopy referring to the transformations of a 'shiny mist': 'vapeur,' 'buée légère comme laiteuse,' 'mousseline flottante,' 'transparences,' 'poussière dorée,' 'poudroiement adouci de rayons,' 'clarté blonde,' 'dentelles.'

At a discursive level, the descriptive segment we have just analysed gives way to a series of other segments where the panoramic view of Paris continues to be described in detail, from the shadows of an early dawn to a sunny morning: 'Le soleil plus haut, dans la gloire triomphante de ses rayons, attaquait victorieusement le brouillard ... Les vapeurs, tout à l'heure si profondes, s'amincissaient, devenaient transparentes en prenant les colorations vives de l'arc-en-ciel ... l'image de Paris s'accentuait et sortait du rêve' (849), and 'Cependant Hélène allait reprendre son livre, lorsque Paris, lentement, apparut ... Et la ville s'étendit sans une ombre, sous le soleil vainqueur ... Paris se déployait, aussi grand que le ciel. Sous cette radieuse matinée, la ville, jaune de soleil, semblait un champ d'épis mûrs; et l'immense tableau avait une simplicité, deux tons seulement, le bleu pâle de l'air et le reflet doré des toits' (850).

The narrative-like characteristics of the first description of Paris become more evident at this moment, since these long descriptive segments can be inscribed into a chronological axis. Furthermore, it is the very changes brought about by natural forces that, together with the book Hélène is reading, will influence her feelings and behaviour.

The impressionistic qualities previously discussed recur in all the descriptive segments about Paris. As Philippe Hamon pointed out in 'A propos de l'impressionisme de Zola' (1967): 'Le romancier, attaché à rendre la fugacité des phénomènes, et à rivaliser avec les possibilités de la couleur, dissout la réalité en une succession de tableaux' (141). However, in this case the impressionistic quality of the descriptive segments is also stressed by references to a pictographic medium and to its techniques, as in the references to an 'immense tableau' (850) or in the following: 'elle [Hélène] distinguait les passants, une foule active de points noirs emportés dans un mouvement de fourmilière' (851); 'une bonne en tablier blanc tachait l'herbe d'une clarté' (851); and 'Les détails si nets aux premiers plans ... s'effaçaient, se chinaient de jaune et de bleu' (853). Indeed, the processes used in *Une Page d'amour* to describe Paris remind us of Monet's eighteen canvases of a frontal view of Rouen Cathedral (1895). In this case, the same subject viewed from the same angle is painted several times according to the gradations of light and colour observable at different times of the day and of the year.

As I mentioned earlier, Paris is described not as a text exclusively based on direct observation but as a set of imaginary impressionistic paintings. From a reader's point of view, the introduction of an 'impressionistic screen' between a given landscape and its literary description, draws our attention to its special status in the overall context of the novel. The long description of Paris acquires, in fact, a metadescriptive and metanarrative quality by shifting our attention from a previous 'narrative mode' to a descriptive one, and by inviting us to engage – as if through a Brechtian effect of 'distanciation' – into a reflection on the types of realistic/naturalistic description used in this novel, thus pointing to the impossibility of any literary direct copies of reality.[10] Consequently, by foregrounding what in chapters 1 to 4 could be considered as background material (complements or aids of narration), this description solicits a rather different type of reading. Narration, which up to this chapter is intended to be read as a clearly concatenated series of actions, becomes in chapter 5 something to be apprehended through a series of discrete descriptive segments.

This emphasis on description as possible narrative material also permeates other segments in this chapter, such as Hélène's thoughts, and particularly the long paragraph where the most important moments of her life pass before her mind's eye (and before the reader) as a number of biographical 'kernels' or turning-points. Indeed, the information about the death of Hélène's husband has already been presented by a 'third-person external narrator' (chapter 2, 815), as a narrative summary establishing a flashback. In this case, although the 'enunciative voice' remains the same, the text is mainly focalized through Hélène, and the narrative summary has given way to what could be designated as a logically concatenated series of 'descriptive summaries':

Alors, évoquée par les pages du roman, sa propre existence se dressa. Elle se vit jeune fille, à Marseille, chez son père, le chapelier Mouret ... Elle vit aussi sa mère, toujours malade, qui la baisait de ses lèvres pâles, sans parler. Jamais elle n'avait aperçu un rayon de soleil dans sa chambre d'enfant ... Puis, c'était tout; jusqu'à son mariage, rien ne tranchait dans cette succession de jours semblables ... Elle avait seize ans, elle était un peu fière de cet amoureux, qu'elle savait d'une famille riche. Mais elle le trouvait laid, elle riait de lui souvent, et dormait des nuits paisibles dans l'ombre de la grande maison humide. Puis, on les avait mariés. Ce mariage l'étonnait encore ... Alors, une vie grise avait recommencé. Pendant douze ans, elle ne se souvenait pas d'une secousse. Elle était très calme et très heureuse, sans une fièvre de la chair ni du cœur, enfoncée dans les soucis quotidiens d'un ménage pauvre ... Rien de plus. Et elle vit brusquement la chambre de l'hôtel du Var, son mari mort, sa robe de veuve étalée sur une chaise. (848)

At a stylistic level, we are dealing with a form of narrating that by the use of the imperfect tense and a concentration of short descriptive sentences manages to convey a character's past through a series of moments in time. It would be tempting to state that narrations in the imperfect make up for 'imperfect narrations,' or for one of those instances where narration and description cannot be as clearly differentiated. In fact, should one in this context entertain the idea of description and narration as a pair of opposites, one would realize the impossibility of such a sharp distinction, since the above passage is both descriptive and narrative. Narration, however, in this case results not from a logical sequence of action verbs but from a sequence of short descriptions that, at a discourse level, allow us to infer a narration. In fact, the only perfective/narrative 'aspects' clearly indicated in this passage (besides the introductory 'sa propre existence se dressa') are marked by the three occurrences of the 'simple past' of *voir*: 'elle vit,' 'elle vit aussi,' and 'elle vit brusquement.' Just as Paris was presented as a sequence of moments in time, Hélène's past is presented to the reader in a similar form, although the descriptive material has been highly condensed, as in the following sentence: 'Et elle vit brusquement la chambre de l'hôtel du Var, son mari mort, sa robe de veuve étalée sur une chaise.' Here, our reading comprehension can easily make a narrative text out of descriptive segments as they are presented as 'kernels' in a sequence.

Given that many narrative segments in this chapter, such as the one we have just analysed, are constructed through a series of short descriptions, we may consider whether this aspect constitutes what Dällenbach designates as a *mise en abyme* of the code. In *Le Récit spéculaire*, referring to this type of *mise en abyme*, Dällenbach informs us that it aims at revealing the functioning of a series of textual structures and mechanisms *'mais sans pour autant mimer le texte qui s'y conforme'* (127), thus, such *mises en abyme* could also be designated as 'textual' or 'metatextual.'

In the case of this chapter, however, such a type of *mise en abyme* works according to a 'specular' effect, whereby the descriptive segments mirror the mechanisms of narration and vice versa. This might lead a more critical reader into a particular form of metatextual reflection, especially since this type of mirroring effect does not occur frequently in nineteenth-century realistic/naturalistic fiction.[11]

The allusions to impressionist painting may also be considered, in this context, as a particular form of *mise en abyme* of the code. As literary descriptions aim to be 'visualizable' as imaginary impressionistic paintings, we become aware of differences and similarities across media and codes. In fact, the knowledge of the impressionist pictorial code we might map onto this reading can only bring to the foreground the literariness of the chapter in question, setting it apart from chapters 1 to 4.

Another type of *mise en abyme* we may find in this chapter is the one Dällenbach designates as 'mise en abyme de l'énoncé,' that is, a *mise en abyme* pertaining to the fictional content.[12] In fact, the long descriptions of Paris do mirror Hélène's feelings and thoughts concerning her life. This, however, does not occur as a 'mimetic reproduction' of all the narrative 'kernels' in the plot summary previously given, but rather as a symbolic transposition: her emotional indifference turns to an almost euphoric enthusiasm, in the same way that the fog over Paris gives way to a shiny mist, and then to a bright sunny morning.

As we have seen, the three types of *mises en abyme* categorized by Dällenbach occur in this brief ten-page chapter. Moreover, direct references to a mirroring effect are sometimes clearly indicated in the text, as in the following passage: 'Il [Paris] était insondable et changeant comme un océan, candide le matin et incendié le soir, prenant les joies et les tristesses des cieux qu'il reflétait' (846).

A further noteworthy aspect of this chapter relates to the descriptive focalization. While in chapters 1 to 4 descriptions of space are mainly focalized through an external third-person narrator/descriptor, here they are focalized by both the external descriptor and Hélène. We are dealing, in fact, with a case of double focalization, since we cannot make sharp distinctions between what has been focalized through Hélène and through a third-person descriptor. Even the text of this chapter reflects this. Never does Hélène make any allusions to Impressionism. The mere fact that she is reading a romantic novel does not justify her seeing Paris as a set of impressionist paintings. Moreover, the long description of Paris refers to well-known landmarks – 'les Champs Élysées,' 'le Palais de l'Industrie,' 'la Madeleine,' 'l'Opéra,' 'la tour Saint-Jacques,' 'les pavillons du nouveau Louvre et des Tuilleries.' However, when near the end of the chapter, Jeanne points through the window, asking her mother the names of some important buildings, Hélène does not know their names. The third-person narrator/descriptor mentions then: 'Elles ne savaient rien de Paris, en effet. Depuis dix-huit mois qu'elles l'avaient sous les yeux à toute heure, elles n'en connaissaient pas une pierre' (854). This clear indication of double focalization leads us to the conclusion of chapter 5, where, as if challenging realistic modes of representation, Hélène's romantic reading material imposes itself over direct observation: 'Les yeux de nouveau levés et perdus, Hélène rêvait profondément. Elle était lady Rowena, elle aimait avec la paix et la profondeur d'une âme noble. Cette matinée de printemps, cette grande ville si douce, ces premières giroflées qui lui parfumaient les genoux, avaient peu à peu fondu son coeur' (855).

Having examined the descriptive characteristics of this chapter and the types of *mise en abyme* that occur in it, we can proceed to a third level of analysis, the functional level, to answer the following questions: Can chapter 5 be considered as a *mise en abyme* of the previous four chapters, and if so, what is its function? To what extent can a predominantly descriptive chapter constitute a *mise en abyme* of previous fictional material where narration (albeit through dialogue) stands for the main 'narrative mode'?

This chapter in fact presents, according to Dällenbach's tripartition of types, a 'mise en abyme de l'énoncé,' that is, the most common type of *mise en abyme* pertaining to the content of fictional information. Referring to this particular type under the heading of 'mises en abyme fictionnelles,' Dällenbach lists the following characteristics:

Les mises en abyme fictionnelles semblent pouvoir, comme les synecdoques, se départager en deux groupes: *particularisantes (modèles réduits)*, elles compriment et restreignent la signification de la fiction; *généralisantes (transpositions)*, elles font subir au contexte une expansion sémantique dont celui-ci n'eût pas été capable par lui-même. Rachetant leur infériorité de taille par leur pouvoir d'investir des sens, ces dernières nous placent en effet devant ce paradoxe: micro-cosmes de la fiction, elles se surimposent, sémantiquement, au macro-cosme qui les contient, le débordent et, d'une certaine manière, finissent par l'englober à son tour. (1977, 81)

Chapter 5 does serve as a 'generalizing synecdoche,' since its function is not to restrict previous meanings or to make them less ambiguous. Quite the contrary. While in the previous chapters the reader is given straightforward narrative information, in chapter 5 he/she is confronted with a highly metaphoric text where narration ceases to be a clearly stated logical sequence of events and becomes a series of descriptive 'tableaux.' It is by linking these descriptive segments that the reader can infer both Hélène's biography and her thoughts about the events that take place in part 1. Because, in this case, the reader can always use his/her knowledge of chapters 1 to 4 to fill in the 'gaps' or the ellipses between descriptive segments, he/she becomes – more than in the previous chapters – a producer of meanings. Furthermore, since in this chapter, which condenses the information of the previous ones, there occurs a clear shift from conventional modes of realistic representation – landscapes being described in terms of imaginary paintings – the text, and consequently its reading, becomes less 'mimetic,' and more 'poetic,' that is, more highly focused on the qualities of language and style. Thus, the function of this chapter is basically to create, through an effect of retrospective *mise en abyme*, an instance where the reader is solicited to *reconsider* previous information while focusing on a series of stylistic and discursive characteristics, namely, on the references to Walter Scott's romantic love story, which function as a metafictional device.

On the other hand, even though the chapter is predominantly descriptive, it can, nevertheless, function as a *mise en abyme* of narration; many of its descriptive segments allow us to infer an implied narration, and the long description of Paris invites us to read, at a more symbolic level, a series of previous events.

Since the organizational structure of part 1 is replicated in the other four parts I shall proceed now to examine how the mechanisms discussed function in parts 2 to 5. Many aspects of my interpretation will become clearer as I proceed from a micro- to a macro-level of analysis.

2. THE NOVEL INSIDE THE NOVEL

In chapters 1 to 4 of part 2, the priest, l'abbé Jouve, tries to persuade Hélène to marry his brother, Mr Rambaud. Hélène is not enthusiastic about the idea since she does not love him. Besides, her daughter, Jeanne, is violently opposed to her mother getting married. One day, when Hélène is at the Deberles' house, Jeanne discloses Jouve's marriage plans in front of Henri Deberle. The doctor is disturbed by the news. During a children's masked ball at his house, he declares his love to Hélène. In a confused emotional state after the doctor's declaration, Hélène leaves the party so as not to reveal her feelings, and takes refuge in her apartment.

Chapter 5 of part 2, as of part 1, starts as Hélène opens a window: 'En haut, dans sa chambre, dans cette douceur cloîtrée qu'elle retouvait, Hélène se sentit étouffer ... Alors, violemment, elle ouvrit une fenêtre, elle s'accouda en face de Paris' (902).

Although this chapter is more narrative than chapter 5 of part 1, with a third-person narrator's account of Hélène's emotional state and a long dialogue in which Jeanne tells her mother about some of the events at the ball, many of the structures already analysed in the previous chapters occur once more. This time, in a state of shock and surprise, Hélène covers her eyes with her hands, refusing to see the landscape, only to be confronted by mental images: 'Bientôt, elle oublia tout. La scène de l'aveu, malgré elle, renaissait. Sur le fond d'un noir d'encre, Henri apparaissait avec une netteté singulière, si vivant, qu'elle distinguait les petits battements nerveux de ses lèvres. Il s'approchait, il se penchait ... Puis, lorsque d'un suprême effort elle avait chassé la vision, elle la voyait se reformer plus lointaine, lentement grossie' (903).

In such a case, we have, no doubt, a concatenation of action verbs: 'Henri apparaissait ... Il s'approchait, il se penchait.' However, this narrative segment is rendered more like description since the verbs are conjugated in the imperfect tense, and since the actions are being imagined by Hélène, who sees them as fixed images deformed by her emotions.

The description of Paris, on the other hand, starts at the moment when Hélène is still closing her eyes; first as a set of non-visual sensations, and then as a memory evoking elements previously mentioned in chapter 5 of part 1: 'Les bruits, les odeurs, jusqu'à la clarté lui battaient le visage, malgré ses mains nerveusement serrées. Par moments, de brusques lueurs semblaient percer ses paupières closes; et, dans ces lueurs, elle croyait voir les monuments, les flèches et les dômes se détacher sur le jour diffus du rêve' (904).

In this chapter Paris is depicted as a series of 'tableaux,' ranging from a late afternoon, described in neutral tones, to a sunset that mirrors, more than any other segment of the long description, Hélène's feelings of passion once she accepts that she returns Henri's love :

Aujourd'hui, elle était à la même place, mais la passion victorieuse la dévorait, tandis que, devant elle, un soleil couchant incendiait la ville ... Une gloire enflamma l'azur. Au fond de l'horizon, l'écroulement de roches crayeuses qui barraient les lointains de Charenton et de Choisy-le-Roi, entassa des blocs de carmin bordés de laque vive; la flotille de petites nuées nageant lentement dans le bleu, au-dessus de Paris, se couvrit de voiles de pourpre; tandis que le mince réseau, le filet de soie blanche tendu au-dessus de Montmartre, parut tout d'un coup fait d'une ganse d'or, dont les mailles régulières allaient prendre les étoiles à leur lever. Et, sous cette voûte embrasée, la ville toute jaune, rayée de grandes ombres s'étendait ... A droite, à gauche les monuments flambaient. Les verrières du Palais de l'Industrie, au milieu des futaies des Champs-Élysées, étalaient un lit de tisons ardents ... Le dôme des Invalides était en feu, si étincelant qu'on pouvait craindre à chaque minute de le voir s'effondrer, en couvrant le quartier des flammèches de sa charpente ... Alors, Paris entier, à mesure que le soleil baissait, s'alluma aux bûchers des monuments ... Bientôt ce fut une fournaise. Paris brûla. Le ciel s'était empourpré davantage, les nuages saignaient au-dessus de l'imense cité rouge et or. (907–9)

If we compare the descriptive segments above with the description of Paris previously analysed, we realize that although in this case we no longer have clearly marked references to impressionist painting, we are, none the less, dealing with a similar metaphorical process and with analogous descriptive characteristics.

At a stylistic level we can discern a large number of action verbs, conjugated in the imperfect tense, and as in part 1, used in a metaphorical sense. The iterative 'aspect' of these imperfects can also be verified in other non-tensed verb forms such as the present participle 'nageant' and the gerund 'en couvrant.' There are also in this description a number of action verbs conjugated in the 'simple past' (for example, *enflammer, entasser, allumer, brûler*); in this case, however, their perfective/punctual 'aspect,' so characteristic of narrative segments, has been toned down or altogether neutralized by the use of a reflexive conjugation ('se couvrit,' 's'alluma'), which lends them an iterative 'aspect' and by their being used in a metaphorical sense. In fact, the only verb in the simple past that is not used metaphorically is the verb *paraître*, as in 'Montmartre, parut tout d'un coup fait d'une ganse d'or'; nevertheless, this verb, which indicates perception, is not an action verb.

At a discursive level many of the segments are linked not only by spatial expressions, typical of a descriptive orientation ('au fond de,' 'à droite, à gauche'), but also by temporal expressions such as 'aujourd'hui,' 'alors,' and 'bientôt.' Although the latter serve to organize the descriptive elements into a temporal sequence, the narrative-like effect of this description results mainly from the way the three main 'semantic isotopies' – 'sunset,' 'fire,' and 'passion' – are entwined into a metaphorical process.

At a functional level, too, the description of Paris contributes once more to create a *mise en abyme* of Hélène's thoughts and feelings, and the whole chapter synthesizes the most important narrative aspects of part 2, constituting, therefore, a *mise en abyme* of a previous fictional content. We can also, at this stage, correlate this chapter 5 with the one in part 1. Although both chapters can be seen as forming distinct units, they are not entirely autonomous, since they are related to each other not only by their theme and structures but also by relations of sequentiality. Chapter 5 in part 2 is a continuation of chapter 5 in part 1, and both constitute a generic *mise en abyme* of what becomes, therefore, the most emphasized narrative contents so far in the novel – the development, from its inception, of Hélène's passion for Henri. Furthermore, if we examine the long descriptions of Paris in both parts of the novel, we notice that, while in part 1 Paris is described from an early dawn to a late morning, in part 2 the description (although later in the year) ranges from late afternoon to sunset and early evening. As we shall see, chapter 5 of part 3 includes a description of Paris at night.

In chapters 1 to 4 of part 3, Hélène gets involved in the religious celebrations of the 'month of Mary' as an escape from the passion she continues to repress. She continues to meet Henri in public, but most of the time she tries to avoid him. Meanwhile, her daughter, Jeanne, becomes very ill. One night, when the doctor saves Jeanne once again from certain death, Hélène declares her love for him. Henri starts to visit Hélène almost every day, but when Jeanne becomes aware of her mother's feelings towards the doctor, the child tries to avoid him by getting sick each time Henri comes to inquire about her health. Jeanne, nevertheless, slowly recuperates from her illness.

Chapter 5 of part 3 begins as Hélène once again opens the window of her apartment: 'La nuit tombait. Du ciel pâli, où brillaient les premières étoiles, une cendre fine semblait pleuvoir sur la grande ville, qu'elle ensevelissait lentement, sans relâche ... Hélène, manquant d'air, souffrant de ces dernières chaleurs de septembre, venait d'ouvrir la fenêtre toute grande, soulagée par cette mer d'ombre, cette immensité noire qui s'étendait devant elle' (964). The chapter differs slightly from those we have analysed so far, since here Hélène is not alone while contemplating a view of Paris but engaged in a conversation with 'l'abbé Jouve,' who, again, tries to persuade her to marry his brother. None the less, the description of Paris still reflects Hélène's feelings of sadness, while the chapter as a whole condenses the most important plot developments of part 3.

The segment describing Paris at dusk, before the lights go on, is of particular interest because here description does not rely on vision but on other forms of perception:

C'était l'Océan, la nuit, avec son élargie au fond des ténèbres, un abîme d'obscurité où l'on devinait un monde. Un souffle énorme et doux venait de la ville invisible. Dans la voix prolongée qui ronflait, des sons montaient encore, affaiblis et distincts, un brusque roulement d'omnibus sur le quai, le sifflement d'un train traversant le pont du Point-du-Jour; et la Seine, grossie par les derniers orages, passait très large avec la respiration forte d'un être vivant, allongé tout en bas, dans un pli d'ombre. Une odeur chaude fumait des toits encore brûlants, tandis que la rivière, dans cette exhalation lente des ardeurs de la journée, mettait de petites haleines fraîches. (965)

Contrary to other descriptions in this novel, elements such as 'la ville,' 'omnibus sur le quai,' 'un train,' and 'la Seine' are perceived as invisible presences communicated through the senses of touch, hearing, and smell. However, after the long description of Paris at night, which is marked by the metaphorical process resulting from the overlapping of two main semantic isotopies – sadness and vastness – the landscape changes to reflect better Hélène's feelings of passion for Henri:

Cependant, sur Paris allumé, une nuée lumineuse montait. On eût dit l'haleine rouge d'un brasier. D'abord, ce ne fut qu'une pâleur dans la nuit, un reflet à peine sensible. Puis, peu à peu, à mesure que la soirée s'avançait, elle devenait saignante; et, suspendue en l'air, immobile au-dessus de la cité, faite de toutes les flammes et de toute la vie grondante qui s'exhalaient d'elle, elle était comme un de ces nuages de foudre et d'incendie qui couronnent la bouche des volcans. (974)

At a symbolic level, one can correlate this segment with previous descriptions. While elements such as 'nuée lumineuse,' 'pâleur dans la nuit,' and 'reflet à peine sensible' evoke the first description of Paris and, therefore, the beginning of Hélène's passion for Henri, elements such as 'haleine rouge d'un brasier,' 'soirée saignante,' 'nuages de foudre et d'incendie,' and 'volcans' evoke the second one in chapter 5, part 2, reasserting Hélène's feelings towards Henri. Thus, the description in part 3, which already functions as a *mise en abyme* of previous fictional contents, also functions as a *mise en abyme* of previous *mises en abyme*. This process, while emphasizing a series of fictional characteristics, also draws our attention to the code – in this case, to the potentialities of description as a 'fictional mode,' able to synthesize, reflect, and produce narration, given the reader's overall knowledge of the previous chapters and parts.

In chapters 1 to 4 of part 4 Hélène discovers that Juliette Deberle is meeting a lover, Malignon, in an apartment he has rented especially for the occasion. Shocked by her discovery, Hélène writes an anonymous letter to Henri, telling him about the secret meeting. However, on the very day Madame Deberle is to meet her lover, Hélène, who fears a violent confrontation, goes to Malignon's apartment to tell Juliette that her husband is on the way there. Malignon and Juliette leave, but Hélène stays in the apartment, waiting for Henri. Ironically, the 'love nest' Malignon had prepared to receive Madame Deberle becomes the place where Hélène and Henri make love for the first time.

Besides this almost farcical plot, which is not mirrored in any way in chapter 5, chapters 1 to 4 of part 3 also focus on Jeanne and on the development of her illness. As a character, Jeanne has functioned as an extension of her mother, a fact that may explain a shift in descriptive focalization. In fact, chapter 5's long description of Paris is focalized mainly through Jeanne; the city is described as if it were a child's drawing, able to reflect her thoughts and feelings: 'Vers la droite, un arc-en-ciel s'allumait. A mesure que le rayon s'élargissait, des hachures roses et bleues peinturluraient l'horizon, d'un bariolage d'aquarelle enfantine. Il y eut un flamboiement, une tombée de neige d'or sur la ville de cristal.

Et le rayon s'éteignit, un nuage avait roulé, le sourire se noyait dans les larmes, Paris s'égouttait avec un long bruit de sanglots, sous le ciel couleur de plomb' (1029).

None the less, unlike the mainly descriptive chapters in parts 1 to 3, this one cannot be read as a retrospective *mise en abyme* of the most important plot moments of part 4. In fact, this chapter functions as a prospective *mise en abyme*, the gloomy tone of many of its descriptive passages foreshadowing Jeanne's death: 'Un jour bas et louche entrait par les fenêtres. Des nuées couleur de suie passaient, qui assombrissaient encore le ciel' (1024), and '[Paris] semblait dépeuplé, pareil à ces villes de cauchemar que l'on aperçoit dans un reflet d'astre mort' (1025). Besides indicating future plot developments, this chapter has three further functions: it is a *mise en abyme* of the code that has been consistently used in the descriptive chapters of parts 1 to 3; a micro-contextual *mise en abyme* of Jeanne's feelings of abandonment and loneliness; and a means of portraying Jeanne not just as an 'actant' (or as a set of descriptive traits), but also as a perceiving consciousness, which, in this case, happens to function very much as a means of stressing her mother's most conformist characteristics.

More than in the previous chapters, we become aware in this description of a type of effacement of the Parisian landscape that seems to point towards a narrative conclusion: 'A travers les vitres, couvertes d'une légère buée, on apercevait un Paris brouillé, effacé dans une vapeur d'eau, avec des lointains perdus dans de grandes fumées' (1024), 'alors, l'immense cité, comme détruite et morte à la suite d'une suprême convulsion, étendit son champ de pierres renversées, sous l'effacement du ciel' (1032–3); 'et c'était, derrière le cristal rayé de ce déluge, un Paris fantôme, aux lignes tremblantes, qui paraissait se dissoudre' (1033). And in the last sentences of the chapter, while Jeanne lies feverish in front of an open window, Paris is described (for the last time through a window) as a landscape that has lost its clear shapes: 'A l'horizon, Paris s'était évanoui comme une ombre de ville, le ciel se confondait dans le chaos brouillé de l'étendue, la pluie grise tombait toujours, entêtée' (1034).

In chapters 1 to 4 of part 5, Hélène continues to see Henri Deberle. Her daughter, however, becomes very ill and dies, looking through the window at the Parisian landscape described in chapter 5 of parts 1 to 4, which have functioned as *mises en abyme*.

Chapter 5 of part 5 begins as Hélène, now married to Mr Rambaud, a man she does not love, and living in Marseille, visits her daughter's grave in Paris two years after the events of parts 1 to 4. Contrary to the other four mainly descriptive chapters, Paris is viewed not from Hélène's apartment window but from the cemetery at Passy. It is a description of a frozen landscape that both accounts for Hélène's emotional state and symbolizes the loss of her passion and her love for Henri:

Au pied du Trocadéro, la ville couleur de plomb semblait morte, sous la tombée lente des derniers brins de neige. C'était, dans l'air devenu immobile, une moucheture pâle sur les fonds sombres, filant avec un balancement insensible et continu ... Les flocons paraissaient ralentir leur vol, à l'approche des toitures; ils se posaient un à un, sans cesse, par millions, avec tant de silence, que les fleurs qui s'effeuillent font plus de bruit; et un oubli de la terre et de la vie, une paix souveraine venait de cette multitude en mouvement, dont on n'entendait pas la marche dans l'espace ... Peu à peu, les îlots éclatants des maisons se détachaient, la ville apparaissait à vol d'oiseau, coupée de ses rues et de ses places, dont les tranchées et les trous d'ombres dessinaient l'ossature géante des quartiers (1083–4)

The city is depicted here as if caught in a motionless movement, when the falling of the snow is characterized by its immense silence. 'La ville ... semblait morte,' 'les fleurs qui s'effeuillent,' 'les trous d'ombres,' and 'ossatures' can be read as referring both to Jeanne's death and to the conclusion of Hélène's love story. In fact, the same mood can be found in the description of Hélène: 'Le sang dormait sous la pâleur reposée des joues, on la sentait rentrée dans la hauteur de son honnêteté. Deux larmes avait roulé de ses paupières, son calme était fait de sa douleur ancienne' (1084).

As the weather changes and blue tones replace grey ones, Hélène, deep in her thoughts, evokes through a series of flashbacks her present life in Marseille and some of the moments she spent with Henri. The landscape, however, regains its dysphoric connotations, stressing once more the sad ending of her love story: 'Maintenant, les mouchetures volantes ne donnaient plus à la ville ce grand frisson, dont les ondes pâles tremblaient sur les façades couleur de rouille. Les maisons sortaient toutes noires des masses blanches où elles dormaient, comme moisies par des siècles d'humidité' (1088) and 'Pas une voix ne montait. Des rues se devinaient à des fentes grises, des carrefours semblaient s'être creusés dans un craquement. Par files entières, les maisons avaient disparu. Seules, les façades voisines étaient reconnaissables aux mille raies de leurs fenêtres' (1091).

In this chapter, Paris is once again not only personified but also constructed as a space able to reflect both the character's feelings and actions: 'Paris était pour elle plein de son passé. C'était avec lui qu'elle avait aimé, avec lui que Jeanne était morte' (1092). The novel ends with a reference to the same general view of Paris: 'Le cimetière était vide, il n'y avait plus que leurs pas sur la neige. Jeanne, morte, restait seule en face de Paris, à jamais' (1092).

The five chapters I have just analysed constitute not only a series of specific *mises en abyme* but also what can be designated as 'a novel inside a novel.' This is made clear in the overall economy of the novel, with the five chapters organized in a sequential order, and linked by a common theme and by a similar function. It is as if the narrative and descriptive voices were presenting us with two versions of the same fictional material: a 'naturalistic' one – comprising chapters 1 to 4 of each part – that develops a story through a main plot and its subplots (Novel 1 or N1); and a 'poetic' version (N2), whereby the main contents and structures of N1 are mirrored, condensed, and semantically expanded. The semantic expansion results, as mentioned above, from the shift that takes place at both a writing and a reading level. In fact, information that is clearly or unambiguously presented in N1, and therefore does not require a complex decoding on the part of the reader, is in N2 transposed or rewritten in such a way as to invite the reader both to expand on previous knowledge through complex mirroring effects, and to question the apparent transparency of the fictional discourse of N1.

According to Mieke Bal in 'Mise en abyme et iconicité' (1971), 'la mise en abyme doit former un tout isolable, constituant une interruption, ou, pour le moins, un changement dans le récit' (124). Dällenbach confirms this opinion in 'L'Oeuvre dans l'oeuvre chez Zola' (1978): 'Simplifiant la complexité de l'original, la réplique fictionnelle convertit le temps en espace, transforme la successivité en contemporanéité et, par là-même, accroît notre pouvoir de *com-prendre*' (130–1).

In the case of *Une Page d'amour*, however, there is no real interruption, at least at a semantic level, but rather a shift, whereby foregrounded linear narration gives way to chapters where descriptive segments that are *mises en abyme* of a previous narrative content become the foregrounded fictional material through which narration can be inferred, reviewed, and expanded. In the descriptive chapters we no longer read in terms of a logical sequence of actions; the reading becomes more 'spatialized,' with the descriptive segments either announcing future developments or inviting us to make specific retrospective connections at a symbolic, iconic, and/or metaphorical level. It is as if our normal patterns for reading a realistic novel had to take into account the type of reading required, for example, by a lyrical poem.

Concerning the *mise en abyme* in general, however, I do not agree with Dällenbach that 'sa propriété essentielle consiste à faire saillir l'intelligibilité et la structure formelle de l'oeuvre' (1977, 16). In *Une Page d'amour* quite the contrary occurs, since the function of the *mises en abyme* is not to restrict or clarify a previous meaning, but rather to expand it through a particular type of metaphorical condensation, sabotaging at times the very structures it highlights.

In 'L'Oeuvre dans l'oeuvre chez Zola' (1978), Dällenbach states, in fact, that this type of *mise en abyme* does not occur in Zola's works: the 'mise en abyme [qui] se préoccupe moins de réduire l'opacité ou la complexité du message que de se muer en *embrayeur d'isotopie* et d'oeuvrer ainsi à la pluralisation du sens.' Justifying his opinion, he continues: '1) la mise en abyme zolienne est toujours le lieu *du* sens et de la lisibilité normative; 2) ce sens est trop totalitaire pour se laisser contester par une seconde isotopie,' and he concludes: 'hanté qu'il est par la transparence, le roman Zolien se veut résolument monosémique – d'où la nette préférence qu'il marque pour les mises en abyme aptes à restreindre le pluriel du texte: les modèles réduits' (131–2).

Such opinions, which the present novel seems to contradict, can probably be explained by the fact that Dällenbach examines *mises en abyme* solely at a restricted micro-level, using a corpus of Zola's novels that does not include *Une Page d'amour*, or, for that matter, novels such as *Thérèse Raquin* (1867) or *La Bête humaine* (1890), which reveal similar types of non-restrictive *mises en abyme* operating mainly through a series of descriptive segments. In a later essay, 'Reflexivity and Reading' (1986), however, Dällenbach is quick to point out that '*mise en abyme* permits us to fill in "blanks" when abundant, [and] form them when scarce' (19). *Une Page d'amour* is, no doubt, a good example of a work where *mise en abyme* creates a higher level of indeterminacy in a text that otherwise would be almost totally unambiguous. It is precisely these indeterminacies that contribute to an increased participation on the part of the reader, and, consequently, to the reader's enjoyment of this particular work by Zola.

The five chapters that form what I have designated as a second version of *Une Page d'amour* (N2), can, to a certain extent, be considered as a predominantly descriptive novel relying not only upon the long descriptions of Paris (which even at a micro-level mirror the inner feelings of Hélène and her daughter), but also upon a series of plot summaries that, at times, use description as the fictional material through which narration can be inferred.

Given the presence of such summaries, and of all the other descriptions of space(s) and character(s) inside and across each of the five chapters, one could speculate that, in fact, N2 *per se* constitutes a novel, the 'experimental' qualities of which can be viewed as precursive of the French New Novel as far as its use of description is concerned.

As Zola himself pointed out in 'De la description,' description does become, in this case, 'un état du milieu qui détermine et complète l'homme' (232). Furthermore, a given view of Paris becomes both an extension of the characters themselves, and, through an almost constant effect of personification, a specific character.

In this case, description is no longer a mere backgrounded 'effet de réel,' ornament, or 'discursive filler,' but the mirror upon which we can see the very inner motor of narration: single frames or slow-motion segments the reader can activate into narrative meaning.

3

Readings of visual images and postcard descriptions in Claude Simon's *Histoire*

> Si la description est impuissante à reproduire les choses et dit toujours
> d'autres objets que les objets que nous percevons autour de nous, les mots
> possèdent par contre ce prodigieux pouvoir de rapprocher et de confronter
> ce qui, sans eux, resterait épars.
>
> Claude Simon[1]

Claude Simon's *Histoire* (1967)[2] is a novel in which the reader feels constantly in the presence of a consciousness generating a text through evocative memory processes. These are both scattered and centred by a range of visual images – postcards, stamps, banknotes, paintings, photographs[3] – that function as modes of suspending a narrative continuum through the introduction of long and detailed descriptions. Thus, memory presents itself as a series of narrative/descriptive segments superimposed upon or juxtaposed against the perceptions of a narrativized present.

The effect is one of 'discohesion' or fragmentation, a type of discourse formed as a shifting mosaic of textual segments with no obvious connection. Through this process, a backgrounded 'narrative present' joining the inscribing of past events, visual images, and other texts,[4] slides along metonymical forms of association that deny Euclidean notions of space and, subsequently, linear story time. In fact, in this novel, as in many of Simon's fictional works, the possible linkages between narrative and descriptive segments do not obey referential forms of discourse coherence, but rather modes of sequencing that are mainly based on paronomastic, semantic, and even morphological similarities. In his preface to *Orion aveugle* (1970) Simon writes: 'Chaque mot en suscite (ou en commande) plusieurs autres, non seulement par la force des images qu'il attire à lui comme un aimant, mais parfois aussi par la seule morphologie, de simples assonances qui, de même que les nécessités formelles de la syntaxe, du rhythme et de la composition, se révèlent souvent aussi fécondes que ses multiples significations.'[5]

In this instance, we become aware of a type of fictional production that, by not relying upon realistic modes of representation for its development, is evocative of the Freudian notion of displacement. This is to say that cross-segmental linkages are established not merely in terms of a general overall semantic coherence, but mainly through discrete features such as rhythm, rhyme, and assonance. Therefore, in *Histoire*, the contiguity established between segments no longer illustrates a connected linearity, but rather the constant shifts operating at the level of a narrator's desire[6] – in this case, an attempt not only to capture or (re)interpret the past, but above all to suspend it by inscribing it forever as text: story and History.

One of the most obvious features in *Histoire* is the narrator's interest in visual material alluded to or described in great detail in all twelve chapters/parts of the novel,[7] particularly the postcards – for which the reader is given not only a transcription of their written text and their respective titles, but also an account of both the illustrated images and of the stamps used on them. The postcards seem to organize, if not mirror, the structure of the novel. As 'framed images' (since they are in this case presented as discrete units) they correlate not only with other descriptive segments in the novel – the house, the garden, the bank – but also with such narrative elements as the narrator's relationship with Hélène, the Spanish Civil War, and De Reixach's death.

The narrative segments are equally 'framed,' since they do not entertain a direct sequential relationship with previous or subsequent textual units. It is noteworthy that one of the narrative voices in *Histoire* points to the way the construction of the novel emphasizes its visual motivation: '(comme dans ces vieux films usés, coupés et raccordés au petit bonheur et dont des tronçons entiers ont été perdus ... usure ciseaux et colle se substituant à la fastidieuse narration du metteur en scène pour restituer à l'action sa foudroyante discontinuité)' (41).

Thus, both narrative and descriptive segments acquire a similar textual status and significance, and their distinctive traits and functions, so obvious in realistic prose fiction, become blurred in the larger context of the entire novel.

Besides determining a structural organization, the postcards, which exist or have existed as elements preceding the writing of *Histoire* (Ricardou 1973, 183; Dällenbach 1988, 107), also pose relevant questions concerning their status as referents in prose fiction. In *Reflections in the Mind's Eye*, Brian T. Fitch devotes an entire chapter to the problematic of the referent in Simon's *Histoire*.[8] According to Fitch, the fact that the postcards are artistic referents preceding the writing of their detailed descriptions is sufficient to determine a very particular mode of reading reception. As far as our present discussion is concerned, if the postcards are the referents of a series of descriptions, as Fitch claims, it is important to stress that they are not faithful copies of reality but carefully planned artistic objects. In fact, even the most instantaneous snapshots reveal the choice of an obligatory single perspective, if not a choice of certain angles of light to provide a particular luminous focus. The descriptor/ narrator, or the 'enunciative voice,'[9] in the description of the postcards, which are mainly photographs, representational paintings, or illustrations,[10] is aware of this, indeed mentioning their deliberate effects and stereotypical qualities: 'photographies de prostituées travesties en documents ethnographiques' or 'paysages radieux, touristiques ou consacrés' (28).[11] The fictional quality of the postcards, particularly those sent by Henri to one who seems to be the narrator's mother, is at times further emphasized by an effect of *mise en abyme*. For example, one of the Egyptian postcards entitled *Arabian Girl* (described at length 200–1), is presented to the reader as a scene in Verdi's *Aida*:

... lorsque le rideau de pourpre peint en trompe-l'oeil s'élève et qu'elle apparaît porteuse d'eau dans le décor stéréotypé de palmiers poussiéreux sur l'azur poussiéreux de la toile de fond ... tandis que l'orchestre attaque le prélude Aïda ou peut-être Aïcha, femme à la vulve cousue au corps de léopard couchée depuis des millénaires dans les sables et ornant les timbres roses safran ou vert Nil ARABIAN GIRL, Lichtenstern et Harari. Cairo No 177, et alors faisant un pas en avant, se détachant du puits s'avançant dans le tintenement de ses lourds bracelets rejetant en arrière son voile vert et commençant à chanter. (56–7)

In this case, as I shall later explain, a series of 'visual lexias' motivates a range of culturally informed patterns of association. These are conveyed to us in terms of an 'Arabian Girl' whose photographic pose evokes both the music and the choreographed gestural language of an opera character.

Even though the postcards can be considered as fictionalized images of a historical period, 'La Belle époque,' they constitute nevertheless the referents of a series of descriptions, that is, visual representations that are transposed,[12] or 'transcoded' (to use Fitch's terminology) from the pictographic into the written medium.

The descriptions in *Histoire*, however, are not mere mimetic or scientific accounts of those images, but rather the process by which the latter may be read and incorporated into fiction as a reported reading. As images, they function, according to Simon, as a 'pre-text,'[13] as generators not only of descriptive segments but of narration. Therefore, each descriptive/narrative segment created through the pictographic referents shows us a mode of describing that is intimately connected to a type of pictographic reading.[14] As Claude DuVerlie states in 'Pictures for Writing: Premises for a Graphopictology' (1981): 'the reader is indeed invited to make numerous observations and rapprochements between visual images and their intellection in a system of words and between the "writing" (écriture) of a painting and of a text' (203).

Having recognized these characteristics, we seek answers to two interrelated questions: How does the 'enunciative voice,' which in the case of *Histoire* is mainly a descriptive one, transpose through written text a series of represented visual images? How does the internal organization of descriptive segments/blocks come to be linked, in this case, to a particular type of visual reading?

Through the proposed interpretations I shall also try to unravel the complex entanglement whereby a *given actuality* (A) is worked into a form of *pictographic representation* (B), which, while undergoing a specific *pictographic reading* (C), becomes a means of encoding a *given description* (D). We must, therefore, read across fictional processes, what leads us from D into an implied and at times 'visualizable' C and B.

The postcards whose descriptions and reported readings I analyse as examples have been chosen according to the following criteria: first, similarity of medium (photographs, representational paintings, illustrations), and second, differences in pictographic readings (for example, more sequential versus more erratic) and, consequently, differences resulting from more cohesive to more 'discohesive' types of discursive organization. Narratological concepts such as 'description' and 'narration' are also taken into account as I propose how certain descriptions become narrativized through the use of certain devices. However, given that the reader of *Histoire* can, in the novel, access in the text a type of pictographic reading, I proceed by establishing a series of parallels across media.

1. READING REPRESENTATIONAL PAINTINGS/PHOTOGRAPHS AND LITERARY DESCRIPTIONS

Representational paintings or 'carefully planned photographs,' as opposed to literary description in prose fiction, do not solicit identical reading activities.[15] Unlike descriptions in literature, a painting/photograph can generally be apprehended by a single gaze, which coincides, to a certain extent, with its mental representation. On the other hand, the mental image or representation evoked by a given literary description (even when the latter strives for an effect of *ekphrasis*, that is, aims at being visualized), is always an after-product – something at which we arrive after having read all its constitutive elements, or after a series of more erratic non-sequential readings. In fact, it is only through these subsequent readings that both paintings/photographs and literary descriptions come to share similar reading processes, even though the visual image is always a reader's construct in the case of literature.

Reading paintings/photographs presupposes, none the less, other activities beyond the initial gaze through which we apprehend them as a totality of simultaneously present elements.[16] As a pictographic text, a painting/photograph can be read in terms of lexias. These can be defined as minimal reading units formed by chains of pictographic signs one generally associates in terms of geometric shape and/or colour.[17] However, unlike literary lexias, pictographic lexias are far more difficult to isolate in terms of sequences of elements, since they do not rely on the syntagmatic arrangement inherent to written language as it is generally presented in a prose fiction text.[18] In *Études sémiologiques: Écritures, peintures*, Louis Marin describes the quasi-arbitrariness that reading a painting in terms of lexias presupposes: 'De plus et c'est là un point essentiel, ce circuit du regard sur la surface plastique est dans le lieu du tableau, un circuit aléatoire: il n'est jamais nécessaire ... En effet, la relative liberté de parcours en impliquant hésitations, retours, différences, n'engage jamais le regard dans un mouvement linéaire irréversible. Le temps de lecture se spatialise par là même, s'étale ou rayonne autour de points stratégiques du tableau' (22). What Marin designates as 'strategic points' translates into the immediate constraints imposed by the internal arrangement of visual signs (Shefer 1969, 189; Marin, 21). These shape an initial perception and trigger possible reading alternatives. For example, bright elements on a dark surface tend to provoke readings based on that very contrast; in the same way, we also tend to associate elements that have similar geometric shapes. Such constraints are particularly obvious in representational painting/photography (for example, the constraints imposed by all the characteristics that determine a mode of presentation, perspective, and point of view).[19] Thus, while in a literary description we tend to make a series of associations based on sound and/or meaning, as they are conveyed through a discursive mode of organization, in a visual aesthetic text the associations are generally determined by a series of 'morphological' similarities.

In literary descriptions, however, the encoded constraints that organize our reading are far less fluid, since we are dealing with a sequential mode of graphic display. Concerning its mode of presentation, a description in prose fiction is presented either as a textual block or as series of descriptive segments capable of being assembled by theme or 'discourse topic' into a single main unit.[20] In fact, no matter its length or mode of presentation, a literary description encodes primarily its type of reading reception through the relation that a number of lexias (or discrete micro-segments) entertain with its main theme.[21] Such micro-segments, when cohesively organized around a general 'discourse topic' – which can correspond to the descriptive title of a painting – give descriptions their inner coherence.

Length of detail for each described object plays, none the less, an important role in terms of coherence in the overall reading reception of each block. In fact, length of detail may provoke a number of shifting reading frames (or frames of reading reference), thus disturbing the apprehensions of each descriptive block as a unity. As I mentioned in chapter 1, at a micro-level of organization, literary descriptions are formed by a succession of discursive segments displayed in a hierarchical order (Hamon 1972, 1981). These function very much as a series of particularizing synecdoches, adding up to the presentation of a single whole. In the case of Simon's postcard descriptions in *Histoire*, this becomes all the more clear for the fact that the descriptor cannot transpose into written language the amount of detailed information existing in a photograph, painting, or illustration. However, as a descriptor, he can always join together through a set of particular choices, elements that in the postcard descriptions, for example, are not organized into clearly defined linguistic lexias. In this case, the description of the postcards results from both a particular choice of elements and a specific type of reading strategy.

Concerning the reading of aesthetic visual texts, Marin also mentions two levels of interpretation: one determined by the pictorial/visual lexias present in the text, and the other by elements *in absentia*, that is, all those extra-textual connections a more informed reader may establish – for example, historical and/or cultural characteristics. These two levels, which generally overlap, are clearly represented in Simon's postcard descriptions as they interact along a continuum where more objective and more subjective types of image reading seem to take place.

The existence of elements *in absentia* is also relevant as they may relate to the concept of *narrative painting/photograph*. This concept, which has been discussed since Lessing's *Laocoön, or On the Limits of Painting and Poetry* (first published in 1766),[22] is expanded by Wendy Steiner in *Pictures of Romance: Form against Context in Painting and Literature* (1988). She designates two specific types of painting: those that depict historical subjects or scenes for which the reader can easily infer a 'before' and 'after' based on a variety of cultural or historiographic texts *in absentia* (as in many of Poussin's paintings); and visual texts that depict events in a sequence, by the use of diptychs or triptychs, by a specific sequence of 'tableaux,' or by representing inside a single frame the same object at different moments in time (as in different stages in the life of a well-known character).[23]

In literary descriptions a similar concept applies. Although descriptions, in the same way as paintings, tend to be deprived of action(s) and are therefore non-narrative by nature, they can nevertheless 'tell stories' or be narrativized: 1) by allowing the reader to infer a before and after (for example, a description of Pompeii at the time of the Vesuvius eruption), or 2) by resorting to a series of discrete segments describing 'the same' at various instants in time. The latter technique is favoured by Robbe-Grillet in his fictional production, and is also used by Simon in a great variety of contexts and descriptions.

In *Histoire*, however, and specifically in the postcard descriptions, the notion of 'descriptive narrativity' becomes more complex, since we are dealing not only with its literary qualities but also with encoded types of pictographic readings. These are reported simultaneously, in the majority of cases, as a set of eye-scanning movements and as a type of reading interpretation caught inside a literary 'transposition.'

2. MOTIONLESS IMAGES AND DYNAMIC READINGS

If all the images in the postcards are, by their nature, motionless fixed instants, their descriptions have, nevertheless, a certain dynamism. This dynamism is accomplished, in the case of *Histoire*, each time the descriptor reads the image in terms of a series of micro-narrations, or whenever he expands on a series of actions presiding at the generation of the visual artistic referent. In the following pages I examine types of description whose movement stems not only from a close reading of the image in terms of visual lexias (as it often occurs in the case of photographs), but also from a reflection on the genesis of the image (mainly in postcards presented as readings of paintings).

If we consider the description 'Les Hautes-Pyrénées. SAHURRE' in a postcard sent by Angèle Lloveras, a housemaid, to the narrator's mother – the first postcard to be described at length in *Histoire* – we shall see that this description, although static in nature, narrates in a detailed manner the descriptor's own visual reading:

La carte représentant la rue d'un village montant en escalier entre des murs de pierres sèches une femme se tenant sur le seuil d'une maison la partie gauche du corps cachée par le montant vertical de la porte, regardant le photographe un poing sur la hanche un seau à ses pieds comme si elle venait juste de le poser et de se relever un chat blanc pelotonné contre la pierre du seuil une petite fille debout un peu plus bas au milieu de la rue vêtue d'un sarrau d'écolière qui lui tombe jusqu'au-dessous des genoux les deux mains jointes sur son bas-ventre les bras en corbeille penchant un peu la tête sur le côté et clignant légèrement des yeux dans le soleil, et immédiatement derrière les toits le flanc abrupt de la montagne s'élevant presque vertical sauvage rocheux et on peut entendre le silence le murmure continu de l'eau glacée qui coule descend le long du caniveau au milieu de la rue en se bousculant, il y a des bûches empilées sous un auvent contre le mur de droite on peut aussi sentir l'odeur du bois l'odeur jaune des bûches coupées montrant leurs tranches leur chair étoilée striée de veines concentriques jaune foncé jaune pâle alternées un peu de neige salie finissant de fondre au pied du tas de bois névé en miniature dessinant une série de pics irréguliers en dents de scie léchant les bûches exhalant l'odeur de violette le parfum glacé coupant de la neige. (21–2)

Here, the perception of the image must have been initially organized by the visual constraints imposed by 'la rue d'un village montant en escalier entre des murs de pierres sèches.' This global description, which sets the main theme of the written block, is then followed by the notation of a perspective focus: 'une femme ... regardant le photographe,' and by the visual syntagm (or lexia) evolving around that perspective, transcoded in the following linguistic terms: 'femme,' 'maison,' 'porte,' 'seau,' 'chat blanc,' 'pierre du seuil,' 'petite fille debout un peu plus bas au milieu de la rue.' This initial syntagm, accounting for part of the first plane of the photograph, is followed by the reading of other planes, going from the nearest elements focused in the perspective to the more distant ones: 'les toits' and 'le flanc abrupt de la montagne.'

It is the main element ('icy water') in the effect of synesthesia – 'on peut entendre le silence le murmure continu de l'eau glacée'[24] – that might have provoked an eye movement from the top of the postcard (the mountain from where the water originates), to other elements in the first plane: 'bûches coupées,' 'un peu de neige salie,' and 'tas de bois névé.' Concerning these last elements, the parallel should be noted between 'flanc abrupt de la montagne' and 'tas de bois névé en miniature dessinant une série de pics irréguliers en dents de scie.' This creates, both at a visual level and in its written account, an effect of *mise en abyme* corresponding to what in the photograph could be considered as a 'visual rhyme,' triggered by similarities in geometric shape that are emphasized by the expression 'en miniature dessinant.'

Other notations of movement, beyond the encoded form of image reading, are given mainly by effects of synesthesia; by the use of certain adverbs – for example, 'et immédiatement'; by the notations of what might have preceded a given instant – 'comme si elle venait juste de le poser et de se relever'; and by the use of the present participles. The synesthesias such as 'le murmure continu de l'eau glacée,' or 'les bûches exhalant l'odeur de violette le parfum glacé coupant de la neige,' transpose the image from the past into a present – that is, from the time the photograph was taken, into the time the image is read and described in terms of a written text. The present participles, a verb form Simon favours in all his novels, create, in this case, the effect of a series of suspended iterative image movements.

The present participle in Simon's writings functions very much as an oxymoron. According to Salvador Jiménez-Fajardo (1971), 'they do suggest an ongoing effort to fixate movement and to give life to the static' (97). In fact, if in the narrative segments of Simon's fiction the present participle gives a concatenation of action verbs a descriptive-like quality, in the descriptive segments, the use of this verb form gives even to stative verbs a dynamic effect.[25]

The postcards initially described in *Histoire* consist of motionless photographic instants whose internal dynamism is mainly the result of a detailed image reading.[26] However, this narrative-like effect can also be created whenever the 'enunciative voice' not only encodes an eye-scanning movement generated by his own reading in terms of visual lexias, but also focuses on the activities through which the image was produced, that is, on an inquiry about the generation of the image. This type of reading is generally associated with paintings, since photographs appearing at the beginning of the century represent mainly a single instant in time – in this case, snapshots that capture a time the descriptor is able to expand beyond its referential linearity. This fact is commented upon by a narrative voice in *Histoire*: '... l'ouverture de l'obturateur, semblent pour ainsi dire nier le temps, donnant l'illusion que la photographie est un de ces instantanés, une de ces coupes lamelliformes pratiquées à l'intérieur de la durée et où les personnages aplatis, enfermés dans des contours précis, sont pour ainsi dire artificiellement isolés de la série des attitudes qui précèdent et qui suivent' (269).

Based on the postcard from Kyoto, sent by Henri to the narrator's mother, we can read a description that also encodes the generation of the visual referent:

Et sur la carte suivante un paysage qui semble fait lui avec des plumes, non pas dessiné mais pour ainsi dire effleuré comme si non pas un crayon ou un pinceau mais des ailes avaient frôlé le carton y laissant des traces délicates floues pervenche pistache antimoine topaze avec des arbres eux-mêmes semblables à des cous sinueux d'oiseaux d'échassiers de hérons un étang des roseaux duveteux balancés par le vent imprécis des roches de cristal rose des joncs bruissants frissonnants de minces pilotis un chuintement transparent léger Karasaki no Matsu near Kyoto. (252–3)

This description starts with the careful notation of the medium and colours used to create the image. A reflection on the medium – pencil or brush used as wings – is going to generate a series of analogies and metaphors both in the painted image and in its written description: 'arbres eux-mêmes semblables à des cous sinueux d'oiseaux,' 'un étang des roseaux duveteux,' 'chuintement transparent.' Even though the image of a landscape is quite briefly described in terms of a series of motionless elements resembling, in this case, exotic birds ('échassiers' or 'hérons'), the medium used for obtaining such an effect presupposes a given amount of work, a 'time of painting.' This implicit time is further stressed, in this description, when it joins a time of image reading encoded through the examination of the medium used in the painting.

3. EXPANSIONS THROUGH DESCRIPTIVE DETAILS AND THE
FRAGMENTED MAIN FRAME

After the description of the previous postcard ('Karasaki no Matsu near
Kyoto'), we are told how the initial image disappears when examined in
its minute details with a magnifying glass: 'les détails de la carte postale
se dissolvant, plus indistincts encore, dans un fin croisillon de losanges
et de points colorés comme une tapisserie' (253). We shall examine now
how an expansion on certain descriptive details may explode the main
descriptive frame – the margins of the descriptive 'tableau' – into a set of
micro-frames no longer perceivable as being generated around the same
main theme or 'discourse topic.'

There are not very many postcard descriptions in *Histoire* inviting a
shifting of successive 'reading frames.' Apart from the description of the
postcard entitled 'The Landing Stage and S. S. Persia,' where a large
amount of detail is generated through a series of 'weaved metaphors'
(57–8),[27] or the description of the postcard entitled 'LES TROUBLES DE
LIMOGES,' where a set of analogically motivated imaginary elements
are blended into an initial visual image (66–7), one of the best examples
of the expansion of image detail and the subsequent fragmentation of its
main frame is to be found in the description of the postcard entitled 'vue
des Grands Boulevards':

Une vue des Grands Boulevards aux bords dégradés en flou artistique, avec une
colonne Morris surmontée de son dôme miniature, décoré d'un oeil-de-boeuf et
recouvert de fausses tuiles en zinc semblables à des écailles de poisson, peintes
en vert sans doute, une horloge marquant dix heures vingt-cinq, et les morts qui
étaient passés là ce jour-là à cette heure-là très exactement: deux chapeautés de
hauts-de-forme gris clair vêtus de redingotes les mains croisées derrière le dos,
en train de regarder les affiches de la colonne: JOB en très grandes lettres
blanches LANGUES ÉTRANGÈRES en oblique de gauche à droite, et une autre
représentant le buste opulent d'une femme coiffée en coques, aux épaules et à la
gorge entourées d'une écharpe aux inflexions d'iris, deux fiacres et une charrette
à bras rangés le long du trottoir, un encaisseur en bicorne sur le refuge au milieu
de la chaussée, une main dans la poche de son pantalon, l'autre bras arrondi
autour de sa sacoche, et un omnibus traîné par des chevaux blancs passant
devant un immeuble sur lequel on peut lire, courant au-dessus des fenêtres du
premier étage, les lettres OURS de DANSE COURS de D, le d et le e minuscules
commençant à pâlir, le dernier D diaphane, à peine visible dans le bord extrême

du dégradé artistique de la photo, tandis qu'entre chaque fenêtre les noms des pas enseignés sont inscrits, superposés par groupes de trois:

SCOTTISH	QUADRILLE
VALSE	POLKA
LANCIERS	MAZURKA

ceux de la ligne supérieure et ceux de la ligne inférieure disposés en arcs de cercle, comme des parenthèses couchées, encadrant ceux du milieu, horizontaux, de sorte que les lettres elles-mêmes ont l'air de composer joyeusement une sorte de figure de danse. (34–5)

This description is organized around a succession of enumerated visual objects: 'colonne Moris,' 'une horloge,' 'deux chapeautés ... en train de regarder les affiches de la colonne,' 'deux fiacres et une charrette,' 'un encaisseur,' 'un omnibus traîné par des cheveaux,' and an 'immeuble sur lequel on peut lire ...' The shifting of 'reading frames' seems to result from: 1) the individualization of the human elements, which is achieved by a detailed description of the way people are dressed, and 2) descriptions of the posters on the column and of the written sign on the building.

All these descriptions contribute to create a series of micro-frames inside a main frame that in this case becomes no longer relevant. In fact, the photograph is referred to as an object 'au bords dégradés,' and when the descriptor mentions the sign on the building, he mentions once more the 'bord extrême du dégradé artistique de la photo.' Represented visual elements in the photograph such as in one of the posters and in the written sign (the latter emphasized by its graphic presentation on the text page), acquire a great deal of importance in this description from the amount of detail conferred on them.

It should be noted that, generally, in an enumerative type of description, details are not expanded but rather synthesized around specific categories. Here, such details help create several micro-descriptions expanded around their respective themes. These then become part of a descriptive segment that therefore is no longer 'visualizable' and cannot be read in terms of a single whole. An interesting effect of *mise en abyme* is once more created, since the attention of the reader is focused both on the characters 'en train de regarder les affiches de la colonne' and on the descriptor reading and writing in great detail about the poster and the sign on the building, thus mirroring the activity of the reader.

The concept of frame, used so far when referring to the mode in which a descriptive segment or block is presented, and to 'frames of reading reference,' can now be expanded so as to encompass also the boundaries that discourse cohesion and coherence may generate in terms of 'readability.' The latter would be a reader's construct resulting not only from the mode in which a given description is presented, but also from its internal cohesion and coherence. As our processing of information tends to shift, in this case, from a main topic to a series of sub-topics, the main frame is eroded, fragmented, or momentarily abolished.[28]

4. FROM DESCRIPTIONS TO NARRATIONS

If almost all postcard descriptions in *Histoire* have a narrative-like quality[29] resulting from stylistic techniques able to convey a certain descriptive dynamism, not all of them are clearly narrativized, or, to use an expression of Jean Rousset's (1981), not every described image is 'mise en récit.' There are, however, in *Histoire* two main modes of transforming written image descriptions into narrative fiction. One of them (as I pointed out previously) consists in imagining a series of activities or enumerated actions preceding or following the images in question, such as the movement of old Chinese armies defending the Great Wall of China ('TONKIN–Doug-Daug–La porte de la Muraille de Chine à Nam-Quan,' [131–2]), or the postcard representing the façade of the Paris Opera (55–6) that we shall examine in a moment. Another less common process consists in expanding a general description into a set of logically concatenated discrete segments, thus creating a series of 'reading frames' and 'micro-tableaux' through which we can read an implied narration.

If we examine the description of the postcard representing the Paris Opera, we observe that after an allusion to the 'ciel bleu au-dessus des muses de bronze' (55) upon which the text of the postcard was written, and after an enumeration of sculpted details on the façade of the building, the description slides into narration. It is no longer a description and/or a reading of the exterior of the building, but the narration of an evening at the Opera; a series of visual elements *in absentia* triggered by the initial image: 'Le soir éclate le scintillement des lustres tandis que les spectateurs les femmes en robes bruissantes gravissent majestueusement les marches disparaissent dans une flamboyante apothéose ... le brouhaha s'apaisant par degrés ... des lustres s'éteignant peu à peu et à la fin plus rien que quelques obscurs reflets palpitant çà et là ... peut-être il murmurait par-dessus son épaule ... et alors ce long frisson, et deux mille paires d'yeux ... suspendant leur respiration dans les ténèbres ... lorsque le rideau de pourpre s'élève et qu'elle apparaît porteuse d'eau dans le décor stéréotypé' (56).

A series of actions, from the moment the spectators enter the building, to the moment the opera starts, is narrated in the present tense, in the imperfect tense, and with the present participle. However, all these verb forms (especially the imperfect and the present participle) give a descriptive-like quality to the actions, while pointing to a series of imaginary activities that could be conceived as a logically concatenated set of images presented in a narrative form.[30]

When we examine the description of a boat leaving Port-Said, we notice that narration is accomplished mainly through a set of descriptive segments:

Puis le long navire plat et bas aux cheminées vomissant d'épais panaches de fumée charboneuse, c'est-à-dire que des deux hauts tubes jumeaux noirs et luisants s'échappent (l'un très droit l'autre légèrement incliné comme chancelant sous son propre poids) deux nuages d'abord étroits ensuite boursouflés crépus faits de volutes tourbillonnantes s'accumulant s'étageant se poussant s'enroulant rapidement sur elles-mêmes comme des bobines se bousculant s'élevant en s'étalant, les sommets des deux panaches s'arrondissant, faîte d'un arbre dont ils imitent le dessin touffu et grumeleux, la fumée enfin se déchirant se séparant en deux masses, une partie continuant à s'élever transparente dans l'air calme l'autre retombant s'affalant se diluant en écharpes cuivrées sur la surface miroitante et plate de la mer où elle étend comme une ombre de deuil, les deux obscurs champignons se reflétant dans l'eau finement crêpée semblable à de l'étain terni ... et tout à coup un plumet blanc apparaît devant la première cheminée bouillonnant quelques secondes puis cessant, le bas la racine du plumet se dissolvant brusquement s'évanouissant puis plus rien et alors seulement le son (le mugissement plaintif lugubre) parvenant, le grand bateau s'ébrouant insensiblement, dans cette première phase de l'appareillage qui est entre l'immobilité et le mouvement (c'est-à-dire qu'on le croit encore immobile alors qu'il a déjà commencé à bouger, et lorsque, le sachant, on cherche à suivre son mouvement il paraît de nouveau immobile), commençant à pivoter lentement sur lui-même ... et quand on regarde de nouveau dans la direction du navire c'est comme s'il s'était soudain réduit, quoique toujours immobile, se présentant de poupe maintenant déjà lointain étroit et haut sous l'énorme champignon cuivré de fumée chavirant au-dessus de lui et on comprend alors qu'il a pris de la vitesse s'éloigne sans rémission solitaire pathétique vers cette ligne irréelle et décevante qui là-bas sépare le ciel de la mer, un sphinx bistre et gras aux yeux allongés de fard fixant d'un regard vide d'invisibles dunes de sable au-delà de la pyramide dessinée en traits pâles à l'arrière-plan au-dessus de la mention POSTES ÉGYPTIENNES. (36–7)

'Le long navire plat et bas aux cheminées vomissant d'épais panaches de fumée charboneuse' constitutes the main theme of this descriptive block and, no doubt, the most important object in the image of the postcard, which seems to be a sepia photograph.[31] The notion of narrative movement is created initially by a narrativized reading of the smoke coming out of the chimneys. This is done in terms of a set of descriptive segments able to convey a narrative-like progression: 'deux nuages *d'abord* étroits *ensuite* boursouflés ... les sommets des deux panaches s'arrondissant ... la fumée *enfin* se déchirant ... une partie continuant à s'élever transparente' (emphasis mine).

In this segment action verbs have a special status, since even verbs such as *arrondir or déchirer* are conjugated reflexively and are presented in the present participle form. This creates the impression of an arrested iterative movement. The narrative effect is none the less accomplished not only by the adverbs 'd'abord,' 'ensuite,' and 'enfin,' but also by a series of fixed images indicating the progression of the smoke. The latter is then read as a contrastive reflection upon the water as a smoke no longer 'transparent dans l'air calme' but as 'ombre de deuil,' a shadow able to evoke the death of the old lady described and narrated in the previous pages of the novel.

The movement of the ocean liner is then presented as a series of captured instants: 'le grand bateau s'ébrouant ... se hâtant ... se rapprochant ... et quand on regarde de nouveau dans la direction du navire c'est comme s'il était soudain réduit, *quoique toujours immobile* se présentant de poupe maintenant déjà lointain' (emphasis mine). The action of leaving the port is presented as a series of perspective changes through which the ocean liner becomes smaller and smaller. No longer in the first plane of the photograph, the objects in 'l'arrière-plan au-dessus de la mention POSTES ÉGYPTIENNES,' become more relevant and are then described.

As some critics have pointed out, this postcard is one of the last sent by Henri to the narrator's mother before he embarks to join her in France. Objects such as 'sphinx bistre et gras,' 'dunes de sable,' and 'pyramide' can thus be read as symbols of all the exotic landscapes and names in the postcards sent by Henri – visual and extremely brief messages that can be assembled into a particular set.[32]

The postcards in *Histoire* are an assemblage of visual images functioning not only as generators of descriptions but also as generators of the whole novel. As motionless framed images of a distant time they symbolize the life of the old lady around whom the story evolves: 'Les dernières des cartes reçues les derniers de ces messages insistants et en quelque sorte brutaux par leur tranquillité même leur régularité leur patient laconisme, jalons dans ce qui n'était pour elle qu'immuable immobilité un temps toujours identique toujours recommencé heures jours semaines non pas se succédant mais simplement se remplaçant dans la sérénité de son immuable univers' (33). When the old lady is on her deathbed, the postcards are mentioned again as a metaphor able to describe her entire life, and as a series of motionless images or detached fragments of a possible discourse: 'Tout était arrêté maintenant présent immobilisé tout là dans un même moment à jamais les images les instants les voix les fragments du temps du monde multiple fastueux inépuisable éparpillés sur un lit de mourante' (385).

In fact, one of the most important means of recovering aspects of the old lady's past life is through a reading of the postcard images able to 'activate' the immobile present of their pictorial representations. Thus, for the 'enunciative voice,' as well as for the reader, the postcards function as modes of capturing, through a subjective reading, an evoked and elusive past. The reported pictographic readings in terms of literary descriptions become, therefore, a mode through which the descriptor tries to recover the forever absent gaze of the old lady. This may account for an effect of double focalization that culminates in the last paragraph of the novel: 'avec ses deux enormes yeux sa tête de ver à soie sa bouche sans dents son front cartilagineux d'insecte, moi?...' (402).

As we have seen, not all postcard descriptions in *Histoire* are clearly narrativized. Nevertheless, no matter how static they may seem, they always encode the dynamics resulting from a specific type of reading. This poses a very specific problem for, if the dynamic descriptions are not necessarily narrative at a discourse level, they become so at a functional one. As we have seen, the most important action in the novel consists in evoking and recreating the life (and even some of the visual perceptions) of the old lady, through a set of postcards abandoned in a random order inside one of her drawers.

As for the narrative present, as I mentioned earlier, it is in fact a mere background: a series of routine tasks performed by a male character after the death of an old lady who is probably his mother, or a literary composite of elderly female family figures. What the novel seems to highlight is how a descriptor of aesthetic visual objects reports his reading experience in literary terms and how we, as readers of prose fiction, can recapture a set of visual representations filtered through an emotional/fictive transcoding.

We are also left with the impression that, paradoxical as it may seem, from a reader's point of view written descriptions generally tend to be more static than paintings or photographs. In fact, if while reading a written description one aims at configuring a series of elements into an imploded simultaneity, the reading of motionless visual texts tends to do quite the contrary, that is, to explode itself around a succession of 'strategic points' and into narrative-like forms of silent or reported readings.

In this specific case, written descriptions become mostly forms of narrating since they imply all the objective, subjective, and cultural dynamics of a reading. Besides, the 'enunciative voice' in *Histoire* tends to erase all clear-cut distinctions between narration and description. At a stylistic level, as mentioned before, the constant use of the present participle functions as a means of diluting such distinctions, thus creating what, at a first glance, can be considered as a pair of oxymoronic designations, that is, 'narrative descriptions' and/or 'descriptive narrations.' In a similar manner, notions of 'backgrounded' vs. 'foregrounded' information are no longer as clear as in realistic types of fictional representation (such as in Zola's *Une Page d'amour*, analysed in chapter 2). As the postcard descriptions seem to illustrate, such grounding dynamics are not, in this case, clearly resolved in the making of the text. They rather occur between text and reader, especially as he/she tries to foreground what in the text of the novel remains backgounded or vice versa: the reading of visual objects in the case of the postcards, and the not-so-relevant daily activities of a character-narrator.

Narration in *Histoire* occurs mainly through its many descriptive segments, which form a central core around which the novel is organized as text, as the ramblings of memories and visual readings in search of a truth that is not beyond fiction but fiction itself, or, more precisely in this case, History and story.

4

The sarcastic descriptor:
Satire and parody in Benito Pérez
Galdós' *La de Bringas*

La mejor ocurrencia del autor, en *La de Bringas,* fue la invención de un
espacio que no es mero escenario, sino ámbito con sustantividad propia.

[The best innovation of the author in *La de Bringas* was the invention of a
space that is not mere background, but rather a context with its own
substantiality.]

Ricardo Gullón[1]

Although humorous descriptions of characters do often occur in nineteenth-century realistic/naturalistic prose fiction (for example, in the
works of Balzac and Dickens), descriptions of space are very seldom
depicted sarcastically or even comically. Commenting on the lack of
humour or sarcasm in the nineteenth-century French and English novel,
Benito Pérez Galdós equated naturalism, which he viewed as a typically
Spanish tendency, not with direct observation (as is often the case with
Zola) but with the fiction of Cervantes and Quevedo, or with Goya's
drawings.[2]
    In this sense, the works of Galdós reveal a different naturalistic prac-
tice. Even in French and English literatures, one would have to go as far
back as the works of Rabelais or Fielding to find something similar to
the humorous sarcasm (*socarronería*) that characterizes many of the
works by this author.[3] This is especially the case in the twenty-four novels under the general title *Novelas españolas contemporáneas* of which *La de
Bringas*, published in May 1884, is the fifth.[4] Indeed, in this novel, at
least at an overall stylistic level, the narrative/descriptive voice is far
closer to Iberian baroque prose fiction, or to the 'golden-age' *comedias*,

than to the works of Zola.[5] The type of Galdosian sarcasm akin to a Menippean 'textual feast,'[6] is not only present through particular traits of character caricaturization, but, moreover, through the means used to describe spaces and objects. Thus, in the case of Galdós, realism/naturalism is not so much the production of an objective and uninvolved persona, but a fictional genre that presents itself as being focalized or filtered through the voice of a narrator, who, very much like the reader, viewer, or spectator, has his/her own biases and ideological standpoints.

My objective in this chapter is to analyse in a comparative realistic context, first, how in several descriptions caricaturization is linked not so much to the way characters are described, but rather to the manner in which settings and objects are depicted; second, how descriptive *mises en abyme* may also become sarcastic ideological devices; and third, how in a nineteenth-century novel with a realistic mode of representation, narration seems to imitate foregrounded description.

Although Galdós' novel has been translated into English under the title *The Spendthrifts* (1952),[7] I present my own translation for this analysis. Even though mine may not be as literary as Gamel Woollsley's, it is, none the less, closer to the Galdosian text. The entire first chapter of the novel can be found in the appendix, 87–8, followed by my English translation.[8]

1. DESCRIPTION AS SUSPENSE

We are all familiar with nineteenth-century realistic novels that begin with a long description – generally a descriptive segment whose function is to inform us about the setting and/or emblematically to set the tone for a specific narrative. What is indeed surprising in this novel by Galdós is that the entire first chapter consists of the detailed description of a rather strange cenotaph. According to *The Unabridged Webster's Third New International Dictionary of the English Language* (1968), a cenotaph (from the Classical Greek *kenós* meaning 'empty,' and *táphos* meaning 'tomb') is 'a monument erected in honour of a person whose body is elsewhere' (361). The cenotaph described in this novel, however, is in no way a monument, but rather a collage accomplished by the painstaking shellacking, aided by fine tweezers, of individual strands of differently coloured human hairs onto a surface that comprises a pre-cut eclectic assemblage of visual motifs.

The opening sentence of the chapter sets the tone for the description that follows: 'Era aquello ... ¿cómo lo diré yo?... un gallardo artificio se-

pulcral de atrevidísima arquitectura' [That thing was – how shall I put it?
– a gallant sepulchral artifice of the most daring architecture]. From the
very beginning, therefore, the reader (or, more precisely, the 'descriptee')
is drawn into a kind of complicity, which is implied not only by the familiar tone one would expect in a sincere and spontaneous judgment, but
also by an absence of any previous reference for the pronoun 'aquello'
[that thing]. Such a beginning presupposes a certain amount of information already shared by both the addresser and the addressee. In *Tormento*,
the novel that preceded *La de Bringas* (the former published in January
1884 and the latter in May), Francisco de Bringas and his wife were
among the main characters. Although the funereal collage we later come
to know as the product of Francisco's patience and kitschy taste is never
alluded to in *Tormento*, from the beginning of *La de Bringas* the addressee
is considered to be already familiar with many of the characters.[9]

In the second part of the passage previously quoted, 'gallardo artificio
sepulcral de atrevidísima arquitectura,' the reader is immediately initiated into the zeugmatic devices that govern the irony (ranging from subtle hint to open sarcasm) that occurs throughout. Zeugma is a rather
ambiguous rhetorical figure operating at both a stylistic and a discursive
level. It does not propel the semantic fusion one would expect of a simile
or a metaphor. Nevertheless, as the initial letter Z itself implies, this figure presupposes a semantic deviation and an almost metonymical
interruption, the effect of which is to surprise by disturbing a sequential
linearity without breaking it. Zeugma brings together not antithetical
pairs but metonymically related incompatibilities which are briefly
short-circuited through its contrastive appeal.[10] In the present case, we
experience the semantic contrast between 'gallardo artificio' [gallant
artifice] and 'sepulcral' [sepulchral], as well as the awkwardness
established by 'atrevidísima arquitectura,' where the Spanish adjective
atrevido/a, meaning both 'bold/daring' and 'uncouth,' comes to qualify
'architecture.' The zeugmatic effect results also from the clash of collo-
quial with stilted literary language. This, of course, engenders a comical
effect that is later expanded as zeugma (mainly at a stylistic and discursive level). Zeugma here is a literary strategy deployed to describe a
realistically represented collage of disparate and extremely conventional
artistic elements.

After the initial sentences of the novel, the descriptor proceeds to
expand on the nature of Francisco de Bringas' 'gallardo artificio': 'grandioso de traza, en ornamentos rico, por una parte severo y rectilíneo a la
manera viñolesca, por otra movido, ondulante y quebradizo a la usanza

gótica, con ciertos atisbos platerescos donde menos se pensaba; y por fin, cresterías semejantes a las del estilo tirolés que prevalece en los quioscos' [grandiose in design, rich in ornament, on the one hand severe and rectilinear in a Vignolesque manner, on the other full of movement, *undulating, discontinued,* and Gothic-like, with certain Plateresque traits where you would least expect them; and, finally, with fretwork similar to the Tyrolean style that prevails in kiosks] (emphasis mine).[11]

As can be seen, the sarcastic descriptor inserts in a prose text a line of chiasmatic alexandrine verse with perfect caesura ('grandioso de traza / / en ornamentos rico'), able to evoke Gongorian constructions and epic themes. This procedure creates a sense of parody,[12] and draws our attention to the fact that the descriptive segment, much like the object it depicts, also combines different literary styles. Emphasizing both these aspects is a reference to a sixteenth-century Italian architect, Giacomo da Vignola, known for his classical buildings. In addition, De Bringas' collage combines other well- and less-known styles from the Gothic to the Plateresque, which are finally summed up by the humorous reference to 'the Tyrolean style that prevails in kiosks.'

At a discursive level, the long single period opening the novel avoids providing a general view of 'aquello' [that thing] by deliberately hindering any immediate effects of visualization. In fact, this description functions very much as a riddle, where, to its highly convoluted literary style, we may add the phony and sarcastic references to an artistic erudition combined with an overworked blending of disparate stylistic tendencies. This communicates to the reader not the sense of a possible artistic object, but a comical effect, that is, the 'fireworks' provoked by zeugmatic forms of adjectival use and discursive construction, which soon leave the reader in the dark.

While continuing to avoid revealing the nature of Francisco de Bringas' 'artificio,' Galdós' sarcastic descriptor goes on to enumerate each of the many elements that constitute the 'artefact.' Thus we read a series of summarized descriptive units with a variety of 'main themes' whose textual montage reflects the nature of the object while keeping in suspense any attempt by the reader at a general view or overall coherence. This is especially the case in the following passage: 'antorchas, urnas, murciélagos, ánforas, búhos, coronas de siemprevivas, aladas clepsidras, guadañas, palmas, anguilas enroscadas y otros emblemas del morir y del vivir eterno' [torches, urns, bats, amphorae, owls, wreaths of everlastings, winged hourglasses, scythes, palm leaves, coiled eels, and other emblems of death and eternal life].

Here several characteristics operate simultaneously. At a stylistic and discursive level is a zeugmatic type of enumeration evocative of baroque poetry, such as the scattering of several not-directly-related elements summed up in a short sentence: 'emblemas del morir y del vivir eterno' [emblems of death and eternal life]. The metaphor 'aladas clepsidras' [winged hourglasses], meaning 'time flies' (and thus representing the well-known Latin cliché *tempus fugit*), although banal, produces a comical effect by taking literally a conventional metaphor through reported visual terms.

From the point of view of a reader's reception, it should also be pointed out that, in this textual segment, each noun, or each discrete element, corresponds to a specific micro-description. This provokes an accelerated sequence of 'reading frames' intended to disorient the reader and to postpone any attempts at a rationalized conclusion. The effect is also triggered by a rather general and confusing spatial orientation: 'Por arriba y por abajo, a izquierda y derecha' [From top to bottom, from left to right].

These micro-descriptions function to the extent that each one is an 'emblem,' or, more precisely, a symbol evocative of artistic styles, as, for example, the satirical reference to Romanticism in the stereotypical allusion to 'urns,' 'bats,' 'owls,' and 'wreaths.' In fact, at a functional level in this reduced context, what we read is mainly a critique of the taste for outdated Romantic themes embedded in a parodic stylistic imitation of Spanish baroque. Once more, the text seems to create the object being described by utilizing a technique borrowed from the visual arts. Although, unlike Francisco's collage or 'hair-picture' (to use Peter Bly's terminology),[13] the descriptor does not assemble an already existing set of textual segments,[14] he can however lend to his 'voice' specific replicating characteristics to be decoded by a 'descriptee' that, in this case, is an entity (a partner?) drawn through humorous 'textual pleasure' into a similar set of references and beliefs.

From the still enigmatic series of 'mind-teasing' micro-descriptive hints about a possible object – where an amount of very detailed work could only correlate with an increasing bad taste – the descriptive voice (as in a cinematic zoom) focuses on a specific central element: 'En el centro del mausoleo, un angelón...' [In the centre of the mausoleum, a big fat angel...]. In this way, the descriptor inscribes onto a general fragmented main frame a minor one containing the description of the angel (ironically referred to as 'angelón'). Such a descriptive process, however, does not strike us as creating an effect of 'discohesion' since the initial overall description of the cenotaph was a confused group of elements pertaining to many different styles and forms. Moreover, the description of the 'angelón' – the term itself is sufficient to evoke the gilded wooden sculptures that often frame baroque altars – functions very much as a *mise en abyme*[15] of both the stylistic and discursive devices used, so far, in this descriptive segment. This is especially the case with the angel's shoes, which are also a strange assemblage of different styles: 'calzaba sus pies de mujer con botitos, coturnos o alpargatas; que de todo había un poco en aquella elegantísima interpretación de la zapataría angelical' [his woman's feet were shod with little boots, high-platform sandals, or espadrilles, for there was something of everything in that most elegant interpretation of angelical footwear].

Once again, a zeugmatic effect is achieved; 'botitos' [little boots] and 'alpargatas' [espadrilles] are familiar types of footwear, while 'coturnos' refers to the type of high-platform sandals used by actors in ancient Greece, especially when performing tragedies. Irony is clear in the expression 'elegantísima interpretación' [most elegant interpretation], where the adjective *elegante* means its opposite. Furthermore, as we have seen concerning the whole cenotaph, the angel also carries an excessive number of objects: 'alas, flores, cintajos y plumas, amén de un relojito de arena,' [wings, flowers, ribbons, feathers, not to mention a little hourglass].

'Pero lo más bonito era quizá el sauce' [But the most beautiful thing of all was, perhaps, the weeping willow]. After this ironic statement we read the description of a tree that, like the angel, has been personified in order to further the descriptor's sarcasm: 'Daban ganas de hacerle oler algún fuerte alcaloide para que se despabilase y volviera en sí de su poético síncope' [One felt like giving it smelling salts to bring it out of its poetic syncope]. Like many of the elements in the chaotic cenotaph, the willow is an emblematic cliché, a symbol of the poetic motifs 'que desde la llegada de la Retórica al mundo viene teniendo una participación más o menos criminal en toda elegía que se comete' [that since the coming of Rhetoric into the world has had a more or less criminal participation in every elegy that is committed].

A parody on elegiac Romantic verse then follows, communicated not only by its semantic content, but also by the rhythm of the sentences and by an inversion of the adjective position (for example, 'ondulado tronco' [*undulating* trunk], and 'altas esparcidas ramas' [*high spreading* branches], emphasis mine). These give this particular descriptive segment a mock-exhortative quality, 'at an age in which the trees of Romanticism had not yet been turned into firewood.'

It is only after an account of the many foregrounded elements that the descriptive voice comes to a notion of perspective: 'El fondo o perspectiva consistía en el progresivo alejamiento de otros sauces de menos talla, que se iban a llorar a moco y baba camino del horizonte' [The sense of depth or perspective consisted in showing a procession of other willows of gradually decreasing size, weeping desperately on their way to the horizon]. The idiomatic expression 'llorar a moco y baba' (literally 'to cry spit and phlegm,' corresponding to the English 'to cry one's eyes out') correlates with the lettering on the tumular inscription: 'letras compungidas, de cuyos trazos inferiores salían unos lagrimones que figuraban resbalar por el mármol al modo de babas escurridizas' [contrite letters from whose lower extremities big tears were falling as if oozing out of the marble itself like sliding spit]. It is interesting however, how the sense of perspective is described as if to evoke, at least visually, the notion of *mise en abyme* through the presence of ever smaller perspective-making willows, which disappear in the clichéd last plane of the collage, where 'mountains,' 'battlements,' and 'Gothic towers' are represented.

This notion of perspective leads us to infer, upon a first reading, that we are dealing with an object similar to a painting, but the notations of colour in De Bringas' cenotaph – 'castaño, negro y *rubio*' (emphasis mine) [brown, black, and *blond*] – strike us not so much as a reference to paint, but as a reference to human hair, which contributes once more to stressing the enigmatic features of the object. In fact, after mentioning its frame, the descriptor poses a question to the reader, inviting him/her to solve at that moment a previously implied riddle: '¿Era talla dulce, aguafuerte, plancha de acero, boj o pacienzuda obra ejecutada a punta de lápiz duro o con pluma a la tinta china?...' [Was it a mezzotint, an etching, a steel engraving, a woodcut, or was it the incredibly patient work of a hard pencil or of a pen dipped in India ink?...]. This false rhetorical question (whose sarcasm mounts in proportion to the amount of specialized vocabulary) is not immediately answered in the text, as the reader is still to be kept in suspense.

The descriptor proceeds then to explain Francisco's intentions: 'El artista había querido expresar el conjunto, no por el conjunto mismo, sino por la suma de pormenores, copiando indoctamente a la Naturaleza' [The artist had wanted to give us a sense of totality, not through the ensemble itself, but through an addition of details, while clumsily copying Nature]. This sentence might lend itself to being read as a metadescriptive observation pointing to a series of intra- and intertextual referents: As 'the artist,' the descriptor also communicates to us, not a 'whole' but an addition of details to be viewed as elements towards the final solution of a riddle. Moreover, by attempting to describe a visual object the components of which proceed from a series of stylistic borrowings, the descriptor assembles a succession of intertexts ranging from the baroque to the Romantic. Curiously, the phrase 'copiando indoctamente a la Naturaleza' [clumsily copying Nature] can be read both as a sarcastic remark on certain aspects of naturalism, and as a reminder that something as real, constant, and present as 'Nature' can only be replicated through the filtering of a sociocultural perspective. In fact, if the descriptor imitates through parody some previous literary styles, he also implicitly mocks the taste for minor details that characterizes many realistic/naturalistic descriptions. Ironically, in this case, minute details, although credible, do not function as mere Barthesian 'effets de réel,' but rather as the sharing of a sarcastic effect capable of backfiring upon the text itself. It is, thus, as if the entire first chapter of *La de Bringas* were also a parody on descriptive naturalism.[16]

Only in the last period of chapter 1, is the reader – having been informed about the identity of the work and his author – finally given the 'main theme' of the whole descriptive block: 'Era, en fin, el tal cenotafio un trabajo de pelo o en pelo, género de arte que tuvo cierta boga, y su autor, don Francisco de Bringas, demonstraba en él habilidad benedictina ...' [In sum, it was a capillary assemblage, a type of art that once had a certain vogue – a work of human hair. Its author, Don Francisco de Bringas, displayed in it a Benedictine ability...]. Only later, however, do we come to know that the cenotaph is not finished but rather a work in progress that, eventually, will cause Francisco's temporary blindness, or, according to the term used by the descriptor/narrator, '[una] jaqueca oftálmica' [an ophthalmic migraine] (49).

In the ensuing two chapters we are informed that the cenotaph is meant as a cheap yet 'impressive' gift to Don Manuel María José del Pez, to mark the first anniversary of his daughter's death. Francisco, who like Manuel del Pez is a bureaucrat, owes the latter some favours, namely a government sinecure Del Pez gave his oldest son Paquito de Bringas (57).

However, aside from the sarcastic detail that the descriptor/narrator uses to describe Francisco's meticulous work, what becomes more relevant is the reader's realization that the collage technique used in the long description of the cenotaph is a pattern upon which the whole novel is generated. None the less, unlike in Zola's *Une Page d'amour* (see chapter 2 of the present work) where descriptive *mise en abyme* mimics previous large narrative blocks, in *La de Bringas* the proleptic *mise en abyme* (constituted by the entire first chapter) becomes a generator of the various 'stylemes' found throughout the novel, of its overall fictional structure, and of the ideological characteristics stemming from both its satirical and parodic bent.

As Peter Bly has observed, it is almost as if the whole novel were contained in its initial description.[17] Indeed, to complicate further an already intricate narrative situation, one could posit (following Ricardo Gullón's accurate historical analysis of *La de Bringas*)[18] that Francisco's cenotaph is not only a *mise en abyme* of the whole novel, but also a device that sarcastically reflects the cultural and socio-economic characteristics of Spain during the last months of the reign of Isabel II, more precisely, from March to September of 1869 (the chronological span of the novel).

Since collage as a technique determines the whole structuring of *La de Bringas*, I shall begin by examining a series of direct and/or more oblique references to this specific pattern.

In chapter 3 we are informed of the source of motifs used in the cenotaph. Thus, the 'weeping willow' is taken from a picture entitled *La tumba de Napoleón en Santa Elena* [*The Tomb of Napoleon at Saint Helen*] (62); the 'big fat angel' from a tomb placed in 'El Escorial para los funerales de una de las mujeres de Fernando VII' [The Escorial for the funeral of one of the wives of Fernando VII] (63);[19] the background from an engraving in a 'librote lamartinesco que era todo un puro jarabe' [Lamartinian booklet that was a complete nonsense] (63); and the flowers from an illustrated book about 'el *Lenguage* de las tales' [the *Language* of such] (63). Once more we find, at a discursive level, a zeugmatic structure for sarcastic purposes, since the descriptive voice metonymically associates historical tombs of absolute monarchs with Lamartinian verse, and with what we can imagine as being a popular book on the 'symbolic language of flowers.'

The hair of different colours required by Francisco to create the cenotaph belongs to both dead and living people of both sexes. Similarly, in its sarcastic intent, the novel can be read as a satire (in this case a *mise en abyme*) of dead and 'present' Spanish political regimes. Indeed, the whole novel functions as a mock-cenotaph, as a commemorative funereal work for someone or something (a type of politics?) whose 'body' lies elsewhere. Furthermore, as we shall see, the novel incorporates historical and purely fictional characters, as well as still existing and equally fictitious places. Zeugma, at a functional level, works here as a form of blending the contrastive 'dead and alive,' 'textual and extratextual referents,' 'history and story.'

Still, at an intratextual level, many of the characters – for example, Don Manuel del Pez, whose dream is to create an administrative government with eighty-six secretariats (187) – appear in at least seven other novels in the series *Novelas españolas contemporáneas*, specifically in three published before *La de Bringas* (*La desheredada* 1881; *El amigo Manso*, 1882; and *Tormento*, 1884). Thus, Don Manuel del Pez functions, to a certain extent, as the collage of a character taken from previous fictional material. This is even emphasized by his physical description: 'Su ropa tenía la virtud de no ajarse ni empolvorarse nunca, y le caía sobre el cuerpo como pintada' [His clothes had the virtue of never appearing worn or dusty, and they fitted him as if they were painted] (107–8). The same applies to Don Francisco de Bringas, also referred to as 'nuestro buen Thiers' [our good Thiers] (57), given his physical similarity to the French politician; and his wife, Rosalía ('la de Bringas'), referred to as 'la ninfa de Rubens' [the Rubens' nymph] (109) – another collage? Both are main characters in *Tormento*.

Up to this point, we have examined a long description where, through the structure of the riddle, a narrative-like suspense is maintained. However, one might also ask to what extent this zeugmatic form of collage pattern functions throughout the novel; and, more important, to what extent narration can be seen to replicate an initial description and its subsequent echoes.

2. PARODIC 'EMBLEMATIZATIONS,' OR WHEN *MISE EN ABYME* ALSO REVERTS TO ITS LITERAL MEANING

Who is doing the describing in *La de Bringas*? In this novel, descriptor and narrator seem to coincide, the same sarcastic tone being common to both. The descriptor/narrator, however, is not a mere exterior third-person entity, but a kind of character-observer (a friend of the family), whose 'voice' occasionally slides into the first person, and who at times (as in the first description we analysed) addresses the reader.

As for the main plot, which only starts to be clearly developed after chapter 9, at this point it consists mainly of the stratagems and tribulations of Rosalía de Bringas as she struggles to satisfy her craving for expensive French fashion, and to pay for all her credit accounts at fancy clothing stores.

It is relevant that several chapters in the novel describe the palace where the De Bringas family, Queen Isabel II of Spain, as well as many other characters in this novel were living. At the eve of the September

Revolution of 1868, the palace is very much a miniature city (sometimes also referred to as 'pueblo' [village]), since all the social classes of nineteenth-century Spain seem to be represented in it: 'Esta ciudad, [el palacio] donde alternan pacíficamente aristocracia, clase media y pueblo, es una real república que los monarcas se han puesto por corona, y engarzadas en su inmenso circuito, guarda muestras diversas de toda clase de personas.' [This Palace-city, where the aristocracy, the middle-class, and the people alternate in peaceful coexistence, is a royal republic the monarchs use as their very crown. Lost inside its immense bowels, one could find several types of people of all classes.] (65). Thus, it would be tempting to say that, in the novel, the royal palace functions as a *mise en abyme* or 'emblematization' of Madrid during the 1860s, if not as a parodic miniature of the whole country.

Like Francisco's work, the palace is described as a labyrinthine architectonic assemblage of renovations and additions:

Hay escaleras que empiezan y no acaban; vestíbulos o plazoletas en que se ven blanqueadas techumbres que fueron de habitaciones inferiores. Hay palomares donde antes hubo salones, y salas que un tiempo fueron caja de una gallarda escalera. Las de caracol se encuentran en varios puntos, sin que se sepa adónde van a parar, y puertas tabicadas, huecos con alambrera, tras los cuales no se ve más que soledad, polvo y tinieblas. (68)

[There are staircases that begin and never end; vestibules and courtyards where one could see whitewashed ceilings that once belonged to rooms on a lower floor. There are dovecotes where before there were only large halls, and drawing rooms that once were stairwells of beautiful staircases. The spiral ones can be found in several places, and one cannot know where they will end. There are also sealed-up doors, hollow spaces covered by wire nets, beyond which one can only perceive solitude, dust, and darkness.]

One has the feeling that, for a moment, sarcasm has given way to amazement as 'reality' starts to become less and less real, with 'staircases,' 'hollow spaces,' and 'sealed-up doors' leading nowhere. Although at a discursive level zeugma is still at work, at a stylistic level this figure of speech is summed up, at the end of the above passage, in the enumeration 'soledad, polvo y tinieblas' [solitude, dust, and darkness], which, none the less, lacks the sarcastic tone of previous descriptions.

Curiously, both the narrator/descriptor and Don Manuel del Pez, while going to visit Francisco, get lost inside the labyrinth. This happens although we are told that Del Pez had a better sense of orientation because he had read several books by Jules Verne (70). This, no doubt, constitutes a more direct sarcastic reference to the scientific and pedagogical aims of a particular type of French naturalism.

However, if the palace is for architecture what the cenotaph is for the visual arts, the notion of *mise en abyme* is further stressed as if through a set of Chinese boxes. In effect, the apartment inside the palace where the De Bringas live is itself a replication of the royal apartment, with each room bearing a similar name (74). In the same way, Rosalía's bedroom in the apartment becomes also a confusing space, as for example in chapter 10, when, with her friend Milagros, she tries to assemble a multiplicity of pieces of cloth to make a dress.

Following an intricate description of the bedroom, the 'implied author' proceeds to represent a dialogue between Rosalía and Milagros. What is striking about the way this conversation is presented is that it not only imitates the writing of a dramatic text (by placing the name of each character followed by parenthetical observations prior to each segment in the dialogue), but also constitutes a linguistic collage of fashion terms in both French and Spanish. The idea of a lexical collage is further emphasized by the following observation: 'Los términos franceses que matizaban este coloquio se desplegaban del tejido de nuestra lengua; pero aunque sea clavándolos con alfileres, los he de sujetar para que el exótico idioma de los trapos no pierda su genealidad castiza.' [The French terms that coloured this colloquium seemed to slide out of the tissue of our language; but, even if I have to pin them down, I shall keep them, so that the exotic idiom of the 'rags' won't lose its genuine authenticity.] (94).

Rosalía's bedroom is again described in chapter 15 when her husband, coming early from work, finds it transformed into an *atelier* for *'haute'-couture*:

Había allí como unas veinticuatro varas de *Mozambique* ... La enorme tira de trapo se arrastraba por la habitación, se encaramaba a las sillas, se colgaba de los brazos del sofá y se extendía en el suelo, para ser dividida en pedazos por la tijera de la oficiala, que, de rodillas, consultaba con patrones de papel antes de cortar. Tiras y recortes de *glasé*, de las más estrañas secciones geométricas, cortados al *bies*, veíanse sobre el baúl, esperando la mano hábil que los combinase con el *Mozambique*. Trozos de brillante raso, de colores vivos, eran los toques calientes, aún no salidos de la paleta, que el bueno de Bringas vio diseminados por toda la pieza, entre mal enroscadas cintas y fragmentos de encaje. (119–20)

[In it, there were some twenty-four yards of 'mozambique' ... The enormous piece of material was crawling throughout the room, jumping over the chairs, hanging from the arms of the sofa, and spreading itself across the floor, to be cut into pieces by the scissors of a sewing woman, who, kneeling down, would check each segment against a paper pattern before cutting. Pieces and designs of bias cut 'glasé' taffeta of the strangest geometrical shapes could be seen on the leather trunk, waiting for the skilled hand that would combine them with the 'mozambique.' Fragments of a shiny, solid, and bright-coloured material were the brilliant touches (not yet out of a pallet) that our good De Bringas saw disseminated throughout the whole bedroom between slightly coiled waistbands and other pieces of cloth ready to be assembled.]

This descriptive block starts with a reference to a large amount of 'mozambique,' a type of silk-chiffon with tiny dots that can prove (in the same way as Francisco's collage) quite disorienting to the eye. The verbs used: *arrastrarse* [to crawl], *encaramarse* [to jump], *colgarse* [to hang], and *estenderse* [to stretch], are all action verbs conjugated reflexively in the imperfect tense and used metaphorically to lend a snake-like quality to the piece of material. Moreover, as in the initial hair collage, the pieces of cloth are cut according to already existing patterns, forming an eclectic composition of different geometric shapes to be assembled. The similarity to a painting (as in Francisco's work), is in this case indicated by a reference to a 'pallet,' while 'mal enroscadas cintas' [slightly coiled waistbands] echo the 'anguilas enroscadas' [coiled eels] in the capillary cenotaph.

Rosalía, in fact, goes about making dresses using the same techniques as her husband. It is also interesting to notice that 'la manteleta' [the short cloak] that, in the novel, represents Rosalía's first temptation and is referred to as '¡Qué pieza, qué manzana de Eva!' [What a piece! What an Eve's apple!] (98), directly correlates with the ophidian animation of the long piece of 'mozambique,' as if in a humorous reference to the book of Genesis.

The idea of baroque-like cluttered spaces filled with a multitude of elements towards a surprising final effect, is also communicated through the nightmares of Isabelita de Bringas – the fragile young daughter – each time she eats rich desserts. This is the case following the Easter ceremonies at the royal court, where, ironically, in a gesture of catholic humbleness, the queen plays waitress to a group of starving beggars, who, once in that situation, miraculously lose their appetites (chapter 7). In Isabelita's nightmare, the Holy Thursday events are transposed into an insidious puppet show that takes place inside her stomach. Relief is only possible by vomiting: a crude form by means of which the descriptor/narrator seems to dispose, in a very literal manner, of the contents of a segment where *mise en abyme* seems also to acquire a very literal meaning.

The second nightmare takes place later in the novel (chapter 34). It involves Isabelita's mother and Don Manuel del Pez, as well as the imminence of an already announced liberal revolution. The sarcastic descriptor also mentions the young girl's collection of useless scraps. This gathering of different materials is encouraged by her father, who tells her to catalogue everything according to a multiplicity of categories.

Los pedacitos de lana de bordar y de sedas y trapo llenaban un cajón. Los botones, las etiquetas de perfumería, las cintas de cigarros, los sellos de correo, las plumas de acero usadas, las cajas de cerillas vacías, las mil cosas informes, fragmentos sin uso ni aplicación, rayaban en lo incalculable. Pero el montón más querido lo componían las estampitas francesas dadas como premio en la escuela, los cromitos del Sagrado Corazón, del Amor Hermoso, de María Alacoque y de Bernardette, pinturillas en que el arte parisiense representaba las cosas santas con el mismo estilo de los figurines de modas. (253)

[Little pieces of wool for embroidery, and bits of silk and cloth filled a large box. Buttons, labels from perfume bottles, bands from cigars, used postage stamps, worn-out steel pens, empty matchboxes, and a thousand and one useless fragments, approached the incalculable. But her favorite pile was composed of French religious prints, which were given to her as prizes at her school – chromos of the Sacred Heart, Holy Love, Maria Alacoque, and Bernardette – little prints in which a Parisian art represented the holy things in the style of fashion plates.]

Here once again an extensive enumeration of items reflects the fashion concerns of the girl's mother, such as the reference to the various pieces of material and to the 'labels of perfume bottles.' Although the first long period of the descriptive block above is not sarcastic, or even ironic, the second part is; the religious objects are referred to as 'pinturillas' [little paintings of no value], and a comparison is made between the representative style of the chromos and the style used in Parisian fashion plates. Implied, as in many other descriptions, is a critique of the Spanish taste for anything French, especially anything from Paris, at a time when all Spanish writers were extensively familiar with realistic/naturalistic French literature.

The idea of cluttered spaces revealing an implicit bad taste appears in many other descriptions in the novel, as for example, in the brief description of the church where Rosalía goes to meet her friend Cándida:

En la iglesia, hecha un ascua de oro, con cortinas de terciopelo del barato, cenefas de papel dorado, candilejas mil, enormes ramilletes de trapo y unos pabellones que parecían de teatro de tercer orden, había tal concurrencia, que era muy difícil penetrar en ella. (134)

[In the church, which looked like a golden ember, with cheap velvet curtains, valances of gilded paper, innumerable lamps, and huge bunches of flowers made of cloth, as well as some tent-shaped curtains that looked as if they had been borrowed for the occasion from a third-rate theatre, there were so many people that it was difficult to get in at all.]

What it looks like is not what it is – as if Madrid as a whole were nothing but a gigantic baroque stage crammed with cheap ornaments, where 'reality' appears as a sort of a deliberate *trompe l'oeil*. At times, in fact, the characters view 'reality' as if it were an artistic construction. Thus, when Rosalía walks with Don Manuel del Pez in the palace terrace, we are told: 'El paseo por sitio tan monumental halagaba la fantasía de la dama, trayéndole reminiscencias de aquellos fondos arquitectónicos que Rubens, Veronés, Vanlóo y otros pintores ponen en sus quadros' [The walk in such a monumental scene stirred the lady's fancy, reminding her of those architectonic backgrounds that Rubens, Veronese, and Van Loo put into their paintings] (106).

The long description of Refugio's apartment, where Rosalía goes to ask desperately for a loan (chapter 45), is another example of a caricaturized space where cheap objects are combined with very expensive ones: 'Sobre la chimenea, un reloj de bronce muy elegante alternaba indignamente con dos perros de porcelana dorados, de malísimo gusto, con las orejas rotas' [On the mantelpiece, a very elegant bronze clock indignantly alternated with two gilded china dogs with broken ears in the worst possible taste] (276).

The notion of text as collage is also communicated in other parts of the novel. Thus, the long sermon Rosalía hears at the church is defined as a 'sermón patético, aflautado, un guisote de lugares comunes con salsa de gestos de teatro' [pathetic and flute-toned sermon, a stew of common-places served with a sauce of theatrical gestures] (134). In a similar man-ner, the journalistic reportage of an official function at the court is said to have '[un] estilo eunuco' [a eunuch style], since Spanish and French sen-tences are mixed indiscriminately.

Although in this chapter I have not analysed character caricaturiza-tions,[20] they can be said to be equally sarcastic. At times they are short anecdotal reports, as, for example, when the descriptor/narrator pre-sents the reader with the bureaucratic speech of Don Manuel del Pez, which consists of a crescendo sequence of more or less synonymous expressions. In a passage where Thiers (that is, Francisco) asks Pez about the present political situation, he answers: 'es imposible, es muy difícil, es arriesgadísimo aventurar juicio alguno.' [it is impossible, it is very dif-ficult, it is extremely risky to hazard any opinion] (108).

It now becomes clear that the long initial description of the cenotaph, due to its privileged position as a first chapter, functions as a proleptic *mise en abyme* of all other subsequent descriptions. Ironically, in this case, *mise en abyme* not only refers to a literary device, but also becomes, very literally, the metaphorical gesture of 'placing into an abyss' a series of representations. However, one might ask, to what extent do these descriptions relate to a main plot?

3. WHEN NARRATION IMITATES DESCRIPTION: LITERARY AND IDEOLOGICAL *MISE EN ABYME*

Although we may be dealing with a realistic linear plot, narration mir-rors, to a certain extent, many of the previously discussed characteristics of descriptions. In a novel composed of fairly short chapters, narration, in the same way as description, evolves as a set of discrete blocks com-parable to a series of anecdotes, and, at times, theatrical sketches.[21]

The main events are triggered by Rosalía de Bringas' obsession with expensive clothing, and by the fact that her husband is a miser who hates to spend money (thus the 'impressive' but cheap cenotaph) and who likes to pay for the family expenses at once and in cash. One day, Rosalía, who according to the narrator has already been 'corrupted' by the expensive dresses Augustín Caballero (a cousin living in France) gave her as a wedding present (chapter 9), and who is tired of having to constantly transform and reassemble her existing wardrobe, sees an expensive cloak at Sobrino Hermanos, one of the fanciest clothing stores in Madrid. Since she has no money of her own besides the meagre allowance her husband gives her for house expenses, Rosalía, encouraged by her friend Milagros, who functions very much as the 'adjuvant' of Rosalía's expensive taste, decides to buy the cloak on credit and pay for it in instalments. To do this, however, she has to borrow from friends. None the less, once she has managed to get the money to pay for the cloak, she is tempted by a very elaborate French hat.

At this point occurs a series of dramatic sketches evocative not only of baroque comedy, but also of the 'make-do' comical plot developments of Spanish picaresque prose.[22] As a way of facilitating such developments, her husband becomes temporarily blind, a result of his composing the very detailed 'obra peluda' [hairy work]. Once he loses his sight, she proceeds to pawn the silver candlesticks, as well as to cut out of a similar type of paper, a ream of banknotes, which she places in the safe that Francisco checks every day by means of his quickly developed sense of touch.

When her husband recovers his sight, however, Rosalía is forced to resort to the services of a moneylender, a greedy man, who, like the famous Spanish inquisitor, is called Torquemada.[23] To pay her debt, she is obliged to humiliate herself by begging money from a former servant, Refugio, who has gone into business by herself. It is with great difficulty that Rosalía convinces Refugio to lend her the money. However, this former servant does not let her go without giving her a sort of 'moral lesson,' which is indirectly aimed at all the political followers and admirers of Queen Isabel II. Thus, Refugio tells her: '¡Ay! qué Madrid éste, todo aparencia. Dice un caballero que yo conozco, que esto es un Carnaval de todos los días, en que los pobres se visten de ricos. Y aquí, salvo media docena, todos son pobres. Facha, señora, y nada más que facha.' [Ah! What a place Madrid is, all make-believe ... A gentleman I know says that the whole thing is a day-to-day Carnival, where the poor dress up as rich people. And here, except for half a dozen families, everyone is poor. Appearance, my dear lady, nothing but appearance.] (283). Later in the following chapter Refugio says to her: '... Un caballero amigo mío ... me ha dicho que aquí todo es pobretería, que aquí no hay aristocracia verdadera, y que la gran mayoría de los que pasan por ricos y calaveras no son más que unos cursis ...' [A gentleman I know ... told me that here there's nothing but disguised poverty, for we don't have a true aristocracy, and the great majority of those who pass for rich and spendthrifts are nothing but a group of phonies ...] (285–6).

It is tempting to assume, as do the annotators of the edition I am using, that the 'gentleman' friend to whom Refugio attributes such opinions is the descriptor/narrator (283, note 118). Indeed, the reported opinions in the above quotations do function as the punch-line of the whole plot, and also as a comment directed at all naïve readers who may quickly identify themselves with the main characters. Such opinions seem to sum up what has occurred in the novel so far, be it through descriptive/narrative segments or through dramatized dialogues. The plot itself is a parodic Carnivalesque transposition of the last months of Isabel's reign, if not of Spain itself in the second half of the nineteenth century: a place where Romantic tendencies combined with outdated baroque bureaucratic structures come face-to-face with the 'wonders' of consumerism.

As previously mentioned, the novel may be read as a *mise en abyme* of a specific political situation. It is interesting to note, following Ricardo Gullón's interpretation in 'La de Bringas' (1970), that the husband of Queen Isabel was also called Francisco, and that he also 'becomes blind' when faced with the excesses of his wife. According to Alda Blanco and Carlos Aguinaga in the preface of their edition, the queen was known to have suggested the auction of the Spanish royal treasure as a means of paying the huge external debt, while securing for her, and for all her government officials, an ostentatious standard of living (13, note 11).

If Rosalía, however, manages to pay all her debts without her husband's knowledge, and acquires in the process a great deal of life experience and independence, the ongoing construction of the cenotaph interrupted by Francisco's 'ophthalmic migraine' is never really concluded; all the characters become caught up in the turmoil of the Liberal Revolution of 1868.[24] At first the reader is tempted to believe that the existing social situation will have to change, but soon comes to realize that everything will remain the same. Even Don Manuel del Pez, a well-paid bureaucrat, finds himself among a family reunion when visiting the new government offices:

Casi todos los individuos que compusieron la Junta eran amigos suyos. Algunos tenían con él parentesco, es decir, que eran algo Peces. En el Gobierno provisional tampoco le faltaban amistades y parentescos y dondequiera que volvía mi amigo los ojos, veía caras pisciformes. Y antes que casualidad, llamaremos a esto Filosofía de la Historia. (304)

[Almost all the people who composed the Junta were friends of Pez (of Mr Fish).

Some of them were actually family relations, which is to say they were some-what Peces (Fishes). He also had a number of friends and relatives in the Provisional Government, and wherever my friend turned his eyes he encountered pisciform faces. And, rather than call such a thing mere chance, let us call it Philosophy of History.]

In this case, aside from a very cynical view of Spanish history, we also find the ironic pun involving the name of one of the main characters: Pez, meaning 'fish,' since he can 'swim' through bureaucracy, as well as through social and political change. It should be noted that other characters also have names that function as 'motivated signs.' Thus, the female friend who is always tempting Rosalía into buying expensive clothes on credit is, ironically, called Milagros, meaning 'miracles.' Similarly, the former servant who constitutes Rosalía's last 'refuge,' and provides the solution for all her credit debts is appropriately called Refugio.

As one would expect in a nineteenth-century realistic novel, in *La de Bringas* there is a strong dialectical relationship between description and narration. In addition, *mise en abyme* comes to acquire less explored meanings, in the light of an overall humorous sarcastic context. In fact, if through description it relates mainly to a series of structural discursive features, narrative *mise en abyme* becomes primarily a mode of replicating, or mirroring for satirical purposes, personally filtered extratextual referents – specifically, the characteristics of a whole political regime.

It could also be argued that, contrary to the assertion of Barthes (1968), descriptive detail in this case is not directly linked to a mere 'effet de réel,' especially when even some of the characters' names seem to be sarcastically motivated. Indeed, minute detail, although credible, creates at times an 'unreal effect,' which is mainly emphasized by the abundant zeugmatic constructions, and, to a lesser extent, by the use of hyperbole, which is known to be prevalent in various forms of caricaturization.

One of the most curious features of this novel, however, is that satire (be it political, literary, or both), although having a very clear ideological and/or pedagogical aim, is always embedded in parody, whether we define the latter as a form of replicating either previous literary texts or contemporaneous socio-cultural structures.

In a novel such as *La de Bringas* where the reader becomes virtually a writer's accomplice, what is created is a type of ironic 'distanciation,' that seems to preclude the parodic characteristics one finds in what has been designated the 'post-modern novel.' Indeed, the post-modern novel might well be seen not only as a recent development but, surprisingly enough, as a continuation of a trend echoing many of the structures and narrative devices already present in baroque prose fiction.

APPENDIX

CAPÍTULO PRIMERO

Era aquello ... ¿como lo diré yo? ... un gallardo artificio sepulcral de atrevidísima arquitectura, grandioso de traza, en ornamentos rico, por una parte severo y rectilíneo a la manera viñolesca, por otra movido, ondulante y quebradizo a la usanza gótica, con ciertos artisbos platerescos donde menos se pensaba; y por fin, cresterías semejantes a las del estilo tirolés que prevalece en los quioscos. Tenía piramidal escalinata, zócalos grecorromanos, y luego machones y paramentos ojivales; con pináculos, gárgolas y doseletes. Por arriba y por abajo, a izquierda y derecha, cantidad de antorchas, urnas, murciélagos, ánforas, búhos, coronas de siemprevivas, aladas clepsidras, guadañas, palmas, anguilas enroscadas y otros emblemas del morir y del vivir eterno. Estos objectos se encaramaban unos sobre otros, cual si se disputasen, pulgada a pulgada, el sitio que habían de ocupar. En el centro del mausoleo, un angelón de buen talle y mejores carnes se inclinaba sobre una lápida, en actitud atribulada y luctuosa, tapándose los ojos con la mano como avergonzado de llorar; de cuya vergüenza se podía colegir que era varón. Tenía este caballerito ala y media de rizadas y finísimas plumas, que le caían por la trasera con desmayada gentileza, y calzaba sus pies de mujer con botitos, coturnos o alpargatas; que de todo había un poco en aquella elegantísima interpretación de la zapatería angelical. Por la cabeza le corría una como guirnalda con cintas, que se enredaban después en su brazo derecho. Si a primera vista se podía sospechar que el tal gimoteaba por la molestia de llevar tanta cosa sobre sí, alas, flores, cintajos y plumas, amén de un relojito de arena, bien pronto se caía en la cuenta de que el motivo de su duelo era la triste memoria de las virginales criaturas encerradas dentro del sarcófago. Publicaban desconsoladamente sus nombres diversas letras compungidas, de cuyos trazos inferiores salían unos lagrimones que figuraban resbalar por el mármol al modo de babas escurridizas. Por tal modo de expresión las afligidas letras contribuían al melancólico efecto del monumento.

Pero lo más bonito era quizá el sauce, ese arbolito sentimental que de antiguo nombran *llorón*, y que desde la llegada de la Retórica al mundo viene teniendo

una participación más o menos criminal en toda elegía que se comete. Su ondulado tronco elevábase junto al cenotafio, y de las altas esparcidas ramas caía la
lluvia de hojitas tenues, desmayadas, agonizantes. Daban ganas de hacerle oler
algún fuerte alcaloide para que se despabilase y volviera en sí de su poético síncope. El tal sauce era irreemplazable en una época en que aún no se hacía leña de
los árboles del romanticismo. El suelo estaba sembrado de graciosas plantas y
flores, que se erguían sobre tallos de diversos tamaños. Había margaritas, pen-
samientos, pasionarias, girasoles, lirios y tulipanes enormes, todos respetuosa-
mente inclinados en señal de tristeza ... El fondo o perspectiva consistía en el
progresivo alejamiento de otros sauces de menos talla, que se iban a llorar a
moco y baba camino del horizonte. Más allá veíanse suaves contornos de mon-
tañas, que ondulaban cayéndose como si estuvieran bebidas; luego había un
poco de mar, otro poco de río, el confuso perfil de una ciudad con góticas torres y
almenas; y arriba, en el espacio destinado al cielo, una oblea que debía de ser la
Luna, a juzgar por los blancos reflejos de ella que esmaltaban las aguas y los
montes.

El color de esta bella obra de arte era castaño, negro y rubio. La gradación
del oscuro al claro servía para producir ilusiones de perspectiva aérea. Estaba
encerrada en un óvalo que podría tener media vara en su diámetro mayor, y
el aspecto de ella no era de mancha, sino de dibujo, hallándose expresado
todo por medio de trazos o puntos. ¿Era talla dulce, aguafuerte, plancha de
acero, boj o pacienzuda obra ejecutada a punta de lápiz duro o con pluma a
la tinta china? ... Reparad en lo nimio, escrupuloso y firme de tan difícil trabajo. Las hojas del sauce se podrían contar una por una. El artista había
querido expresar el conjunto, no por el conjunto mismo, sino por la suma de
pormenores, copiando indoctamente a la Naturaleza; y para obtener el follaje,
tuvo la santa calma de calzarse las hojitas todas una después de la otra.
Habíalas tan diminutas, que no se podían ver sino con microscopio. Todo el
claroscuro del selpulcro consistía en menudos órdenes de bien agrupadas
líneas, formando peine y enrejados más o menos ligeros según la diferente
intensidad de los valores. En el modelado del angelote había tintas tan delica-
das, que sólo se formaban de una nebulosa de puntos pequeñísimos. Parecía
que había caído arenilla sobre el fondo blanco. Los tales puntos, imitando el
estilo de la talla dulce, se espesaban en los oscuros, se ramificaban y desv-
anecían en los claros, dando de sí, con esta alterna y bien distribuida masa, la
ilusión del relieve ...

Era, en fin, el tal cenotafio un trabajo de pelo o en pelo, género de arte que
tuvo cierta boga, y su autor, don Francisco de Bringas, demostraba en él habilidad benedictina, una limpieza de manos y una seguridad de vista que rayaban
en lo maravilloso, si no un poquito más allá. (53–6)

FIRST CHAPTER

That thing was – how shall I put it? – a gallant sepulchral artifice of the most daring architecture: grandiose in design, rich in ornament, on the one hand severe and rectilinear in a Vignolesque manner, on the other full of movement, undulating, discontinued, and Gothic-like, with certain Plateresque traits where you would least expect them; and, finally, with fretwork similar to the Tyrolean style that prevails in kiosks. It had pyramidal ramps and Graeco-Roman foundations, and, at the same time, buttresses with pinnacles, ogival ornaments, gargoyles, and cupolas. From top to bottom, from left to right, it had a quantity of torches, urns, bats, amphorae, owls, wreaths of everlastings, winged hourglasses, scythes, palm leaves, coiled eels, and other emblems of death and eternal life. These objects were so crowded together that they seemed to be disputing inch by inch the space they were to occupy. In the centre of the mausoleum there was a big fat angel of robust physique, leaning upon a gravestone in an afflicted mourning manner, covering his eyes as if he were ashamed of crying – from whose attitude one could infer he was a male. This young gentleman had a wing and a half of very find curling feathers trailing down his back with fainting softness, and his woman's feet were shod with little boots, high-platform sandals, or espadrilles, for there was something of everything in that most elegant interpretation of angelical footwear. Surrounding his head, there was a sort of garland of ribbons which curled around his right arm. If at a first glance it appeared that he was groaning under his burdens (since he was carrying wings, flowers, ribbons, feathers, not to mention a little hourglass), a second look revealed that the real motive of his grief was the sad memory of the virginal creatures buried in the sarcophagus. Their names were sadly published in various contrite letters from whose lower extremities big tears were falling as if oozing out of the marble itself like sliding spit. In this expressive way, the grieving lettering contributed to the melancholic effect of the monument.

But the most beautiful thing of all was, perhaps, the weeping willow, the sentimental little tree that, given its age, is known to cry, and, that since the coming of Rhetoric into the world has had a more or less criminal participation in every elegy that is committed. Its undulating trunk rose up beside the cenotaph, and from its high spreading branches fell a rain of tenuous faint dying leaves. One felt like giving it smelling salts to bring it out of its poetic syncope. Such a weeping willow was irreplaceable at an age in which the trees of Romanticism had not yet been turned into firewood. The ground beneath it was sown with lovely plants and flowers which rose from stalks of varying heights. There were daisies, pansies, passion flowers, sunflowers, lilies, and huge tulips, all respectfully bending down in a sign of grief ... The sense of depth or perspective consisted in showing a procession of other willows of gradually decreasing size, weeping desperately on their way to the horizon. In the distance, one could see the soft outlines of mountains, collapsing as if they had been drinking; there were also a little sea, a bit of river, the disorienting skyline of a city with Gothic towers and battlements; and, up there, in the space reserved for the sky, a wafer which was probably the moon, judging from its white reflexes shimmering upon the waters and the hills.

The colours in this beautiful work of art were brown, black, and blond, the gradations from darker to lighter shades serving to produce the illusion of an aerial perspective. The work, delimited by an oval frame that might have had eighteen inches in its greater diameter, seemed to be not so much a painting but a drawing where everything was expressed through hues and dots. Was it a mezzotint, an etching, a steel engraving, a woodcut, or was it the incredibly patient work of a hard pencil or of a pen dipped in India ink? ... For observe the excessive, scrupulous, and deliberate amount of detail in such a difficult work! The leaves of the willow could be counted one by one. The artist had wanted to give us a sense of totality, not through the ensemble itself, but through an addition of details, while clumsily copying Nature. Indeed, to obtain the foliage, he had had the holy calm of imbuing with colour each single leaf. Some of these were so tiny that could only be seen under a microscope. The chiaroscuro of the sepulchre had been secured by minute variations in the arrangement of lines forming shades and cross-hatchings growing thinner and thicker according to the intensity of the values. In the modeling of the poor angel there were tints so delicate that were only arrived at through a mist of very tiny dots, as if fine sand had fallen upon a white background. These fine dots, imitating the style of a mezzotint, expressed themselves through the shadings while spreading to become fainter in the more clear areas, thus giving us an illusion of relief, owing to their impeccable distribution ...

In sum, it was a capillary assemblage, a type of art that once had a certain vogue -- a work of human hair. Its author, Don Francisco de Bringas, displayed in it a Benedictine ability, a steadiness of hand and sharpness of eye which approached the marvellous, if not something slightly beyond it.

5

Description and modes of representation in Cornélio Penna's *A Menina Morta*

Não existe na literatura brasileira um romance mais sombrio que
A Menina morta, nem outro mais alheio à desenvoltura da peripécia.

[There is not in the Brazilian literature a novel more somber than
A Menina morta, nor one as reticent with regards plot development.]

Luiz Costa Lima[1]

Cornélio Penna's *A Menina Morta* (1954)[2] is a Brazilian novel that seems
to elude all labels categorizing novelistic genres: it has the descriptiveness of the French New Novel, some of the historiographic metafictional
qualities of post-modern fiction,[3] and yet at the same time it manages to
convey, at least on first reading, an overall realistic mode of representation. These characteristics, together with the fact that the novel does not
follow either the 'modernistic' or the 'regionalistic' trends of the Brazilian fiction of the 1950s, may explain why it has remained practically
unknown.[4]

It should be mentioned that Penna's work is out of print at the time I
write.[5] With the exception of the Brazilian critic Luiz Costa Lima, no one
has given this novel the attention it deserves. Costa Lima has written
extensively on Penna's fictional work, particularly on the symbolic and
sociological meanings that permeate a geometry of fictional spaces in *A
Menina Morta*.[6]

This novel, whose action takes place on a big coffee plantation in the second half of the nineteenth century, evolves along a linear chronological
axis, starting with the death of the 'menina' (the young daughter of the

landowner, and the principal character in the book)[7] and ending with the gradual decay of the plantation. However, the reader soon realizes that what could be considered as a plot, albeit linear, is merely a mechanism to facilitate and motivate the inclusion of long descriptive segments. The latter exist along the semantic complexities of a 'representational continuum' that ceases to be entirely homogeneous when we analyse the descriptive segments (even some of the most obviously realistic) at a symbolic and functional level. Furthermore, the sequential logic of what seems to be a fairly realistic plot is continually sabotaged through the inclusion of a great number of ellipses. These devices, however, do not create an immediate effect of 'discohesion,' but rather a series of narrative dead-ends or truncated subplots whose resolutions cannot be inferred through textual information (for example, why has Dona Mariana – the landowner's wife – taken a trip that ends inexplicably at a clearing in the middle of the jungle?). In a similar vein, it is difficult, if not altogether impossible, to pinpoint at times what motivates the characters' actions (for example, why were the slaves and some of the people living on the plantation forbidden to attend the young girl's funeral?).

The characteristics just mentioned seem, in fact, to background what could be considered as a main plot, which, although chronologically linear in its progression, functions merely as a means of bringing together and further contextualizing a set of descriptions.

We should also bear in mind, while analysing this novel, that Cornélio Penna was not only a writer, but also a painter and an illustrator of some of his own fictional works[8] and that *A Menina Morta* (although devoid of illustrations) seems to have been generated around an extratextual referent briefly described in the novel: an oil painting inherited by Penna, representing in a rather naïve style a dead young girl.[9] This painting, the existence of which precedes the writing of the book, is also referred to by the author as 'o retrato da menina morta' [the portrait of the dead young girl]; although the novel is not organized through a set of visual referents (as in the case of Claude Simon's *Histoire*, analysed in chapter 3), it seems none the less to have been constructed as an imitation of pictographic texts, or rather, of cinematic sequences. Confirming this hypothesis are several characteristics: 1) the fact that the novel is organized as a montage of several described spaces; 2) the effect of *ekphrasis*, or visualization, inherent in almost all of its descriptions; and 3) a series of metapictorial references that, in this case, acquire a metanarrative/descriptive relevance.

Since in this text narration, with its mechanisms of logical sequentiality, is frequently put on hold through ellipses during which description takes over, and since as Costa Lima states in one of his essays: 'seria contraditório com a estrutura dos romances de Cornélio Penna que um elemento da peripécia tivesse relevância'[10] [the existence of relevant plot elements would contradict the structure of Cornélio Penna's novels], I have chosen, as previously, a mode of inquiry that focuses mainly on descriptive characteristics. However, besides the analytical framework I have applied to the novels examined in previous chapters, I now take into consideration how the majority of descriptive segments illustrate at least two different types of fictional representation. Therefore, my present analysis attempts to answer the following questions: 1) How can descriptive segments/blocks be conceived of along a 'representational continuum' whose boundaries range from the most realistic to the most 'symbolic' and quasi-fantastic; and 2) how does the main character (the 'menina' who dies before the beginning of the novel) come to be present not only through a series of references in the speeches of other characters, but, above all, through the mode in which certain descriptions of space are represented throughout the novel?

As far as the macrostructure of the text is concerned, we are constantly confronted in *A Menina Morta* with a form of descriptive sequencing for which the best exemplifying rhetorical figure (as Costa Lima has pointed out in reference to the whole novel) is chiasmus rather than antithesis.[11] It is as if there were a peculiar effect taking place across descriptive segments, precipitating the more realistically represented against the more symbolic and vice versa, while the point where both types would intersect or overlap (as in a metaphor working at a macrotextual level) is deliberately kept hidden by recurrent ellipses. This creates a series of non-existent textual spaces that Costa Lima (1976, 1989) reads as the marks of an oppressive interdiction whereby an access to knowledge seems to be constantly postponed. Thus, in the same way as the principal female characters cannot bring together their experiences and information in terms of a coherent whole, the reader cannot map with certainty, through explicit or implicit information, many of the mechanisms of a realistically embedded plot.

A constant dialectic, nevertheless, is established between historically determined spaces and the actions or reactions of the characters, as if the sociohistorical environment depicted in the novel were both a product and a production of the characters themselves, and the latter, mere elements that function as symbolic and/or metaphorical representations of their own environment. To these characteristics I should add that an exterior narrative/descriptive voice follows, almost systematically, the point of view of the characters whose particular gaze it seems to inscribe. It is this constant crisscrossing, or inversions of points of view, that contributes not only to the construction of ideological traces (for example, the point of view of the slaves as opposed to that of the masters), but also to the diversification of the monological qualities of an exterior third-person narrative/descriptive voice.

In *A Perversão do Trapesista*, Luiz Costa Lima states that, from the beginning of the novel, the reader is faced with an obsessive enumeration of details, which communicate an oppressive effect; that is, with something that, in spite of the high ceilings of the Grotão (the labyrinthine mansion on the plantation),[12] is able to create a claustrophobic or a progressively asphyxiating space. Such an effect, however, seems to result not just from a mere enumeration of objects or from the silences and prohibitions the characters impose on themselves, but, above all, from a descriptive technique whereby a series of illuminated objects is juxtaposed against others that, remaining in darkness, can only be conceived of as hypothetical presences:

Não havia ali nenhuma luz natural, pois não existia clarabóia e as bandeiras das portas eram guarnecidas de tela de arame, de tal forma que quando estavam fechadas não deixavam passar sequer réstia luminosa que tornasse visível a grande cômoda de embutidos, a marquesa e as duas canastras que a mobilavam. (chap. 4, 740)

[There was no natural light in there, since there were no skylights and the fanlights above the doors were provided with a wire gauze, so that when they were closed they would not allow a single ray of sunshine that might have made visible the commode with inlaid work, the ottoman, and the two leather trunks that furnished the room.]

Or, later in the novel:

O clarão palpitante das velas não vencia o escuro dos cantos e ora se tornava mais forte, ora enfraquecia de modo a fazer com que os vultos se destacassem ou esmaecessem caprichosamente. Muitas vêzes os rostos pálidos e atentos das duas irmãs, Inacinha e Sinhá-Rôla, surgiam, e seus olhos tinham brilhos repentinos, pois talvez a luz refletisse as lágrimas. Outras vêzes Carlota sentia a impressão de estar só no grande canapé de palha entre duas sombras sem vida, sem fisionomias logo depois reveladas quando eram alumiadas, os traços bem marcados de Dona Virgínia e os empastamentos do rosto de Dona Mariana Violante, ladeados por brincos de diamantes reluzentes e de grandes dimensões. (chap. 66, 1042)

[The palpitating glimmer of the candles could not overcome the darkness of the corners, and either it would grow stronger, or it would grow fainter, so as to highlight human shapes that would whimsically fade way. Many times, the pale and attentive faces of both sisters, Inacinha and Sinhá-Rôla, would appear, and their eyes had a sudden sparkle, for perhaps the light could only reflect the tears. Other times, Carlota would have the sensation of being alone upon the long straw chair, between two lifeless shadows whose absent features would appear in a flash, the well-marked traces of Dona Virgínea, and the two swathes of hair framing the face of Dona Mariana Violante, flanked by earrings studded with huge glittering diamonds.]

One of the most surprising effects in the quotations above resides in how certain absences come to acquire the weight of hidden revelations. It is precisely what is kept in darkness that seems to alter, offset, and enclose an enumeration of visualized objects, as if the materiality of the gaze could only regain its object, and its own reverberating echo, once it had been filtered through a non-visible space. In a similar manner, it is the presence of the 'menina,' be it as a 'personagem sem interioridade'[13] [character with no internal make-up] or as the 'presence of an absence,' that contributes towards the creation of the oppressive effect we find in a large number of descriptions where she is named or merely felt as a haunting presence by the other characters and by the reader.

These particular descriptions achieve within the written text a pictorial effect of chiaroscuro able to evoke baroque paintings typical of an interaction between a set of illuminated objects and the ones that insinuate themselves through shadows and darkness (for example, many of the paintings by Caravaggio). However, they may also alert us to other similar patterns in the novel. Another example is the constant oscillation between realism and symbolism among its descriptive segments.

It should be stressed, however, that such an oscillation able to evoke different gradations of light (the descriptions that tend towards a more realistic representational pole presuppose a brightly illuminated environment while the more symbolic relate to a more shady or dark setting) does not operate as it would in a text revealing a fantastic mode of representation. While in a 'fantastic' text one generally finds a contrast between verisimilar and non-verisimilar strata, in *A Menina Morta* we never totally abandon an overall mode of realistic representation. In fact, elements that in certain descriptions could be characterized by their quasi-hallucinatory qualities, come to be justified or explained in the text itself either as memories, as invocations, or as the desire for the presence of the dead and absent 'menina.' In sum, it is as if such elements were psychological traces, revealing a given point of view, where several forms of perception seem to oscillate equally between an exterior objectivity and the feelings such an objectivity may provoke.

From this chiasmatic effect, which occurs constantly in the novel, originate two different but not antithetic forms of descriptive 'modalization': the kind that through several extra- or intratextual references relates more directly to a series of accurate sociohistorical and/or ethnographic data,[14] and the kind that through intra- or intertextual references is more closely related to an aesthetic practice. One should notice, however, that in the same way as description in the social sciences can be, at times, literary,[15] no description in literature is entirely devoid of marks of historicity since the marks in question seem to be inherent in their very own linguistic make-up.

In the case of *A Menina Morta*, the notion of descriptive polarities in a dialectic interaction not only facilitates a reading of this novel, but also our proposed mode of inquiry.

1. SEMANTIC POLARITIES AND DESCRIPTIVE 'MODALIZATIONS'

As mentioned before, the narrative axis in *A Menina Morta* becomes a means to foreground a large amount of descriptive information, but, unlike in a nineteenth-century novel (such as Zola's *Une Page d'amour*, analysed in chapter 2), one cannot establish a sharp distinction between foregrounded and backgrounded descriptive material, and, subsequently, between more versus less meaningful descriptive blocks. In this case, we are constantly confronted (almost as if in a cinematographic text) with the caption of a series of well-identified spaces, where characters seem to move and talk erratically while engaging in activities that may not necessarily contribute to the main plot.

We tend, therefore, to assign an equal value not only to all descriptions in this novel, but also to many narrative blocks that have a descriptive-like function. While all of these segments do not share the same stylistic, discursive, and functional characteristics, their differences and/or similarities can be made more explicit, if we conceive of a 'representational continuum' able to reveal an oscillation between two main types of semantic 'modalizations.'

As the main corpus on which to elaborate our analysis, I have chosen two long descriptive blocks that exemplify well the chiasmatic inversions that constantly take place at a representational level. In addition, we shall be examining one of the narrative episodes to demonstrate that what could be designated as narration at a stylistic and discursive level, comes in this case to acquire a descriptive function.

Segment 1:

E tôdas olharam ao mesmo tempo para o quadrado, pois chegavam os três grupos de escravos que iniciavam a colheita, na escolha dos primeiros grãos maduros do café. Na frente vinham as negras com os grandes balaios cheios de frutas ainda salpintadas de prêto e de escarlate, e logo seguidas pelos homens que traziam dois ou três cestos superpostos, em altas tôrres, acompanhados pelos tomadores de conta dos eitos. Fechavam o cortejo mulatas gordas, que traziam nos ombros os paus das barracas enrolados na lona grossa, e samburás com latas e garrafas destinadas ao leite dos negrinhos e aos refrescos, acompanhadas por moleques e meninas em desabrida algazarra, com pequenos sacos às costas. O quadrado todo se animou de vida, pelos panos brancos, pelas côres ousadas dos saiotes, pela tez escura e de variados cambiantes, e parecia o mercado de cidade do extremo oriente ou o pátio de grande caravanseralho. Vieram todos até perto do alpendre e ali foram dispostos em semicírculo os recepientes tecidos de taquara e de cipó, para contagem e verificação do pêso. O Sr. Justino, vindo apressado da mangueira onde ficara ainda muito tempo com o veterinário, sentou-se no banco de ferro da pequena varanda e gritou logo que deveriam fazer tudo em silêncio. Não era possível porém conter a agitação e falatório dos negros, na ânsia febril de receber a recompensa de seu trabalho, e assim o zunzum era de ensurdecer apesar dos esforços do feitor, postado nos primeiros degraus com o grande chicote em riste. Entretanto logo tudo se acalmou, quando começaram a trazer os primeiros cêstos para a verificação e a entrega das chapinhas de metal àqueles que haviam colhído além da tarefa de que tinham sido incumbidos. As negras escondiam precipitadamente no seio as rodelas amarelas, com a marca do Senhor gravada no cobre, entre a pele e a camisa de algodão grosso, e os homens as recebiam gravemente e as guardavam com displicência afetada nos bolsos das calças, mas todos logo em seguida corriam para a senzala, depois de terem dado alguns passos com estudada lentidão. Eram muitos os balaios e depois foram levados até a tulha de onde sairiam, já despejados, para o correr alpendrado das casas de fora, onde esperariam a continuação da safra. Os grandes terreiros calçados de lajes enormes já tinham sido limpos e tôdas as ervas arrancadas, para seca do café a se iniciar logo no dia seguinte, pois naquele ano a colheita prometia ser copiosa. (chap. 32, 893–4)

[And they all looked at the same time towards the square, since three groups of slaves were arriving to initiate the harvest by choosing the first ripe grains of coffee. In the front, the black women were coming with great baskets full of fruit that still showed some black and red speckles; they were immediately followed by men who were carrying two or three superimposed baskets forming high towers. The men were walking together with the people in charge of measuring the amount gathered by each worker. This procession ended with a group of fat mulatto women who were carrying their tent frames rolled in thick canvas upon their shoulders, and baskets with cans and bottles for the milk and refreshments of the black children. These women were walking together with young black boys and girls who were carrying little bags over their shoulders and engaging in an unrestrained uproar. The whole square came to life given the white pieces of cloth, the daring colours of the skirts, and the various tones of dark skin. And it looked like a market in a city of the Far East, or the patio of a huge inn for caravan travellers. They all came towards the porch, and there, in a semicircle, the containers made of bamboo and tropical vines were presented for the counting and verification of their weight. Senhor Justino, who was rushing from under a mango tree where he had stayed a long time with the veterinarian, sat down upon the iron bench in the small veranda, and immediately shouted that they should go about it in silence. However, it was not possible to restrain the agitation and chatter of the blacks in their feverish desire to receive the rewards of their work. Therefore, the loud hubbub was deafening in spite of the efforts of the foreman placed on the front steps with a whip in his hand. Meanwhile, everything calmed down when they started to bring the first baskets for verification and for the distribution of small metal tokens to those who had gathered more than the amount they had been ordered to. The black women would hastily hide in their breasts the yellow tokens with the mark of the master engraved on copper, and the men would respectfully receive these and discreetly keep in the pockets of their trousers. But soon, after some studied slow steps, they all ran towards the slave quarters. There were many baskets and they were then taken to a granary from whence they would emerge already empty to be placed in the porches of the outer houses. There, they would await the continuation of the harvest. The large terraces, paved with enormous slabs, had already been cleaned and had all the weeds removed so that the coffee could start drying on the following day, because in that year the harvest promised to be abundant.]

At a lexical level, one notices, particularly, nouns such as 'balaios' [baskets], 'mangueira' [mango tree]; 'moleque' [young black boy], and 'senzala' [slave quarters] (two words of Quimbundo origin)[16]; borrowings from the native South-American Tupi language that are typically Brazilian, such as 'samburá' [an elongated type of basket used for fishing], 'taquara' [bamboo], and 'cipó' [a type of tropical vine]; as well as a Black Creole adaptation of a Portuguese word, such as 'Sinhá' instead of 'Senhora' [lady/Mrs]. By using such lexical items among a variety of more formal Portuguese vocabulary and grammatical constructions, the descriptive voice is creating a more realistic (or credible) effect, thus opting for a range of terms that better illustrate the historical 'scene' it recreates.

At a stylistic level this 'scene,' whose visual and documentary-like qualities almost transpose into written language the impression of a filmic excerpt (for nothing in it behaves as in a static image), does not contain a large number of figures of speech that could hinder its ekphrastic qualities.[17] Apart from the sparse occurrence of similes or implied comparisons (for example, 'cêstos superpostos, em altas torres' [superimposed baskets forming high towers], or 'parecia o mercado ...' [it looked like the market ...]), one can only register metaphors already built into common linguistic expressions, such as 'o quadrado todo se animou de vida' [the whole square came to life]. Furthermore, and still to facilitate its ekphrastic effect, the long sentences used in this case inside a single paragraph, are brought together by a flowing and undisturbed rhythm and by a very careful type of punctuation that strongly conveys the 'schematization' that shapes its reading reception.

At a discursive level, if we examine all the 'finite verb forms' used in this segment (that is, the ones that are conjugated), we notice an almost equal balance between 'perfective' and 'imperfective' verbal aspects. This may surprise us, since the imperfective aspect is usually far more commonly used in descriptive segments. Another uncommon characteristic may also lie in the fact that, although this segment aims at an effect of *ekphrasis*, verbs related to visual perception, such as *olhar* [to look / to watch] and *parecer* [to look like], are quite rare, since the implied mechanism of visualization does not hinge, in this case, on a set of discrete images but on the logical sequence they bring forth in terms of everyday forms of visual perception.

In fact, as we examine the internal organization of this segment, we find its narrative structure can be synthesized in the following manner:

a) 'chegavam os três grupos de escravos'
   [the three groups of slaves were arriving]

b) 'Vieram todos até perto do alpendre'
   [they all came towards the porch]

c) 'O Sr. Justino ... sentou-se ... e gritou logo que deveriam fazer tudo
   em silêncio'
   [Senhor Justino ... sat down ... and immediately shouted that they
   should go about it in silence]

d) 'Entretanto logo tudo se acalmou, quando começaram a trazer os
   primeiros cêstos para a verificação e a entrega das chapinhas de
   metal'
   [Meanwhile, everything calmed down when they started to bring
   the first baskets for verification and for the distribution of small
   metal tokens]

e) 'As negras escondiam ... no seio as rodelas amarelas'
   [The black women were hiding ... in their breasts the round yellow tokens]

f) 'os homens as recebiam ... e as guardavam ... logo em seguida corriam para a senzala'
   [The men would receive these and keep them ... after ... they ran
   towards the slave quarters]

This type of structure, where the descriptive elements have been sup-
pressed as much as possible, makes it easier to verify that, in segment 1,
description imitates a narrative program, that is, a logical sequence of
actions from (a) to (f). This is stressed not only by a concatenation of
action verbs, but also by adverbial expressions that render a series of
enumerations less arbitrary and more logically connected: 'Na frente vinham as negras ... logo seguidas pelos homens ...' [In the front, the black
women were coming ... immediately followed by men ...] (emphasis
mine). These characteristics allow us, no doubt, to read this segment as if
it were a narrative passage. In fact, there are other elements that contribute towards a dynamic effect although they do not constitute a sequence
of actions, as for example, certain micro-segments that, in this context,
imply movement: 'moleques e meninas em desabrida algazarra' [young

black boys and girls *in an unrestrained uproar*], 'a agitação e falatório dos negros' [*the agitation and chatter* of the blacks], 'o zunzum era de ensurdecer' [*the loud hubbub* was deafening], and 'as negras escondiam *precipitadamente* ...' [the black women would *hastily* hide ...] (emphasis mine).

Although at a stylistic and discursive level segment 1 uses a number of narrative-like devices, at a functional level it works very much as a description. In fact, this passage occurs in a chapter where Celestina and the two sisters, Inacinha and Sinhá-Rôla, are talking about Dona Mariana, and, therefore, does not relate directly to any previous information.

The passage inserted in the text: 'E todas olharam ao mesmo tempo para o quadrado' [And they all looked at the same time towards the square], together with the final comment in a subsequent paragraph: 'Esse espetáculo realizado diante das três senhoras com rapidez, grande ruído e vivacidade exuberante, as distraía do que conversavam ...' [That scene carried out in front of the three ladies, with swiftness, great noise, and exuberant animation, distracted them from what they were talking about ...] (chap. 32, 895), function very much as a sort of illustrative tableau (an animated *tableau vivant*) whose immediate framing is established by the 'square' itself.

In addition, the previously mentioned series of actions through which this description becomes narrativized at a discursive level bear no relation to the main narrative axis of the novel, except at a general semantic level. In fact, its notations of sound and colour, together with a very particular type of discursive montage emphasizing its visual aspects, contribute towards a more 'mimetic' or realistic type of representation. Besides, it is its most descriptive aspects, contained in the historical and/or ethnographic data it recreates, that inscribe in the novel the marks of a specific historicity – something that could not be arrived at through a bare sequence of actions.

However, segment 1, while being focalized through the gaze of the three female characters, also constitutes a 'scene' able to provoke in Celestina mental flashbacks related to the dead 'menina.' Thus, when in the same brief chapter the collective point of view is reduced to Celestina's, we read:

Recordava-se [Celestina] da menina, que vinha sentar-se na sua cadeirinha ao lado do Sr. Justino ou então nos degraus da escada e, com habilidade, furtava algumas chapinhas para dar disfarçadamente às negras, quando vinham receber o seu quinhão. (chap. 32, 895)

[Celestina would recall the young girl who used to sit in her little chair beside Senhor Justino, or upon the steps, and, discreetly, would steal some small tokens she would give, surreptitiously, to the black women, when they came to receive their share.]

These memories do, in fact, set the scene for another description one could almost read as pertaining to the 'fantastic mode.'[18] However, it should be stressed that in the context of the novel, remembering becomes, to a certain extent, a form of seeing or of making present a former visual perception.

A môça *via distintamente* a figura da menina, com seus vestidos esvoaçantes, com o cabelo de tons fulvos rebrilhantes ao sol, as pernas a balançarem sob as rendas e babados, como um milagre de doçura e de pureza ... (chap. 32, 895, emphasis mine).

[The young woman could *see distinctively* the figure of the little girl, with her fluttering gowns, with her red hair intensely glowing in the sun, her legs swinging under the lace and the frills, like a miracle of sweetness and purity ...]

Although the adverb 'distintamente' [distinctively] brings an almost eerie quality to this segment, it is not as if the dead 'menina' had taken the appearance of a ghost, but were rather the projection of a previous memory suddenly made present due to Celestina's nostalgic mood.

These examples reveal that Celestina, after being the focalizer of a realistically represented 'scene' involving the slaves, ends up seeing something that is not 'really' there, or that does not belong to the same time-space frame: the icon-like image of the 'menina.' Similarly, we can notice as readers how a very realistic descriptive segment seems to attract a more 'symbolic' one.

In sum, although segment 1 inscribes the vision of a presence in a way that is characteristically 'mimetic,' or simply constitutes a mode of realistic representation, it also evokes and paves the way for the inclusion of other descriptive segments pertaining to the dead 'menina' as the 'presence of an absence.' In fact, what the characters see is later replaced by an impression of *déjà vu* (the phantasmagoric vision of a past invading the present), or by the prediction of future misfortunes metonymically related to the little girl's death. This event, which occurs before the beginning of the first chapter, constantly works not only as a destabilizing element in the life of the big plantation, but also as a haunting presence able to challenge the more realistic representational qualities of the novel.

Another example of mimetic description that seems to announce future deaths is a passage where, as in segment 1, we are dealing with the depiction of an activity that also informs us about the daily life on the plantation: the dyeing of woven materials kept in stock. After an accurate and detailed description of all the objects needed for the preparation of the dyes, a dialogue between Sinhá-Rôla and Joana Tintureira [Joana the dye-maker] takes place:

– Braúna é para fazer tinta prêta, não é? – perguntou Sinhá-Rôla, que logo acrescentou: – Para quê mais luto? Nós tôdas já temos vestidos pretos suficientes para o tempo que vai ser preciso. Quem mandou ferver braúna? –

– Não foi ninguém não senhora, minha Nhanhã ... mas eu tinha ido buscar braúna e pensei que fôsse preciso muita roupa preta. (chap. 34, 906)

['"Braúna"[19] is to make black dye, isn't it?' asked Sinhá-Rôla, who immediately added: 'Why more mourning outfits? We all have sufficient black dresses to last us for the rest of our lives. Who asked for "braúna" to be boiled?'

'Nobody did, my lady, my dearest lady ... but I had gone to fetch "braúna" and I thought that a lot of black clothing might be needed.']

The allusion to black clothing not only brings to mind the mourning for the 'menina' but also foreshadows future deaths and misfortunes: the deaths of Celestina, her father, and her younger brother, as well as the fact that when Dona Mariana returns to the Grotão mansion, after a long and unexplained absence, she has already gone mad.

We are now in a position to analyse segment 2, which I have chosen as a descriptive example that can be placed at the other end of the 'representational continuum' previously mentioned.

In this segment, Celestina, unable to fall asleep, and 'convencida de que as tábuas do corredor estalavam debaixo do pêso de alguém em sua passagem furtiva' [convinced that the wooden boards in the corridor were cracking under the weight of somebody who passed furtively by] (292), goes down to the garden where she sees what seems to be Carlota's shape.

Segment 2:

Finalmente chegou à pequena aberta formada pelo recanto onde estava o banco, e deteve-se para não sair em plena luz do luar, que livre dos galhos das árvores ali batia em sua plenitude e pelo contraste tornava impossível de se reconhecer os traços do vulto sempre imóvel e alheio a tudo que se passava em derredor. Celestina começou a sentir-se gelada e teve ímpetos de gritar, de alertar aquela visão, para que se denunciasse ou se desvanecesse, porque compreendia não ser possível não ter ela ainda percebido a sua presença ali, tão próxima, e sua respiração se fazia alta e irregular. Conseguiu porém conter-se e dando ágil passo, quase salto, alcançou o banco, para nêle se sentar e ficou separada da sombra pelo espaço do assento ainda livre, onde a luz se reflectia muito branca.

Foi então que percebeu não estar o vulto imóvel. No banco iluminado ela viu passar a sua mão muito pálida, e parecia varrer a superfície com seus dedos contraídos. Esse gesto se repetia com regularidade, sempre o mesmo, mas não havia ali nada para tirar, para fazer cair no chão ... E Celestina acompanhou fascinada aquêle movimento regular, sem ânimo de erguer os olhos e procurar distinguir a quem pertencia aquela mão, que semelhava ela própria pequeno fantasma, independente do corpo tão próximo, e ficou assim por muito tempo sem saber se não devia fugir. Tudo em tôrno dela perdera inteiramente a sua significação, e era como se o mundo tivesse desabado silenciosamente e só ela escapara, prêsa àquela mão que raspava sem cessar alguma nódoa invisível ali existente, e que ela não sabia explicar. Entretanto a luz da lua continuava o seu giro, e agora a copa das árvores se interpunha entre ela e o lugar onde estavam, que se tornou assim sombrio. Então Celestina compreendeu, talvez mesmo sem ouvir, que a pessoa ao seu lado murmurava baixinho algumas palavras sôltas ...

Tinha certeza agora de ser Carlota quem ali ficara, sem a ver, sem a sentir, completamente alheada. De súbito perdeu o mêdo e examinou-a sem preocupação alguma, na curiosidade de duas viajantes que se encontram lado a lado na banqueta da diligência, e não pôde afirmar ser ela mesma, pois na penumbra não era possível fixar seus traços, e todo o seu corpo mantinha aquela atitude irreal, flutuante, e apenas tomara o banco como apoio. Havia vaga auréola de sobrenatural em tôrno de seu rosto, cujo perfil perdido ela apenas distinguia, e não via nem sequer o ritmo de sua respiração erguer o seu peito, coberto pelo cabeção branco, muito liso, de aspecto monacal. (chap. 107, 1217–18)

[Finally, she arrived at a small opening formed by the recessed area where the bench was, and she stopped so as not to come out into the moonlight that, away from the tree branches, was being reflected upon that surface in all its plenitude. Due to the contrast of light and shade, it was impossible to recognize the traces of the human shape, forever immobile and far removed from whatever was happening around it. Celestina was feeling the frozen cold, anxious to scream and to alert that vision, so that it would either betray itself or simply fade away. Because she could not understand that it did not acknowledge her presence there, so very near, her breathing was now becoming heavy and irregular. She could, however, get hold of her senses, and with an agile step, almost a jump, she reached the bench to sit down on it, and she stayed there, separated from the shadow by the still empty space on the bench where a very pale light was falling.

Only then she realized that the human shape was not immobile. Upon the illuminated bench she saw its very pale hand with contracted fingers that seemed to go back and forth upon the empty surface between them. That gesture, always the same, repeated itself with regularity, but there was nothing on that surface that could possibly have been taken hold of, or thrown upon the ground ... And Celestina, in her fascination, followed that regular movement with hardly the courage to raise her eyes and find out to whom that hand belonged. The hand was in itself similar to a small ghost, independent from that other body, so near, and Celestina remained there for a long time without knowing if she should run away... Everything around her had suddenly lost its meaning, and it was as if the world itself had crumbled and she were the only survivor attached to that hand that incessantly scratched or rattled over some invisible stain, for the presence of which she could not find an explanation. Meanwhile, the light of the moon was following its course, and now, the treetops were reflected between her and the bench where they sat suddenly enveloped by the same shadows. Then, Celestina understood, perhaps without even listening, that the person beside her was murmuring softly some random words ...

Now, she was certain that it was Carlota who had remained there without seeing her, without having noticed her, completely removed as she was from their present surroundings. And then she finally lost her fear and examined the other person with no special preoccupation, with the curiosity of two travellers who find themselves side by side upon the bench of a stagecoach, and she could not affirm with certainty that it was Carlota, since, in the penumbra surrounding them, it was not possible to make out her shape, and her whole body maintained an unreal and floating aspect, for she had only taken that bench as a place on which to lean. There was a vague supernatural halo around her face, of which she could only distinguish her fading profile, and she could not even perceive the breathing movement of the other woman's chest, which was covered by a very smooth and short white cape that had a monastic appearance.]

If we compare at a stylistic level this segment with segment 1, we can find several differences: first, in this large block we are no longer dealing with the typical Brazilian lexical items that added realism to segment 1; second, while in the first segment one presupposed an illuminated space where actions could be easily visualized, in segment 2 the depicted space is sombre or faintly lit; third, although this description has fewer figures of speech that segment 1, apart from a very few implied comparisons, its general theme hinges on the ambiguities of a perception, which, to a certain extent, makes it more complex and not so immediately realistic. In fact, in this case we are dealing with a different 'texture,' and with a mode of representation that no longer relies on a large amount of explicit information. Consequently, segment 2 invites a type of reception responsive to more implicit and more symbolic meanings.

At a discursive level, if we look at the range of verb tenses used in segment 2, we find that the majority of action verbs are conjugated in the imperfect tense, that is, have an 'imperfective aspect' that, at times, is further stressed by the use of reflexive conjugations (for example, 'se fazia' [was becoming], and 'se interpunha' [was coming between]).

On the other hand, the large number of verbs that do have a 'perfective aspect' (that is, verbs conjugated in the perfect and/or the pluperfect) do not indicate action. Many, in fact, are either 'stative verbs' (for example, *deter-se* [to detain oneself/to stop], and *ficar* [to stay/to remain]); or verbs that indicate perception, such as *perceber* [to understand/to perceive], *distinguir* [to distinguish], *ver* [to see], *parecer* [to look like], and *examinar* [to examine]). Furthermore, beyond their aspectual characteristics, many of the action verbs either function as common types of metaphor built into everyday language, or have inanimate subjects (for example, 'luar, que ... ali batia,' [literally, 'moonlight, that ... was beating there'], 'a luz da lua continuava o seu giro' [the light of the moon was following its course], and 'a copa das árvores se interpunha entre ela e o lugar onde estavam' [literally, 'the treetops were coming between her and the bench where they sat'].

There is no doubt that segment 2 is a description. However, it is neither entirely static nor devoid of temporality. Were we to summarize the narrative-like information contained, for example, in the first paragraph of this segment, we could do it in the following manner:

a) '[Celestina] chegou à pequena aberta'
    [Celestina arrived at a small opening]

b) 'deteve-se'
    [she stopped]

c) 'dando ágil passo, quase salto, alcançou o banco'
    [with an agile step, almost a jump, she reached the bench]

d) 'ficou separada da sombra'
    [she was separated from the shadow]

However, unlike in segment 1, here there is no logically concatenated series of actions. (A) does not imply (b), nor can we read (c) as the consequence of (a) and (b). In the same way, (d) does not represent a logical conclusion for some of the actions initiated in (a).

In fact, in spite of indications of action and/or movement, we are in this case no longer dealing with a 'narrativized description,' since the main events account solely for the several stages of an ongoing observation. Temporality, none the less, is expressed through other means: first, by the adverbs in the opening of each paragraph – '*Finalmente* chegou' [*Finally*, she arrived], 'Foi *então* que percebeu' [Only *then* she realized], and 'Tinha certeza *agora*' [*Now*, she was certain] (emphasis added); and second, by the effect of chiaroscuro, which in this case does not depend, as in a painting, on a fixed source of light, but on the natural movement of the moon – which implies an indeterminate temporal span.

Besides, if we consider the graphic presentation of this carefully punctuated description, we realize that each successive paragraph of the three does not reflect a specific change of content, nor does it follow stylistic conventions. We might speculate about the possibility that the two blanks between paragraphs mirror the two suspension marks present in this descriptive block, both as signs of a lapse of time, and as indicators of an elliptical effect that, occurring discretely between minor discursive segments, contributed to the inscribing of a time span. One of the best examples of the latter can be found in the last paragraph of segment 2, where two contradictory sentences seem to cancel each other out: 'Tinha certeza agora de ser Carlota quem ali ficara' [She was now certain that it was Carlota], and 'não pôde afirmar ser ela mesma' [She could not affirm with certainty that it was Carlota]. In fact, however, instead of establishing a contradiction, the sentences presuppose an ongoing perceptive adjustment along an unspecified time continuum.

The subtle ellipses, the staccato we may be hearing beneath a flowing rhythm, pertain mostly to the semantic qualities of this description, for it is at a semantic level that this segment becomes more significant.[20]

As I mentioned before, we are dealing here with an effect of chiaroscuro that, unlike in previous quotations, cannot be compared to the fixedness of a painting. What remains in darkness versus what becomes highlighted reveals (even more in this case) a specific choice on the part of an exterior descriptive voice.

Both characters in this description remain in the dark: Carlota, who is later identified, and Celestina, who tries to perceive the presence of the former. Curiously, the light falls first on the empty space on the bench where they both sat, and it is inside the limits of that vacant space that Celestina sees Carlota's hand 'que semelhava ela própria pequeno fantasma' [similar to a small ghost], engaged in an uncontrollable movement, trying to scratch out or to erase a stain, a mark, or something with no physical volume that she could not 'fazer cair no chão' [throw upon the ground] or get rid of. Later, this illuminated 'emptiness' is covered by the shadow of the trees, and the light shifts to become a 'vaga auréola de sobrenatural' [vague supernatural halo] around Carlota's face.

What is highlighted, in this case, is the empty space between both women – a void where Celestina, the focalizer of this description, sees a phantasmagoric presence. As such, it evokes in this context the absence of the main character: the dead 'menina,' who, since the beginning of the novel, seems to be everywhere as a haunting presence. Similarly, at a structural level, if the 'menina' is represented as a major ellipsis, we as readers tend to feel her presence not only through the eerie quality of some of the descriptions of space, or simply as a construction built through the dialogue of the various female characters, but, above all, as that which inhabits a series of recurrent 'gaps,' which cannot be filled through implied data or by the reader's imagination. Furthermore, as an oxymoronic absent-present main character, the 'menina' installs a progressively elliptical mechanism that, as in segment 2, gradually drains the characters' sense of identity by tainting the colours and the shapes of the 'reality' that surrounds them. Another reference to the dead 'menina' can also be found when Celestina examines Carlota 'na curiosidade de duas viajantes que se encontram lado a lado na banqueta da diligência' [with the curiosity of two travellers who find themselves side by side upon the bench of a stagecoach]. This reference brings to mind the fact that the young girl's coffin was taken to the church on Celestina's lap and inside a stagecoach. Moreover, the garden mentioned in this description is a place where the 'menina' used to play, and where the slave Libânia – her wet-nurse – had buried the baby girl's umbilical cord.

It should be noted that, although this segment seems to have characteristics one generally finds in 'fantastic' literature, such an effect is cancelled by some of the contextual information. In fact, Celestina has already contracted tuberculosis, which may explain the nature of her hypersensitive perceptions. On the other hand, Carlota is, at that time, in a state of psychological depression brought about not only by the unexplained events taking place around her, but also by the fact that her father has promised her in marriage to a man she hardly knows. Once back from a college in Rio de Janeiro, Carlota becomes the 'menina' on the plantation, which, to a certain extent, leads her to assimilate some of the characteristics attributed to her dead sister.

As was previously mentioned, we can now better observe how the literary descriptions in *A Menina Morta*, although characterized by an overall realistic mode of representation, seem to oscillate systematically between two poles: a 'more mimetic' and a 'more symbolic' one.

It is this polarization that paves the way for the chiasmatic effect created by the semantic 'modalizations' that take place mainly through the descriptive aspects of this novel. This can be more easily explained if we consider segments 1 and 2 at a functional level. While the first relates to the fictional recreation of a large amount of well-researched historical and ethnographic data, the second is more closely connected to the aesthetic devices that shape a particular type of discourse. Furthermore, segment 2 echoes not only all the descriptive passages in which the absent 'menina' becomes a presence, but also narrative episodes that, by their specific nature, acquire a descriptive-like function.

2. DESCRIPTIVE NARRATIONS

Certain descriptions may, at times, reveal narrative characteristics (for example, segment 1) or may be read as implied narrations whenever a series of purely descriptive micro-segments can be placed into a logical sequence (for example., some of the postcard descriptions in Simon's *Histoire*, analysed in chapter 3). Conversely, narrative passages, although retaining their narrative characteristics at a stylistic and discursive level, can sometimes function as descriptions. This generally occurs when they cannot be read as part of an explicit main plot, and acquire the functions of expanding on the characteristics of a described character (for example, a digressive narrative episode or anecdotal report accentuating the psychological traits or the mode of behaviour of a given character); and adding to what the Anglo-American 'new critics' used to designate vaguely as 'atmosphere.'

It is important, however, to stress that while descriptive segments can encode narrative characteristics at a discursive level, narrative segments only become descriptive-like if we take into consideration their function in the wider context in which they occur.

In the case of *A Menina Morta*, some narrative episodes or passages become descriptive by means of an elliptical mechanism whereby previous or subsequent information has been omitted in such a way as to depict them as an almost erratic, unexplained, and unmotivated series of actions.

The predominantly narrative episode I have chosen to illustrate this point constitutes the entire chapter 31 (887–91) and tells us about Dona Mariana's trip to a mysterious place in the jungle that surrounded the well-kept plantation.

As the absent-present 'menina,' Dona Mariana, her mother (who later abandons the plantation to return as a mad woman with whom communication is no longer possible), acts through the absence that her silent and enigmatic presence establishes, as a hole or a blank, superimposed upon the realistic representation of the daily routines on the plantation. Portrayed like her dead daughter, she becomes an unreachable presence, described from the beginning of the novel as a theatrical figure upon a courtly stage (chap. 3, 738–9).

The chapter opens in a way reminiscent of the beginning of a traditional oral story: 'Pela estrada em direção oposta a Pôrto Novo, muito além do vale misterioso e fechado da fazenda, corria pequena caleça guiada por uma mulata, e nela viajava elegante senhora.' [Through the road, in the opposite direction to Pôrto Novo, beyond the mysterious and closed valley where the plantation was, there ran a small chariot guided by a mulatto woman, and in it travelled an elegant lady] (chap. 31, 887).

The fact that the two main action verbs, *correr* [to run] and *viajar* [to travel], occur in the imperfect tense frames this narrative episode into a mythic-like time beyond the main temporal axis of the novel. Soon we realize that what promised to be the beginning of a story is in fact a means to facilitate the inclusion of descriptive segments: first, a depiction of the cultivated land surrounding the mansion, then the endless coffee fields where the harvest has started, and finally the jungle that surrounds the whole plantation.

Dona Mariana and her slave, Ângela, finally arrive at a clearing in the jungle where they see a hut similar to the ones used by the foremen. Inside, however, is a huge wooden cross, surrounded by stones upon which traces of candle wax can be seen. Could it be a place where the slaves have initiated a cult around the memory of the dead young girl? But no explicit or implicit answers are given in this chapter, or in other parts of the text.

Dona Mariana, who has not spoken during the whole trip, kneels and prays silently, detached from her surroundings, while Ângela gathers medicinal plants. Meanwhile, the whole clearing becomes tainted with an uncanny aura: 'O silêncio era absoluto, e até os pássaros pareciam evitar aquêle lugar taciturno, onde a sensação de vazio e de ausência se fazia sentir de forma insidiosa, que subia do coração ao cérebro, sufocando primeiro a garganta, como nos envenenamentos da beladona.' [There was an absolute silence, and even the birds seemed to avoid that taciturn spot, where an impression of absence and of void could be felt as something insidious that, coming up from the heart to the brain, would first suffocate the throat as in poisoning by deadly nightshade.] (chap. 31, 889). Then, they both hear something, like 'uma gargalhada louca que esturgia ali perto, sôbre-humana, infernal' [a mad superhuman infernal laughter that crackled nearby] (889). Dona Mariana orders the slave to take her back home.

The trip, although constituting a predominantly narrative chapter, could not have been more uneventful. As a sequence of actions delaying a possible main narrative axis, it behaves very much as a digressive episode whose main function is to characterize the unpredictable behaviour of Dona Mariana, and to add to all the sombre empty spaces where the presence of the 'menina' can generally be felt. Indeed, if the clearing constitutes, *per se*, an ellipsis inscribed onto the very jungle and into the meaning of the chapter, the fact that we never know what the hut similar to a shrine stands for, or why Dona Mariana has taken a trip to a space filled with emptiness, seems to drain this narrative passage of its very narrativity. Narration becomes in this case (as in some instances of Claude Simon's fiction previously analysed) an *ancilla descriptionis*, that is, a backgrounded device bringing to the fore the more significant descriptive passages. Thus narration, by absorbing in this case the characteristics of the descriptive segments it highlights, comes to acquire the same secondary functions description may generally take on in a text revealing an overall realistic mode of representation.

We may now examine how, in *A Menina Morta*, the main character establishes, *ab initio*, the presence of her absence to become a naughty and childish entity playing with the representational characteristics of the novel and, consequently, with the reader's expectations. But how does a non-acting dead character draw a disparate series of meanings within the elliptical holes created by her omnipresent absence?

3. THE 'MENINA' AS A FILLED ELLIPSIS

For the female characters residing on the plantation and depending on the financial support of the rich landowner (Celestina, Inacinha, Sinhá-Rôla, and Virgínia), the 'menina' constitutes a symbol of 'sweetness,' 'purity,' and salvation. For the other female main characters, her sister and her mother, (Carlota and Dona Mariana), she seems to have no special meaning until they both become, somehow, the embodiments of her soul. For the male characters, especially her father, the 'menina' constitutes an indefinable power able to challenge or disrupt his patriarchal authority. For the large population of black slaves (that have been deliberately grouped according to the differences in their African native languages so as to render communication among them practically impossible), the blond 'menina' becomes a religious icon, someone who, because of the innocence of her young age, can cross the well-marked space divisions that exist between mansion and slave quarters, gardens and coffee fields, plantation and jungle, as well as all the imposing social barriers.

As Luiz Costa Lima has pointed out, the 'menina' functions as a 'floating signifier,' able to channel different types of representation (1989, 268-9). However, if when she was alive she constituted a focus of hope and joy, especially for all the powerless male and female characters who saw her as an escape for their personal frustrations, after her death the 'menina' becomes an uncanny presence, a strong but invisible entity vampirizing those who most remember her.[21] She thus becomes a potent ellipsis able to implode a variety of meanings into a filled and inexplicable emptiness.

The 'menina' as a mysterious force is mentioned from the beginning of the novel:

O Senhor parou petrificado quando viu que ao ser tirada a mesa onde estivera exposto o corpo da menina tinham ficado algumas marcas dos pés do móvel que era todo de jacarandá maciço, e os riscos pareciam sinais de luta como se tivessem arrastado alguém que se agarrasse a tudo em selvagem defesa e resistência. (chap. 13, 787)

[The Master stopped as if petrified, when he saw that when they took out the table upon which the body of the young girl had been laid out, there were some marks in the solid jacaranda piece of furniture, and the scratches looked like traces of a fight, as if someone who had tried to hold on to everything as he savagely resisted in self-defence, had been finally dragged out.].

Similarly, we read that, shortly after the girl's death, Dona Virgínia felt that 'uma pequena divindade confusa vivia agora em seu coração e quem sabe seria a da vingança, muito longa e muito sutil ...' [A little confused divinity was living in her heart, and who knew if it were the instrument of a long and very subtle revenge] (chap. 18, 812–13). In addition, many other characters in the novel tell us how the absent 'menina' becomes a presence in their lives and in the familiar places that thus become more and more unfamiliar.

None the less, it is mainly as an ellipsis that the 'menina' becomes the main character. In fact, if in many descriptions of space she joins a series of present but non-visible objects, she is clearly represented as a particular type of ellipsis through many other representations: 1) in the clearing in the middle of the jungle; 2) in the legend told by Libânia where a black female slave who has no face 'só cabelo e pescoço' [just hair and neck] (chap. 26, 866), walks into the rooms of the wife of a former plantation owner; and 3) in the references to the painting where the 'menina' was represented after her death.

Concerning the portrait of the dead young girl, although the novel is highly descriptive, the painting itself is not described in great detail: 'Nela, estendido sôbre a mesa, o corpinho da menina com vestido de brocado branco entertecido de flôres de prata, destacava-se do fundo escuro, com a cabeça adornada de pequeninas rosas, levemente coloridas.' [In it, stretched out upon the table, the small body of the young girl with a white brocade dress embroidered with silver flowers, loomed out of a dark surface, with her head adorned by small, softly coloured roses.] (chap. 21, 836). What is curious is that the painting that nobody seems to notice starts to become more meaningful after the master orders it off the wall, under the pretext that it was not well executed (chap. 52, 1060). The empty space that is left evokes more than ever the removed object, especially for Carlota, who at the end of the novel realizes that she is the real 'menina morta' [dead young girl] (chap. 125, 1296).

As the elliptical 'gap' between light and darkness, the explicit and the implicit, the clearly represented and the unrepresentable, the character of the 'menina' leads us to reflect on how we, as readers, tend to perceive her so clearly through the textual spaces where she is not; especially through a set of descriptions where she is just an indefinable tone, a semantic shading, or the 'presence' that overlaps the 'voice' of a specific focalizer.

We have seen how the 'menina,' through her elliptical presence, disturbs the overall realistic mode of representation of this novel, and how all its descriptive aspects oscillate along a representational continuum.

None the less, such representational characteristics should not be confused with what is generally labelled as 'nineteenth-century realism.' Surprisingly, this novel has some characteristics of the French New Novel. The fact that in *A Menina Morta* great emphasis is placed on types of description that seem to imitate pictographic and cinematographic referents, no doubt brings to mind the fictional production of Claude Simon, who, like Cornélio Penna, is also a painter who became a writer.

A parallel with post-modern fiction can also be drawn, mainly by reason of the fact that in its historical recreations, we never find what could be designated as an 'omniscient narrator,' that is, an authoritative 'voice' in full control of the information it reveals. In this case, we are dealing with a descriptive voice that is diversified through multiple points of view. In all the descriptions, there is always the implied vision of the characters; whenever these are not the main focalizers (as, for example, in chapters 5, 12, and 16), a space is described in pictographic or cinematographic terms. Thus, a series of cross-media references become, in this case, metadescriptive, as if the 'enunciative voice' were very subtly to draw our attention to the fact that, as a painting or even as a motion picture, a fictional written text is always a fabrication.

Furthermore, the realistic mode of representation found in this novel is not based on forms of direct observation (as in many instances of Zola's fiction), but results principally from a dialogue between text and reader. Thus, it is especially through a constant effect of visualization, where the works of the imagination of a given period have been historically inscribed, that we arrive at a realistic mode of representation, even in spite of the semantic polarities we find across descriptive segments.

As the narrative/descriptive voice, we are invited, in this case, to revisit and reinterpret an imperial Brazil that, much like the dead 'menina' represented in one of the portraits of the Grotão mansion, is nothing but a set of traces frozen in time, upon which we try to map out a certain form of coherence.

6

The impossible 'mimesis': Description and metadescription in Carlos de Oliveira's *Finisterra*

La reproduction du réel devient elle-même, à partir d'un certain niveau de recherche, aussi opaque – aussi peu lisible – que le réel lui-même.

João Camilo dos Santos[1]

Although the early poems and novels by Carlos de Oliveira can be viewed as works of Portuguese 'neo-realism' (a trend that spans from the 1940s to the 1960s),[2] his literary production as a whole still remains one of the most difficult to place among the canons of a literary school. His first four novels – *Casa na Duna* (1943), *Alcateia* (1944), *Pequenos Burgueses* (1948), and *Uma Abelha na Chuva* (1953) – although 'neo-realistic' when first published, underwent (with the exception of *Alcateia*) extensive revisions and transformations. In fact, what started as a series of minor stylistic modifications (basically changes in punctuation as well as omission, addition, and substitution of words and short segments), soon expanded into the fusion of chapters, and major changes in mode of fictional representation.

If, for example, we compare the first edition of *Uma Abelha na Chuva* (1953) to the fourth and subsequent ones, we soon realize, as João Camilo dos Santos has pointed out, that 'telling' becomes more a way of 'showing' as far as the narrative segments are concerned.[3] It is as if the narrative voice were trying to relinquish its own authority by toning down narration and by becoming more of a descriptive voice. Thus, in chapter 12 of a recent edition, for example, a sequence of verbs conjugated in the preterite, has given way (especially after revisions including and following the fourth edition), to a sequence of infinitives; through a simple stylistic change a previously narrative segment acquires a pictographic quality.

A span of twenty-five years separates the first edition of *Uma Abelha na Chuva* and *Finisterra: Paisagem e Povoamento* (1978), written shortly before the author's death. During this period Oliveira wrote no other novels, but produced several books of poems and a book of chronicles, as well as revising and modifying three of his first four novels. Like his previous fictional works, *Finisterra* underwent minor modifications in a second and definitive edition that I use in this study.[4] However, in *Finisterra* more than in the final editions of Oliveira's previous novels, we are dealing not with a neo-realistic fictional text but rather with an elusive biographical-like novel, which some Portuguese critics hesitate even to classify as a novel in the traditional sense of the term.[5]

The text does not simply portray a central male character from childhood into adult life, but the ways through which a main narrative/descriptive voice tries to recollect various life-moments through a range of texts and documents belonging to different media and genres.[6]

In fact, what seems at a first approach to be 'biographical,' if not 'autobiographical' (not in the sense of a physical life, but pertaining to the developments in Carlos de Oliveira's own writing), becomes, among other aspects, and after more analytical subsequent readings, a metatextual yet lyrical reflection on the shortcomings of 'mimesis' as a mode of reproduction. Given the particular concerns of the present study, the novel can also be seen as an analytical reflection on the accuracy of descriptions and on the impossibility of their completeness.

Faced with *Finisterra*, for a brief but revealing moment we tend to hesitate. Are we dealing with a long narrativized prose poem, with an essay on fictional representation disguised as a novel, with a specific form of (auto)biography? Or, on the other hand, are we dealing with an author whose emphasis on neo/social realism led him from ideologically clad forms of realistic representation to the scientific-like description of micro-details, whereby realism is lost only to reappear with the 'objectal' or 'reificational' qualities we find in many of the poems of Francis Ponge?

It is useful to consider these speculative questions, for they enable us to focus our analysis, especially if we place *Finisterra* in the context of the complete works of Carlos de Oliveira. *Finisterra* is one of the most hermetic Portuguese novels of the twentieth century. Although it is constructed as a set of descriptions and dialogues, the reader is never absolutely sure who is speaking – the man, the child, the father, the uncle? The novel lacks any clear form of temporal orientation. Story-time tends, in fact, to become reading-time, with the result that the reader is obliged to perceive, through an effect of simultaneity, a series of different textual strata or layers. These, once superimposed, form a complex metaphorical mechanism that becomes more and more allegorical even as we concentrate, as in the present case, mainly on the descriptive aspects of the novel. Furthermore, it is only after reading the main body of this fictional work that we arrive at a 'Nota final' [final note] (n.p.), where in smaller print we are told by an 'implied author,' or by the 'enunciative voice' the text itself produces, that:

Imitando um dos narradores deste livro (coincidência e necessidade), também o autor coligiu numa única pasta velhos papéis dispersos: alguns, dactilografados; outros, manuscritos e às vezes (quase) ilegíveis. Decifrou a letra emaranhada, reconstituiu lacunas, ordenou tudo pelas diferenças caligráficas, a cor da tinta, os caracteres (mais ou menos nítidos) da máquina: sinais de um trabalho intermitente ... Aqui está o romance (um dos romances) escrito e anunciado há anos, sem garantia de terem aparecido todos os papéis ... no capítulo XI, transcreve (ipsis verbis, diria a criança) um certo número de frases colhidas na monografia do padre João Rezende sobre a região ... Lembra-se ainda doutra (sua) casa destruída: obsessões pessoais e sociais idênticas? Não lhe parece grave, dada a frequência com que sucede aos romancistas repetirem o essencial (para eles) em vários enredos. Grave seria, com certeza, não as ter aprofundado um pouco. (n.p.)

[Imitating one of the narrators in this book (coincidence and necessity), the author has also gathered old and dispersed papers within a single briefcase: some were typed, others handwritten, and, at times (almost) illegible. He has deciphered the convoluted handwriting, reconstituted lacunas, and collated everything according to the calligraphic differences, the colour of the ink, the characters (more or less clear) of the typewriter: signs of an intermittent work ... Here is the novel (one of the novels) written and announced for some years, but it cannot be guaranteed that all the papers have appeared ... in chapter 11, he transcribed (*ipsis verbis*, the child would say) a certain number of sentences taken from the priest João Resende's monograph on the region ... The author still recalls another (his) destroyed house: identical personal and social obsessions? It does not seem very serious to him, given the frequency with which novelists repeat the essential (for them) through several plots. It would, no doubt, have been serious not to have perfected them further.]

As in Faulkner's *The Sound and the Fury* (1931), only at the end can we as readers understand some of the aspects that, up to then, have remained enigmatic. Temporal disconnections and a large degree of fragmentation become now clearer since the 'implied author,' 'imitating one of the narrators' in the novel, has taken upon himself to collate and assemble not only a group of literary fragments written at different times previously, but also other types of texts such as the priest's monograph.

The assembling of the different materials does not reflect a traditional narrative concern, but rather a method akin to the visual arts, whereby segments are brought together according to similarities of shape and colour, which, in this particular case, can also indicate a series of changes across time able to mirror different phases, moments, and concerns in the written production of a given author. Unlike in the Faulkner novel, however, on second reading we still lack much necessary information; we feel as though we are stepping into a void each time we abandon a close reading in search of an overall coherence or general interpretation. In returning to chapter 11, where the 'voice' of the ethnographer-priest could have been transposed *ipsis verbis*, we find that his writings have been incorporated and fused together in such a way as to render impossible any type of stylistic and/or semantic distinctiveness.

If one searches for an explicit plot – something that posed no major problems in Oliveira's previous four novels – even a second reading may prove frustrating. None the less, with a text that keeps demanding (especially through subsequent readings) closer attention, the reader starts to focus more on aesthetic qualities. It is as if we were reading not a novel, in the traditional sense, but a series of prose poems the thematics of which resounds throughout the text: first as an allegorical search for the most rigorous and comprehensive form of replicating descriptiveness, and second, as a pedagogical attempt at demonstrating the impossibility of the latter.

In fact, the reader familiar with Oliveira's previous four novels (where description takes on the familiar emblematic role we find in nineteenth-century fiction – for example, in Flaubert or Zola – or even in the twentieth-century works by Jorge Amado and Mario Vargas Llosa), tends to search for the narrative foreground that descriptive passages would highlight or expand. However, the reader soon realizes that *Finisterra*, like Oliveira's non-neo-realistic poems, is mainly about the impossibility of imploding into a completed or finalized fictional work, a lifetime search for a given standard of literary perfection.

Imitating one of the 'enunciative voices' in *Finisterra*, and its 'implied author,' the reader is also left to make a coherent whole out of a series of dialogues and descriptive segments, some of the meanings of which we shall explore. However, since the novel is highly descriptive, following the suggestive subtitle of *Finisterra: Paisagem e Povoamento* [Landscape and Settlement], I focus mainly on the various descriptions of a particular landscape surrounding the family house.

This obsessively described landscape is first presented as a painting framed by one of the windows of the house, focalized through the gaze of the main male character-narrator/descriptor, as he tries to recall a familiar view. The same landscape is later presented (following the syntagmatic arrangement of the novel): 1) as a photograph the child perceives; 2) as a pyrography executed on a leather cushion by the child's mother; 3) as one of the child's drawings; 4) as the same drawing observed with a magnifying glass by the adult the child became; 5) as a filmic excerpt where some of the elements in the child's drawing become animated; 6) as it could have been clearly perceived through the window; and 7) as a scrupulously made-to-scale replica capable of incorporating not only the natural topography and the plants of the landscape, but the very mineral components that account for its geological characteristics.

Unlike in the Claude Simon example analysed previously, we are not concerned with the existence of specific extratextual referents, although referentiality in general comes to be problematized in the novel. In this instance, it is not as relevant to know if the child's drawing, the photograph, or the made-to-scale model ever existed outside the written novel, since the main emphasis in Carlos de Oliveira's text is not so much on the reading or on the written transposition of specific extratextual referents, but on the ability of a text to make real something that no longer exists: the destroyed family house and surrounding places, as well as the family documents and photographs the father ends up throwing into the fire (chapter 27, 150).

In this specific case, we are, in fact, dealing with eight variations on a lost landscape, and as we shall later discover, the cross-media references through drawing, photograph, film, and sculpture function mainly as a stylistic exercise through which a time past is recaptured in terms of a series of spatial settings.

1. EIGHT VARIATIONS ON A LANDSCAPE

As mentioned before, the main character–'enunciative-voice' recalls the landscape he saw through the window of his home when he was a child:

A primeira zona de areia (mancha a ferver num hálito prateado, como o sal dos velhos itinerários: ruivo por dentro, alvo por fora) ocupa o terço inferior da aridez que a janela enquadra.

Segue-se uma faixa estreita de gramíneas: a evaporação da lagoa (juncos densamente roxos) submerge-as num tom mais carregado que o da própria água. Esta área, no entanto, é bastante instável: sob a declinação do sol, as cores mudam com frequência de intensidade; basta um sopro de vento, a ondulação pouco perceptível que provoca, para clarear ou escurecer as gramíneas.

Na outra margem, a linha das dunas reflecte o movimento dessa ondulação (sinusóide ténue demarcando a altura da segunda grande zona de areia) e serve de limite ao terço intermédio da paisagem.

O último terço acaba na linha superior do caixilho: formam-no as dunas distantes (recorte acentuado, revérberos de cal, como a auréola, a inquietação, que as estrelas irradiam fixamente). Ao fundo, uma nesga de azul pode parecer ao mesmo tempo céu e mar; placa de zinco a incendiar-se; ou apenas um reflexo turvo da luz. (7–8)

[The first zone of sand (stain boiling out of a silvery breath as the salt of old itineraries: reddish on the inside, white on the outside) occupies the inferior third of the barrenness the window itself frames.

There follows a narrow ribbon of graminaceous plants: the evaporation of the lagoon (densely purple rushes) submerges them in a tone deeper than the water. This area, none the less, is very unstable: with the declining of the sun, the colours change frequently in intensity; a breath of wind, and the slightly perceptible undulation, is enough to brighten or darken the graminaceous plants.

On the other margin, the line of the dunes reflects the movement of that undulation (a tenuous sinusoid demarcating the height of the second large sand zone) functioning as the limit for the intermediary third of the landscape.

The last third ends in the top line of the frame: it is made of distant dunes (accentuated cut, reverberation of lime, as the aureola the twitching of the stars fixedly irradiate). Beyond, a dash of blue can stand for both sky and sea: a zinc plaque beginning to burn, or just the opaque reflection of the light.]

At a stylistic level, if we examine the verb tenses in this passage, we find that a distinction between action versus stative verbs is no longer relevant, because all the verbs have unanimated (non-human) subjects. Thus, verbs such as *seguir* [to follow], *submergir* [to submerge], *provocar* [to provoke], and *incendiar* [to burn/to set on fire] are devoid of the actions they generally indicate, in that they are used as metaphors to represent an immobile landscape; something that is further stressed to the extent that the view is described in terms of a representational painting framed by the window itself. Such framing also functions, at a discursive level, as a means to organize a distribution of elements that are described both from the bottom to the top, and from the nearest to the farthest. This type of syntagmatic structure is not entirely arbitrary, for time in this novel is mainly conceived as a cumulative series of layers and mineral residues.

The reference to 'a primeira zona de areia' [the first zone of sand] can be seen as accounting for the most remote memory around which (as in the formation of a crystal) other memories are generated as successive layers both expanding and encasing an initial core. This notion is further highlighted through several related metaphors: 'mancha a ferver num hálito prateado' [stain boiling out of a silvery breath] evoking the natural process according to which the water of the lagoon evaporates under the intense light of the day, to leave as a residue 'o sal dos velhos itinerários' [the salt of old itineraries], a mineral component described as something able to encase the light 'ruivo por dentro, alvo por fora' [reddish on the inside, white on the outside].

It should be noted that the adjective *ruivo*, translated in this case as 'reddish,' is generally used to refer to people with red hair, a shade of colour that can be better observed under the light of the sun. On the other hand, *alvo* [white] is an archaic form from the Latin *albus*, used instead of the modern Portuguese adjective *branco*. 'Alvo,' none the less, still survives in some local dialects to designate 'white bread' (pão alvo). In this case, the use of an archaism not only suggests local dialects, but also relates to the notion contained in 'velhos itinerários' [old itineraries], which, in turn, highlights the fact that this description is about a remote memory or experience.

As in other novels by Oliveira, the landscape is arid: sand, rushes, and 'gramíneas' [graminaceous plants]. The latter is a rare noun that, like some others in the novel, such as 'vinhático' [Brazilian mahogany], and 'gisandra' (the name of an invented plant that cannot be found in any dictionary or botanical book), is used mainly as an aesthetic signifier, and as a way of impeding any immediate effect of referentiality.

The landscape is not fixed, however, as its being described as a painting could have led us to assume, but proves to be 'bastante instável' [very unstable]. The overall visual metaphor that was initially presented as a means to frame both visible and emotional impressions, becomes at the same time a way of pointing out the representational shortcomings of a given medium: a painting cannot represent different gradations of light occurring at ongoing moments in time due to the 'declinação do sol' [declining of the sun]; it cannot represent a change of colours, nor the 'ondulação pouco perceptível' [imperceptible undulation] provoked by a breath of wind. The desire, however, to capture that first memory, as if in a painting, seems to provoke, at a discursive level, a 'visual rhyme': as the contour of the dunes mirrors the undulation of the water through a similar 'sinusóide ténue' [tenuous sinusoid] which is able, at the same time, to conjure up the almost illegible written manuscripts referred to by the 'implied author' in the 'final note.'

This description, although extremely cohesive and coherent in spite of the depiction of its own impossibility, ends with an apparent contradiction: 'placa de zinco a incendiar-se; ou apenas um reflexo turvo da luz' [zinc plaque beginning to burn, or just the opaque reflection of the light], that is, with the inscription of two distinct moments whose descriptions could not have coexisted simultaneously in a representational painting.

Immediately following the previous quotation, the same view is described as a photograph:

Levanta-se e examina também a ampliação fotográfica, suspensa na parede (perto da janela), que reproduz esta mesma paisagem: a moldura dá-lhe um enquadramento semelhante; falta-lhe porém a cor real, e o tempo destingiu a imagem: os contrastes são pouco visíveis, desaparecem as três zonas distintas, dissolvem-se numa única mancha castanha (quase sépia) à medida que os anos (e a réstia de sol batendo na parede pelo fim da tarde) devoram linha a linha a nitidez dos contornos. Reconhece-se ainda a paisagem, mas há sobre as coisas o resíduo dum luar lento que se esconde (como nas sanguíneas oitocentistas) para lá das últimas dunas. (8–9)

[He stands up to also examine the photographic enlargement hanging on a wall (near the window), which reproduces this same landscape: the wooden mould gives it a similar framing; however, the photograph has no real colour, time has taken the tones out of the image: the contrasts are less visible, the three distinct zones have now disappeared, dissolved into a single brown stain (almost sepia) as the years (and the sunshine upon the wall in the late afternoons) keep devouring, line by line, the outlining shapes. The landscape is still recognizable, but upon everything there is the residue of a slow moonlight, which hides itself (as in eighteenth-century red pencil drawings) beyond the last dunes.]

At a stylistic and discursive level, this passage is very similar to the one previously analysed. As before, action verbs such as *desaparecer* [to disappear], *dissolver* [to dissolve], or *devorar* [to devour] are used metaphorically as a means of expressing an ongoing action in an indeterminate time.

What may surprise us in this case, however, is that photography fails to transmit the realistic accuracy one tends to associate with this medium. What was distinct or made precise in a text based on a distant memory: 'as três zonas distintas' [the three distinct zones], or 'a nitidez dos contornos' [the clarity of the outlining shapes] is here presented as something lacking 'cor real' [real colour] and dissolved 'numa única mancha castanha' [into a single brown stain]. It should also be noticed that the object in question is not simply described as a photograph or a snapshot but as a 'ampliação fotográfica' [photographic enlargement], which may lead us to infer that it is, in fact, a mimetic copy of a reproduction of reality. However, once the medium has captured a given reality, according to the same perspective – a snapshot always reveals its own referent – that same 'reality' starts to acquire an autonomous identity, as the photograph starts to reflect its own ageing process and its 'objectal' qualities rather than the view it was suppose to illustrate.

Ironically, what was supposed to reflect reality with a wealth of shapes, tones, and details no written text can ever capture in the same way, becomes more and more similar to a monochromatic eighteenth-century drawing, where elements become entrapped by the 'luar lento' [slow moonlight] of an indefinable time hiding the clear outlining shapes, which become an indistinguishable mass.

Once more, as in the description first quoted, we are led to reflect on the means of reproducing reality, to be confronted, in this case, with the inadequacies of what is generally labelled as 'photographic realism.' Both of the descriptions previously cited thus start to acquire a metadescriptive quality, as the reference to different media becomes a mode of highlighting the shortcomings if not the impossibility of a totalizing and all-encompassing form of literary description.

The medium, none the less, seems to determine, and at the same time, to limit, in this specific case, a form of reproduction and our access to it. In fact, the medium becomes akin to an implied general metaphor, since it presupposes an 'as-if' preceding a 'reality' one would imagine to be immediately accessible. This is especially the case of the pyrographed version of the same landscape executed by the child's mother:

Lavrado a fogo, o sulco do estilete nunca se interrompe, tece a teia castanho escura no castanho mais aberto do material, sugere uma gravura abstracta, repete com rigor o traço das dunas, as margens da lagoa, a rede confusa das gramíneas, equilibrando geometricamente superfícies, volumes, relações de espaço: a arquitectura real (?) da paisagem. (9)

[Engraved with fire, the furrow of the stylus is never interrupted, it weaves a dark-brown web upon the lighter brown of the material, it suggests an abstract engraving, it repeats with rigour the shape of the dunes, the margins of the lagoon, the confused net of graminaceous plants balancing off, geometrically, against surfaces, volumes, relations of space: the real (?) architecture of the land-scape.]

Unlike in the previous descriptions, here we have an almost scientific account of an image. Not a single personal pronoun is used in this passage and the only focalizing mark is merely transmitted by the verbal form 'sugere' [it suggests]. However, if our comments at a stylistic and discursive level prove to be, in this case, quite unnecessary, at a functional level this description brings us closer to problems concerning the reproduction of reality. Paradoxically, the written account of the pyrographed landscape becomes less subjective and almost devoid of similes and/or metaphors when that same initial view becomes 'uma gravura abstracta' [an abstract engraving].

Metaphors, none the less, operating at a reading level, become more obvious, if not in this isolatable block *per se*, then in the way in which this same segment coheres with the ones previously analysed. What in the first description we subjectively analysed as a possible reference to writing, the 'sinusóide ténue' [tenuous sinusoid], alluded to in the second description as the 'linha ... dos contornos' [line ... of the outlining shapes], has now become a type of calligraphy, something able to evoke a form of cursive writing where 'o sulco do estilete nunca se interrompe' [the furrow of the stylus is never interrupted], weaving a web, or more precisely, a network of depicted 'volumes' and 'relations of space.' Implied is, no doubt, an oblique reference to the written manuscripts alluded to in the 'final note,' and a rather strange metatextual reflection: one that (following a type of critical analysis pertaining to the visual arts) would try to connect different handwritten styles with the content of the handwritten material (as if one's handwriting could also become a motivated sign).

The production of the red-hot stylus (like the pen?) ends up, however, representing not an objective reality, but rather a series of replicating intentions that result from the constraints imposed by a specific medium. In fact, elements in the fictionalized pyrographed text are not described as being transposed for the sake of a mere preoccupation with descriptive accuracy. '[A] rede confusa das gramíneas' [the confused net of graminaceous plants] is not inscribed with the aim of replicating, but solely to balance off against a set of 'superfícies geométricas' [geometrical surfaces]. This leads us once again to the metadescriptive aspects I have been emphasizing and to the rare nouns previously mentioned, such as 'gramíneas' [graminaceous plants] a term that, albeit botanically accurate, can only conjure up (especially for a literary critic) not the object itself, but a series of subjective mental images suggested by the signifier.

Shortly after the above description, the landscape is described as a child's drawing:

A obsessão da família continua: a criança, sentada no osso de baleia, tentou também reproduzir a paisagem, sem se empenhar numa cópia excessiva. Desenhava de cór, entre flores selvagens, movido pelo revérbero que fendeu as nuvens.

Lápis alteraram as proporções e os tons (demasiado azul, muito vermelho, algum roxo, nenhum amarelo), mas povoaram esta desolação (areia, água, sol ou luar fotográfico): surgem recortados a negro (excepto as cabeças que são laivos de fogo) os primeiros homens, cavalos, bois, carneiros, caminhando a custo entre grãos de areia grandes como penedias: Procuram matar a sede na lagoa pouco maior que uma gota de chuva. Ao alto, sobre as dunas distantes, com as asas rente às margens do papel, pairam aves brancas, esperando com certeza a sua vez de beber.

A luz do halo (que retarda a ameaça em torno da casa), o próprio tinir das goteiras, dão agora ao desenho um fulgor de fósforo. (9–10)

[The family obsession continues: the child sitting upon the whale bone, has also tried to reproduce the landscape, without any concern for an overdetailed copy. He was drawing by heart, between wild flowers, moved by the reverberation that split the clouds.

Pencils altered the proportions and the tones (too much blue, a lot of red, some purple, no yellow), but such colours are enough to fill this desolation (sand, water, sun, or photographic moonlight): the first men appear, cut out in black (except for the heads, which are strings of fire), horses, oxen, sheep, walk painfully between grains of sand as big as cliffs. They are all trying to quench their thirst in the lagoon no bigger than a drop of rain. High above, upon the distant dunes, with their wings right against the margins of the paper, white birds hover, waiting, no doubt, for their turn to drink.

The light of the halo (which retards the menace around the house), the very tinkling of the eaves, lend now to the drawing a phosphorous glow.]

Once again, this description expands and reframes the ones previously analysed. Although at a stylistic and discursive level this is a very straightforward descriptive block – since its immediate context has been clearly stated – one should notice the following hyperboles: 'grãos de areia grandes como penedias' [grains of sand as big as cliffs], and 'lagoa pouco maior que uma gota de chuva' [lagoon no bigger than a drop of rain]. These expressions function only as such at a sentence level. In fact, once we realize that this version basically describes a child's drawing, what we read is not so much two hyperboles, but a faithful account of the 'reality' of the drawing.

As with the previous versions of the landscape, what seems to be more relevant, in this case, is not the discrete overall organization of a specific segment, but the way in which we, as readers, concretize that same segment. Although we are dealing with a set of isolatable descriptive blocks, we recognize they all constitute variants of the same theme – a kind of kaleidoscopic combination and recombination of elements to which we should add the changes in contextual framing brought about by references to different media.

Unlike what occurs in the previous descriptions, however, the child is not (as are the adults in the family) interested in 'uma cópia excessiva' [an overdetailed copy]. Thus, the child tries to replicate not what he sees but what he feels, based of the potential of his own technical abilities, which explains why the pencils alter 'as proporções e os tons' [the proportions and the tones]. None the less, we are not dealing here with an adult reading of an actual drawing, but with a child's version of the same landscape. This becomes clearer as the descriptive voice seems to point very subtly to processes pertaining to our own reading of this passage. Thus, the references to the colours used by the child, 'demasiado azul, muito vermelho, algum roxo, nenhum amarelo' [too much blue, a lot of red, some purple, no yellow] can also be read as metadescriptive references. In the same way as blue mixed with red makes purple (a different colour), we perceive this description, having superimposed in our minds the reading of the descriptive variants previously analysed. In fact, this segment makes a clear reference to the previous three versions of the same landscape when 'esta desolação' [this desolation] is equated with the following parenthetical descriptive summary: '(areia, água, sol ou luar fotográfico)' [(sand, water, sun, or photographic moonlight)].

Thus, while the reference to 'desolation' points to the barrenness of the view being described (something common to all the previous versions), it also points to semantic characteristics that can be associated with the descriptive segments analysed so far; especially with the rigorous economy of stylistic means and with the 'minimalism' that shapes a printed literary product that one may imagine to have been exhaustively worked and revised. It is through this type of work that the descriptive voice, no longer keeping an emotional tone towards its written content, can thus look at itself, as if in an imaginary mirror, with the degree of 'distanciation' the text, conversely, places between itself and the reader.

References to other versions are also made in this description, such as 'dunas distantes' [distant dunes] and the hovering birds, which will also appear in subsequent versions. However, what this specific description adds to the previous ones is: 1) the presence of human elements and the grazing animals that, in a peasant economy, tend to become an integral part of life; and 2) the mentioning of a present of self-reading that precedes our own. The latter can be seen in the reference to the 'tinir das goteiras' [tinkling of the eaves] that supposedly deforms or reshapes a visual perception, adding to the drawing something that is not 'really' there: 'um fulgor de fósforo' [a phosphorous glow].

In the following version, the description of the same drawing is made more objective but far less mimetic as the main character–descriptor observes it through the power of a magnifying glass. It is interesting to notice that, out of the eight descriptive versions, this one is the longest, and thus, to a certain extent, may be set apart from the other descriptions:

Traços densos sulcam o papel, tão unidos que formam uma pasta de espessura sem falhas. Cristais microscópicos de lápis faíscam, dão à superfície negra o fulgor de certos minérios. Corpos compactos, do mesmo tamanho (refiro-me aos camponeses). Gestos dum ritual perto do fim: braços que pendem, para equilibrar a marcha, pernas flectidas torneando os rochedos, dificilmente, a caminho da água.

Os bichos, esses, variam de corpulência. Carneiros maiores que bois; cavalos de rastos, como serpentes. Mas não custa muito reconhecê-los. Pelas cabeças: chifres retorcidos, cornos de curvatura só insinuada, crinas erguidas ao céu. Tudo isto a arder em vários tons: roxo com vermelho por cima, laranja, açafrão, tijolo.

Nas cabeças humanas o fogo é mais intenso, as chamas mais altas, e a disposição das cores (sobrepostas com fúria) esconde tons indecifráveis. Aproximo, afasto a lupa (várias vezes), tentando surpreendê-los. Não consigo. Um incêndio

uniforme paira a dois ou três metros do chão, e conduz os corpos (já carboniza-
dos? apenas com sede?) à gota azul da lagoa.

Na primeira zona de areia (parte inferior do desenho), grãos com a altura, a
rugosidade, dos penedos (castanho-rubro-arroxeado). A seguir, um pouco por
toda a parte, gramíneas emaranhando-se ao acaso. Tufos (muito azul-algum
verde) sem o arrumo das plantas reais que se abrigam na margem da lagoa onde
a água tem mais profundidade; patas de aranha, inúmeras, peludas: riscos à
pressa contra os grânulos do papel; e o felpo, o resíduo, doutros riscos menores
(laterais) que o lápis a tropeçar deixa atrás de si.

Na zona superior do desenho, aves pairam sobre dunas. Cores que se opõem à
violência do resto (a nesga de zinco, muito longe, não as perturba). Substâncias
claras; talvez um esboço de nuvens. (17–18)

[The paper is ploughed by thick traces, so close together that they form a paste
whose thickness has no flaws. Microscopic lead crystals sparkle, lending to the
black surface the effulgence of certain ores. Compact bodies have the same size (I
am referring to the peasants). Gestures of a ritual approaching its end: arms that
dangle to balance the gait, bent legs painfully going around the cliffs, in search
for water.

The animals, however, vary in body size. Sheep bigger than oxen; horses
crawling like serpents. But it is not difficult to recognize them by their heads:
twisted horns, horns whose curves are only suggested, manes towards the skies.
And all these things burning through several tones: purple with red above,
orange, saffron, brick.

Upon the human heads the fire is more intense, the flames are higher, and the
disposition of colours (furiously superimposed) hides indecipherable shades. I
bring the magnifying glass closer and farther away (several times) trying to surprise them. I cannot. An uniform fire hovers two or three metres above the
ground, and guides the bodies (already carbonized? just thirsty?) to the blue
drop representing the lagoon.

In the first zone of sand (the lower part of the drawing), there are grains with
the height and the roughness of cliffs (brown-red-hot-purplish); after, and everywhere, graminaceous plants entangled at random. Tufts (a lot of blue, some
green) without the arrangement of the real plants that find shelter in the margins
of the lagoon where the water is deeper; spider legs, countless and hairy: quick
traces against the small grain of the paper; and the down, the residue of the other
minor (lateral) traces the stumbling pencil leaves behind.

On the top part of the drawing, birds glide above the dunes. Colours that contrast with the remaining violence (the dash of zinc, far away, does not disturb the
birds). Clear substances; probably a sketch of clouds.]

More than in the previous descriptive variations, language here acquires a particular literary quality, apparent in its metaphoric structure and the number of alliterations.[7] In relation to a mimetic or immediate replication, we are dealing with two stages of distortion. The first is inherent in the drawing of the child, which, as we have seen, is not in any way a faithful representation of an actual reality, and the second operates on the level of a detailed observation of the same drawing but blown up by a magnifying glass.

What in the previous description was a set of discrete pencil traces, becomes now 'uma pasta de espessura sem falhas' [a paste whose thickness has no flaws], revealing not so much what they represent, but the nature of their very own mineral composition, that is, a series of 'cristais microscópicos' [microscopic crystals]. However, if a very detailed and close observation can only capture a certain type of uniformity, or degree of neutrality, the peasants, on the other hand, become more clearly identified as they engage in purposeful gestures (that is, as they search for water). These characters, therefore, lend a narrative-like quality to the segment, although this segment practically omits action verbs in favour of the depiction of a logically concatenated series of gestures.

Metonymically related to the peasants, the domestic animals are then described as they appear in the child's drawing, that is, through similes and metaphors capable of explaining how the drawing deviates from an assumed concept of 'mimesis' as a direct transposition or replication. An observation of details with a magnifying glass gives way then to two distinct visual fields: the one that is constituted by the drawing being observed, and another that, as if on the surface of the magnifying glass itself, gives the impression of a different plane of vision randomly superimposed on the first one. This may explain why a set of complementary colours, such as 'red,' 'orange,' 'saffron,' and 'brick,' can be seen (given the movement of the hand holding the magnifying glass) as forming 'um incêndio uniforme' [a uniform fire] hovering 'a dois ou três metros do chão' [two or three metres above the ground], that is, on the different visual field created by the magnifying glass above the surface of the drawing.

As we follow the composition of this descriptive segment, the peasants, who were previously depicted while searching for water, become burnt bodies, not in the drawing itself, but in the movements of the character-descriptor's hand as he seeks a more or less close magnifying reading. In fact, it is due to a closer observation – 'Aproximo, afasto a lupa (várias vezes)' [I bring the magnifying glass closer and farther away (several times)], that motionless descriptive material, such as the drawing, ultimately reveals its narrative qualities.

The fourth paragraph of this descriptive block emphasizes once more the same microscopic or micro-segmental observation, not only of the child's drawing but also of the previous versions or variations. This is announced by the repetition of the first line of the first description, to which a preposition has been added: 'Na primeira zona de areia' [In the first zone of sand] (my emphasis). The reference to the graminaceous plants in the first description, not alluded to in the first account of the child's drawing, surfaces once more, this time as 'patas de aranha, inúmeras, peludas' [spider legs, countless and hairy], that is, as a metaphor reminding us of: 1) the convoluted traces in the child's drawing; 2) its perception through a magnifying glass; and 3) the entanglement resulting from our reformulation of the former descriptions. The latter leads to the evocation of the 'riscos menores (laterais) que o lápis a tropeçar deixa atrás de si' [minor (lateral) traces the stumbling pencil leaves behind], that is, to a writing that becomes also a form of reading or vice versa.

As was mentioned previously, it is the child's drawing, as it deviates from the mimetic processes that, to a certain extent, characterize an adult transposition of a distant memory into writing (as well as into a representational painting, a photograph, and a pyrography), that are transposed in terms of a filmic text:

Os peregrinos deslizam nas paredes. Silhuetas a arder sobre um fundo rugoso. O gado atrás: cavalos rastejando, os carneiros maiores que os bois. Sobem barrancos de estuque, películas de cal inchadas pela humidade; afundam-se em manchas de bolor; alongam-se ao dobrar os quatro cantos da sala, que os flectem, projectam para diante. Nas portadas da janela, as figuras tornam-se quase ruivas: a luz do halo atravessa a madeira e o seu poder continua. Caminham com o movimento articulado duma lanterna mágica, que não esfuma os contornos. Ao contrário: vultos de grande nitidez marcham num gráfico anguloso mas firme. E de súbito, param. Não tropeçam, nem se atropelam uns aos outros, param simplesmente no relevo do écran. (39–40)

[The pilgrims slide over the walls. Burning silhouettes against a crumpled background. The cattle behind: horses crawling, the sheep bigger than the oxen. They go up ravines of stucco. Scales of lime swollen by humidity sink into mould stains; they get more elongated once they have crossed the four corners of the room that reflects and projects them forwards. Upon the portals of the window the figures become almost reddish: the light of the halo goes through the wood and its power continues. They walk with the articulated movement of a magic lantern, which does not efface their outlines. Inverted, very clear human shapes slide over an angular but stable graphic, and, all of a sudden, they stop. They do not stumble, nor do they run over each other, they simply stop upon the distinctness of the screen. High above, clouds (invisible) caught by the wires of a stage setting also linger.]

Since in this case we are dealing with a description of the child's drawing as if it were a film, this version, more than the others previously analysed, acquires a narrative quality that can best be summarized once we isolate the following micro-segments:

1) 'Os peregrinos deslizam nas paredes'
   [The pilgrims slide over the walls],

2) 'o gado atrás: cavalos rastejando'
   [the cattle behind: horses crawling],

3) 'sobem barrancos de estuque'
   [they go up ravines of stucco],

4) 'alongam-se ao dobrar os quatro cantos da sala'
   [they get more elongated once they have crossed the four corners of the room],

5) 'caminham com o movimento articulado duma lanterna mágica'
   [they walk with the articulated movement of a magic lantern],

6) 'de súbito, param'
   [all of a sudden, they stop].

For a moment, some hesitation may occur and raise the question of whether we are, in fact, dealing with a description or with a narration to which descriptive elements have been added. The answer, in this instance, is not as obvious as in the case of other narrativized descriptions analysed in previous chapters, since a choice between 'highly descriptive narration' and 'narrativized description' does not depend solely on the specificities of this particular segment, but on our reading perspective.

In this case, I have opted for its being designated as a 'narrativized description' in the light of the following characteristics: 1) the animation (or 'narrativization') of the drawing is not represented as having occurred; that is, although at a discursive level we may be examining a series of action verbs whose actions are not metaphorical in an immediate context, those same actions occur under the heading of a rhetorical 'as-if'; 2) the action sequence that transforms the pilgrims and the cattle into agents does not relate to major plot lines in the novel but to other descriptions; and, most important, 3) the micro-narration, in this particular descriptive block, has been backgrounded by the descriptive material where it is embedded, behaving very much as a description at a functional level.

Indeed, what seems more important from the point of view of my own interpretation, is not the fact of realizing that the drawing has been redescribed as if it were a film, but rather that it is being projected upon a particular type of screen. In this case, the film is not being reflected merely off an empty white smooth surface (evocative of a Leibnitzean *tabula rasa*) but off a previously mentioned area formed by the walls of the room, where the window, now closed, would open upon the same obsessively described landscape. Indeed, what we end up perceiving is not so much the twice described version of the child's drawing as he tries to replicate the view, but the foregrounding of the background constituted by the unusual projection surface, and also by the screen that we as readers have created in light of our knowledge of the previously described versions. In this case, there exists a 'reading-screen' of retrospections and expectations capable of altering or deforming the fixedness of the moving images. The projection surface that, in this specific segment, also reflects the degradation of the house – 'películas de cal inchadas pela humidade' [scales of lime swollen by humidity], 'manchas de bolor' [mould stains] – becomes a complex metaphor, or rather, an allegorical representation of the general referentiality against which writing and reading take place.

It is only after the six complex versions of the same view that we arrive at a description of the landscape in question as it could have been objectively perceived through the window of the house:

A paisagem visível (o seu enquadramento) não corresponde à fotografia, nem ao almofadão pirogravado ou ao desenho da criança: lagoa, faixa de gramíneas, dunas que se desdobram (à esquerda) contra o horizonte, desaparecem; ficam apenas as dunas mais ao sul, cortadas em baixo pelo muro que rodeia o jardim e, em cima, pelo caixilho da janela, uma linha passando junto do socalco onde ela esteve sentada: neste espaço cabe o seu itinerário (repetido agora todas as madrugadas) entre pequenos declives e vertentes a pique. (75–6)

[The visible landscape (its own framing) does not correspond to the photograph, nor to the pyrographed cushion, nor to the child's drawing: lagoon, strip of graminaceous plants, dunes that unfold (to the left) against the horizon, disappear; only the most southern dunes remain, cut underneath by the wall that surrounds the garden, and above, through the window frame, a line passing through the terrace where she had sat: her itinerary (now repeated in the very early dawns) fits inside this space, between descents and steep slopes.]

Curiously, the 'visible landscape,' the view that could have been made 'real' through an effect of immediate visualization (as in many cases of nineteenth- and twentieth-century prose fiction) exists only as a deviation from the previous descriptive accounts of it, especially the photograph, the pyrography, and the child's drawing. The 'visible landscape' is, moreover, quite bare and empty – 'dunas ... cortadas em baixo pelo muro que rodeia o jardim' [dunes ... cut underneath by the wall that surrounds the garden] – with no other characteristics than the ones previously built through descriptive accounts obsessed with a most accurate form of literary replication. The cross-media-framed descriptive passages have, to a great extent, created the landscape by means of a paradoxical process of addition through erasure, or, more precisely, as an abstract configuration resulting from our superimposition of the previous versions upon one another. The 'visible landscape' thus ends up by becoming invisible, since it undergoes a process similar to the one used by cubist painters. This is a process whereby the same object comes to be perceived through a multiplicity of angles and geometrical representations so as to lose or vaguely to insinuate its outlining shapes in a final but rather abstract depiction.

The 'visible' or 'real' landscape, however, constitutes the space where the mother of the character-descriptor takes erratic walks: 'neste espaço cabe o seu itinerário' [her itinerary fits inside this space]. It is also the space where, among the dunes, she loses a cross made of glass. Such an occurrence leads the character-descriptor to replicate the same landscape, this time as a faithful three-dimensional made-to-scale model, where he expects to find the cross, as if a replication of space would automatically entail a replication of time.

Vou modelando as dunas sobre o tampo da mesa. Materiais de trabalho: areia (quatro sacos), cinza (um balde) e sal (meia panela). Para uma noção perfeita da escala, faltam-me cálculos, medições, instrumentos (mesmo rudimentares). Reproduzo a paisagem que o suporte das florestas soterradas mantém a flutuar. Volumes, linhas, etc. A substância, como disse, é igual: areia colhida nas próprias dunas. As florestas (embora existam), subentendo-as por comodidade: teoricamente, erguem-se do soalho e alcançam a face inferior do tampo; este representa a camada argilosa do subsolo. Elementos que não se vêem, basta considerar-lhes a existência. Posso, claro está, imitá-los com suficiente naturalismo: lenha carbonizada na lareira e barro autêntico (o estrato geológico que separa as dunas, ostras e árvores). Mas sinto-me cansado e o barro exige escavações morosas. Deixemos as coisas assim. (77–8)

[I start modelling the dunes upon the table top. Working materials: sand (four bags), ash (a pail), and salt (half a pan). For a perfect notion of scale I am still missing some calculations, measurements, instruments (even the rudimentary ones). I reproduce the landscape that the underpinning of buried forests maintains afloat. Volumes, lines, etc. The substance, as I said, is the same: sand gathered in the very dunes. The forests (although they may exist) will rather be inferred so as to facilitate my task: theoretically, they raise themselves from the wooden floor to reach the underside of the table top. This one represents the argillaceous layer of the subsoil. Elements that cannot be seen, since it is enough to consider their existence. I can, of course, imitate them with sufficient naturalism: carbonized wood in the fireplace and real clay (the geological stratum that separates dunes, oysters, and trees). But I am tired and the clay calls for long excavations. Let us leave things as they are.]

In this instance, we are left with a list of ingredients, as in a recipe, with which the character-descriptor aims at reproducing the landscape 'com suficiente naturalismo' [with sufficient naturalism]. The model, initially alluded to in the above segment, is supposed to replicate with scientific precision not only the 'visible landscape,' but the very nature of its subsoil. Thus, materials such as clay, sand, fossils, and even plants, are gathered *in loco*, so as to recreate more precisely the actual components of the landscape. Only one element seems to stand in the way of the character's attempt to replicate the landscape: the forests that reach 'a face inferior do tampo' [the underside of the table top]. This passage can be read as a representation of an ongoing actual time, something that cannot be as easily frozen or captured as the outlining shapes. The lack of 'cálculos, medições, instrumentos (mesmo rudimentares)' [calculations, measurements, instruments (even the rudimentary ones)] is later surpassed as the model-maker engages in a series of careful measurements: 'reduzo os metros a milímetros' [I reduce metres to millimetres], and goes so far as to inscribe his mother's footsteps on the surface of the model: 'marco os passos com o bico do lápis na areia da maquete' [I mark the footsteps with the tip of my pencil upon the sand of the model]. This is done in an attempt to recover his mother's lost cross: 'Submersa ou não, a cruz de vidro espera, algures, junto desse rasto' [Submerged or not, the glass cross waits, somewhere, near the traces of her footsteps] (78).

The replicating intent, however, does not stop with the making of the model, since this one has to be exposed to comparable temperature variations and lighting conditions. Concerning the latter, the model-maker (the character-descriptor) goes so far as to install miniaturized planets and light sources hovering above the model (133). Although we are told that 'o modelo copia o real sem o deturpar' [the model copies reality without distorting it] (80), the final result is only to be expected. The cross is never 'really' found, since it only existed as a textual metaphor; in the same way, the model that so faithfully replicated nature takes on a life of its own as the sculpted masses start to break up, and the miniature plants start to take root and grow (133).

These latter examples point to a technical impasse that is thematized throughout this novel. A given landscape undergoes eight descriptive variations, each capable of adjusting or expanding upon a previous account, while pointing to the shortcomings of a 'naturalistic' realism, or, more precisely, of description as a form of 'mimesis.'

2. DESCRIPTIVE/NARRATIVE VERSUS DIALOGICAL 'MIMETIC' REPRESENTATIONS

The question arises of how these descriptive variations, which read both as lyrical poetical texts and allegoric essay-like reflections on 'mimesis' as a form of replication, relate to the other parts of the novel.

I have mentioned how narration in *Finisterra* does not obey mimetic mechanisms, and does not develop a logically concatenated plot line. Indeed, what could be viewed as the narrative scheme of the novel is, beyond an attempt at recapturing the history of a family house, very much a reader's construction stemming from a large set of descriptions, metatextual comments, dialogues, and other dispersed segments.

However, it is not by chance that such a novel, obsessed by modes of accurate (albeit segmental) replication, exhibits a large amount of direct speech (dialogues and monologues), which at times practically make up entire chapters.

From a Platonic and Aristotelian point of view, direct speech (dialogue in particular) as it was represented to a live audience by actors on a stage was the most perfect form of 'mimesis.' Scenery, setting, background (that is, description) were not as important, since the actors were to mimic a series of actions (to narrate) against a background assumed as common knowledge. From a formalist and structuralist perspective, direct speech (where both description and narration may occur) still conveys the notion of an almost absolute time-space where 'story time,' 'time of narration' (including arrested time through backgrounded descriptive pauses), and 'reading time' seem to coincide perfectly. This may, in effect, be true, provided that direct speech occurs inside a contextual frame of verisimilitude where characters *clearly* speak. However, in a novel such as *Finisterra*, this is seldom the case.

As previously noted, the reader is not always sure who is speaking. Dialogues and other marks of direct speech are rarely introduced by an initial dash or by other consistent graphic conventions, nor can we count on final external commentaries of the type 'he/she said.' Moreover, to the extent that we cannot pinpoint a 'story time,' 'time of narration' as well as 'time or non-time of description' become rather vague, if not identical. In addition, many of the dialogues in *Finisterra* are built so as to account clearly for, and identify, the metatextual processes occurring throughout the novel (namely, in descriptive passages). In fact, many dialogues, or other marks of direct speech, are inserted in the text in order to elucidate the reason why characters (including the 'enunciative voice') engage in types of artistic and/or scientific replication. This is the case, for example, when the father interrogates the child about his drawing:

Example 1

Na paisagem, na fotografia, na almofada, não havia ninguém.
Pois não. E eu povoei-as. Quer dizer, povoei o desenho a pensar nelas. (12).

[In the landscape, in the photograph, in the cushion there was nobody. That's right. And I filled them with people. I mean, I filled the drawing with people as I thought about them.]

This is also the case when the mother speaks about her pyrography:

Example 2

Quando lavro a fogo, na carneira duma almofada, a paisagem que as lentes fotografam (areia, gramíneas, lagoa, céu e nuvens), não espero que a minha imaginação se desprenda da paisagem. Espero (talvez) um estímulo de fora. Nas relações sujeito-objecto, o sujeito faz parte da realidade e sem ele (que sente as coisas) nada teria sentido. (30-1)

[When I engrave with fire upon the leather of a cushion the landscape that the lenses photograph (sand, graminaceous plants, lagoon, sky, and clouds) I do not expect my imagination to detach itself from the landscape. I expect (probably) an outside stimulus. In the relations between subject and object, the subject is part of reality and without him (the one who feels) nothing would make sense.]

And this is so even when someone (probably the father) inquires about the name of the 'film' after the cinematic-like description previously analysed:

Example 3

Como se chama o filme?
Não respondem.
Peregrinação?
Silêncio.
Finis terrae? (40).

[What is the name of the film?
No answer.
Pilgrimage?
Silence.
Finis terrae?]

Nothing is, in fact, less 'real,' less 'mimetic,' than these apparently straightforward marks of direct speech, which are just a small sample of the dialogical characteristics of the novel. As can be seen, such marks of direct speech only occur through the metatextual focalization of the character–'enunciative voice.' A span of several years may even have taken place between question and answer, as in example 1, where the child's response appears filtered through an adult realization; or in example 3, where possible names for the 'film' evoke early seventeenth-century Portuguese travel literature (Fernão Mendes Pinto's *Peregrinação*, 1614), and point to a Latin translation of the title of the very novel at hand. Example 2, however, seems even more complex, since here the mother is not speaking about something akin to an actual pyrography, but about the descriptions previously created by the character–'enunciative voice.' Although in this case we may tend to conceive dialogues or other marks of direct speech as having occurred in a narrative historical past, they are only metafictional segments commenting not on a series of possible situations but on the fictional text as it is being written.

The characters become, thus, less and less mimetic as their voices acquire a ghost-like quality inside a purely textual space, given that their speeches do not truly occur in any time besides the one created through our own interpretation. Therefore, as direct speech flows into previous or subsequent reading material (especially into descriptions), it carries with it, in its clear statements, an allegorical echo. It inscribes both an expansion and a delay, a subjective or 'subjectivized' instance narrating not a sequence of actions in a conventional plot, but the reflection and the appropriation that (through a cluster of mental and textual images) take place between self-reflective writing and self-reflective reading. The latter, in turn, is also put into question as the text continuously makes present the traps of replication and, conversely, what could be designated as 'critical mimesis,' that is, how our critical reading of a text and our writing about it tends, to a certain extent, to mimic the form and the predetermined meanings of other critical discourses. This, no doubt, brings us closer to notions of referentiality in general, and to how and why the fictional descriptions previously analysed pose problems concerning not specific extratextual referents (as in the case of Claude Simon) but literary referentiality as a dialectical reader-writer construction.[8]

3. IMPOSSIBLE REPLICATIONS AND SLIDING REFERENTS

The eight descriptive variations we have analysed evoke similar ones in Oliveira's other fictional works. However, a clear difference emerges between descriptions in *Finisterra* and those in his previous four novels. Although descriptive segments in his earlier fictional works tend to have a symbolic and/or emblematic function, they remain part of a 'neo-realistic' context, which is to say, of a specific logical and ideological framework capable of encouraging a rather direct and unproblematic appropriation. This presupposes a more conventional type of 'mimesis,' through which both writer and reader can automatically create or recreate a shared familiar referent, namely, through effects of immediate visualization.

It is in light of the 'significance' of Oliveira's previous novels that I have approached *Finisterra* to comment on the eight descriptive variations above. When one places this novel in the context of all the fictional works published under the author's name, however, an adjustment to and a redefinition of our perception take place. We become suspicious of the immediate 'transparency' assumed in his previous 'neo-realistic' descriptions. In fact, *Finisterra* not only thematizes modes of referentiality in fiction and the impossibility of 'mimesis' as replication, but also invites us to reconsider Oliveira's 'neo-realistic' production as a whole. One wonders, indeed, whether *Finisterra* may not be said to function as a kind of final chapter both to his previous four novels (where the actions take place in the same region of Portugal – the Gândara – and where, at times, the same characters appear in different novels) and to all his literary works.

At the heart of *Finisterra* lie the contradictions (if not the impossibilities) inherent in any 'realistic' project. Such a project tends to 'naturalize' and domesticate 'the real' to the extent that we, as readers or spectators, attempt not to establish necessary distinctions between reality and its replications. In Peter V. Zima's words, 'discourse merely produces object constructions which are to be treated and tested as hypotheses about the real.'[9]

In *Finisterra*, as the title itself suggests, we approach not only the end of conventionalized forms of realistic representation, but also the end of mass reception (the one 'neo-realists' had dreamt of). It is, therefore, as 'hypotheses about the real' that we are invited to perceive the eight descriptive variations that constitute one of the principal concerns of the main character–'enunciative voice' in this novel. Fictional description, however, very seldom presents itself this way.

In this specific case, we have a series of descriptive segments that seem to have, at least at first sight, a rather unusual and ambiguous status. As fictional descriptions, they are presented very much as lyrical poems, thus pointing to a type of referentiality that can only occur inside a metaphorical framework (as Paul Ricoeur suggests when referring to 'narrativité et référence.')[10] At the same time, it is precisely through the metaphorical dimensions of the text itself, and through how we stand in relation to our own reading, that those descriptions become metadescriptions – in this case, instances highlighting the shortcomings of Aristotelian 'mimesis,' or the failure of any illusions of accuracy pertaining to direct or immediate forms of replication. In turn, these metadescriptive characteristics bring to what was initially presented as something akin to lyrical poems, essay-like traits, as if in *Finisterra* descriptions were allegoric vignettes of/in a theoretical discussion. This brings any possible imaginary referents into the text itself, or, more precisely, referents that are mainly constructed through other texts: the descriptions in Oliveira's previous 'neo-realistic' novels; many of his poetical works, for example, *Micropaisagem* (1969); those chronicles in *O Aprendiz de Feiticeiro* (1973) that can be identified as earlier versions of some of the passages in the present novel;[11] and, at a contextual level, the descriptions analysed in this chapter, as the eight variations keep referring to one another.

A question, none the less, remains to be addressed: If these metadescriptions become less like description – since they foreground not so much what one would expect in a fictional work, but rather a theoretical problematization – are they, at the same time, metanarrative? The answer would seem to be obvious, since in this case those same (meta)descriptions constitute the core of the narrative program of the whole novel: the self-reflective capturing of a lived past revealing itself, more and more, as a fictional construction.

Distinctions between narration and description seem not to apply, or to be quite irrelevant, in a context where direct speech reveals its indirectness, and where the 'final note' of the 'implied author' (however graphically detached) diffuses its meaning into the very centre of an 'ex-centred' novel. One is therefore led to reflect on the operative model for the analysis of fictional description I proposed in chapter 1.

From this perspective we are left in much the same situation as the character–'enunciative voice' in *Finisterra*, as he examines the descriptive function of a drawing with a magnifying glass. In effect, what seems descriptive at a micro-segmental stylistic level, may become narrative at a discursive level, to become once again descriptive or metadescriptive at a functional level. In the end, and very much as in a filmic text one could move fast-forward/backward, or arrest into a series of immobile frames, a fictional text (be it a lyrical or 'concrete' poem, or something pertaining to a prose fiction genre) ends up, in fact, presenting us with a vast array of descriptions which, eventually, allow for, or open out on to a potential narration.

Conclusion

Avec Balzac ... on voit apparaître de longues et minutieuses descriptions de lieux ou de personnages, descriptions qui au cours du siècle se feront non seulement de plus en plus nombreuses mais, au lieu d'être confinées au commencement du récit ou à l'apparition des personnages, vont se fractionner, se mêler à doses plus ou moins massives au récit de l'action, au point qu'à la fin elles vont jouer le rôle d'une sorte de cheval de Troie et expulser tout simplement la fable à laquelle elles étaient censées donner corps.

Claude Simon[1]

After detailed analysis of five novels belonging to different cultures and periods and illustrating various problems concerning the nature and the uses of literary description in prose fiction, it is now possible to summarize the findings, following both synchronic and diachronic approaches. I begin such a synthesis with a brief reexamination of the theoretical framework proposed in chapter 1. Then, departing from traditional distinctions between description and narration (or, from a discourse linguistics point of view, between 'backgrounded' and 'foregrounded material'), I shall consider several cases where such dichotomies prove to be awkward, inapplicable, or altogether irrelevant, even in the context of certain realistic/naturalistic novels.

1. STYLISTIC, DISCURSIVE, AND FUNCTIONAL LEVELS

Popularized or traditional distinctions between description and narration could only be challenged as one proceeded from a micro- to a macro-context of analysis, while taking into consideration not only the stylistic and discursive characteristics of targeted descriptive and narrative segments, but also their functions within given works. These levels of inquiry (which can be conceived of as a series of transparent layers viewed through a specific but variable lens), enabled us to engage in possible redefinitions of an initial perception or impression. It was easier, therefore, to realize that descriptive/narrative distinctions were only possible as frozen frames belonging to the zooming in/out characteristics of reading, and critical interpretation of a given text.

In the present study, fictional examples in both Simon's and Oliveira's novels allegorize the instances when an aesthetic object is observed with the aid of lenses or magnifying glasses. Similarly, we have seen in a variety of texts that what appeared to be narrative at one level could become descriptive at another, and vice versa. We can conclude, therefore, that specifically focused points of view can be shattered by multiple perceptions able to bring into a new configuration both 'estrangement' and familiarity, certainty and doubt, the descriptive and the narrative. Only then can paradoxical concepts, or apparently oxymoronic terms, such as 'descriptive narrations' or 'narrative descriptions,' be explained.

Concerning some of the relevant findings, we have observed how at a stylistic level, a distinction between action and stative verbs proves to be quite unreliable as an indicator of a contrast between descriptive and narrative segments. In both nineteenth-century and more recent works of prose fiction, description can contain a series of logically concatenated action verbs; narration, on the other hand, can sometimes avoid the use of the latter altogether to present us with a series of micro-descriptive segments, or with a single existing state able to imply a series of events. Examples of this occur, respectively, in the excerpt concerning the life of Hélène before she came to Paris, in Zola's *Une Page d'amour* (quoted in chapter 2), and the body of a murdered woman in Robbe-Grillet's 'La Chambre secrète.'[2]

A focus on the aspectual characteristics of verb tenses, as suggested by discourse-linguists such as Dry (1983) and Fleischman (1985 and 1990), proved to be more helpful, especially in the context of realistic/naturalistic prose fiction. In fact, action verbs in descriptive segments tend to reveal an imperfective 'aspect,' or, quite often, the iterative movement that may result from their being reflexively conjugated. By contrast, in narrative segments, action verbs have a 'punctual' perfective 'aspect,' able to convey the notion of 'accomplishment and achievement,' which, according to Dry, accounts for 'the illusion of time movement' (1983, 31), since verbs, in this case, have a well-defined temporal frame resulting from the fact that they imply 'a culminating point and an outcome' (24).

Although, at a discursive level, aspectual characteristics prove helpful for immediate distinctions between description and narration, especially if the material in question presents a realistic mode of representation, problems do arise from a possible generalization solely based on aspectual considerations: 1) What takes place if a logical string of verbs expressing punctual actions, and therefore accounting for a clearly identifiable narrative segment, is used metaphorically or allegorically (as is often the case in *mises en abyme*)?; 2) What if we are confronted with a fictional text that uses the same verb tense and 'aspect' to both narrate and describe (for example, the present participle in Simon's fiction, or the present tense in Oliveira's *Finisterra*)?

The 'punctuality' of the perfective 'aspect' is only possible within a realistic mode of representation, and even then, reported dreams, fantasies, or hypothetical situations present narrative material that has lost its dynamic performative qualities once the actions they indicate cannot be conceived of as having actually occurred. Narrations, in this case, lose their 'factuality' and become, strangely but not surprisingly, closer to descriptions and digressions as more complex semantic characteristics soon dislodge any 'illusion of time movement.' In fact, it is often only at a functional level that narrative segments of this kind function as descriptions, because they generally tend to expand on the significance of a given character or place, and do not directly impinge upon the time-sequence of a main plot. Together with this type of narrative segments, one could also include those that, while not forming a subplot *per se*, have an equal descriptive function because they also generally highlight the characteristics or attributes of a character (for example, Dona Mariana's trip to a clearing in the jungle, in Penna's *A Menina Morta*).

In more recent prose fiction, such as Oliveira's *Finisterra*, however, we are often dealing with segments that, at a discursive and at a functional level, reveal themselves as being highly metaphorical or allegorical, and for which a narrative/descriptive distinction is no longer possible. In fact, the whole novel uses an ambiguous historical present throughout, as the 'enunciative voice' ponders on the construction and representational possibilities of a text being created as if before our eyes. Action, in this case, becomes closer to the development of arguments and examples in an essay, than to explicit or implicit forms of storytelling.

Apart from the cases mentioned above, it should also be noted that a 'text-type'[3] such as the 'interior monologue' – particularly when it presents itself as 'stream of consciousness' – seems to dilute (especially at a stylistic and discursive level) any distinctions between narration and description. In Virginia Woolf's *The Waves* (1931), and in many instances in Simon's *Histoire*, for example, implied or explicitly narrated information is intimately linked to the representation of acts such as remembering and recalling, and is thus not bound by constraints of discourse logic or sequential time frames. Narrated events acquire, therefore, a more descriptive quality.

These characteristics, which can be seen as the result of a historical shift from realism to modernism and post-modernism, are, however, not enough to invalidate completely critical distinctions between narration and description. If, in many twentieth-century texts, such distinctions prove to be irrelevant or pertain only to a specific level of analysis, they are, nevertheless, very applicable to a great variety of more traditionally structured fictional works, be they nineteenth-century novels or the majority of current best-seller fiction.

Concepts relating to grounding distinctions prove, however, to be more generally applicable and more useful, since they imply a set of textual characteristics (of salient features) in terms of their reception. Through this notion, the reader may challenge common assumptions, since different 'text-types' (for example, narrations, descriptions, dialogues, digressions, epigraphs, quotations, etc) do not function in all fictional texts in the same way. For example, a main plot may be of secondary importance while a digression containing an emblematic effect of *mise en abyme* may be more relevant than the actions of a given character. Similarly, as I have demonstrated, description can not only complement and aid narration, but also dislodge it altogether by assuming its very functions. When this occurs, however, description, by transforming the narrative voice into a 'reader's voice,' performs, very literally, what in the discourse of phenomenological hermeneutics could have been perceived as mere metaphors: the *reader-writer*, the reader as the narrator, or as the character the text itself fictionalizes.[4]

2. FOREGROUNDED VERSUS BACKGROUNDED DESCRIPTIONS: A DIACHRONICAL OVERVIEW

From a chronological perspective, descriptions evolve from a rhetorical topos,[5] whose function is mainly to provide a number of aesthetic pauses for the reader engaged in processing a main plot to a far more complex text-type. Although some classical, baroque, or romantic novels may reveal an abundant use of descriptive passages, description, both as a fundamental part of the fictional text and as a critical concept, only begins to be more consistently used and discussed in the nineteenth century. In fact – to use French literature as an example – ever since Rousseau's and Chateaubriand's romantic fiction, descriptions of space, in particular, cease to be mere background to reflect some of the characteristics of *mises en abyme*. These devices, which always foreground the 'text-types' where they may occur, enable descriptions to mirror not only the mood and psychological concerns of the characters, but also (at an oblique metaphorical level) the main events in the story. With Balzac's fiction, these characteristics become even more salient in novels such as *Eugénie Grandet* (1833), where description becomes an extension of the characters themselves. However, it is with the emergence of the naturalistic school, especially with the works of Zola, that description becomes a ubiquitous feature of narrative. In many instances Zola's novels are, in effect, lengthy descriptions cohesively and coherently bound together by a plot that quite often constitutes a fictional mode of presenting sociohistorical, and even medical information.[6] One of the best examples of foregrounded description in Zola, is, no doubt, the five long depictions of Paris in *Une Page d'amour*. In this case, description becomes a salient feature since it systematically constitutes a *mise en abyme* of the plot.

By the end of the nineteenth century, as Elrud Ibsch points out,[7] in novels such as Huysmans' *A Rebours* (1884), the act of describing has clearly become a form of storytelling. Indeed, what is being narrated, in this case, is mainly how a main character (Des Esseintes) builds for himself a specific setting/scenery able to reflect his psychological traits and life concerns. Such a process, no doubt, brings us closer to the fiction of French New Novelists such as Simon and Robbe-Grillet. These writers have taken description a step further by quite often creating 'tableaux,' which form long descriptive segments that can be organized chronologically so that one may infer a possible narration. It is as if the audience were given a series of randomly assembled photographs, slides, or cinematic clips, and asked to constitute the narrative connections of the story. The reader, in this case, is engaged in a form of fictional montage, which is, in fact, necessary if sense is to be made out of a number of fragmented 'discohesive' blocks. One of the best examples of how descriptive information can form the building blocks of a possible narration is Robbe-Grillet's short story 'La Chambre secrète,' a text Seymour Chatman comments upon and analyses at the end of the second chapter of

Coming to Terms.[8] Other similar examples, however, have been analysed in the present work, particularly in chapter 3.

If such types of fiction writing clearly foreground description, the contrary procedure is also possible. Thus, narrative segments that one might at first assume to be foregrounded can ultimately reveal themselves as examples of backgrounded descriptions. The most extreme example of this process is Robbe-Grillet's *La Maison de rendez-vous* (1965). In this novel, the reader is confronted with many multiple incomplete and contradictory versions of a series of events, which, therefore, cannot be read as elements in a main plot. One has the strong impression that Robbe-Grillet has here deliberately inverted one of his fictional techniques; instead of using description to narrate, as in many of his previous novels (for example, *Le Voyeur*, or *La Jalousie*) he has used action-packed narrative segments to describe. In fact, *La Maison de rendez-vous* leaves a reader with illogical and achronological material evocative of a random assemblage of narrative filmic segments. In the end, the reader can only bring together a number of recurrent themes that, given their very nature and function, cannot represent *per se* a narrative development. Surprisingly enough, what at a stylistic and discursive level looks and reads like narrative segments, comes to constitute, at a functional level, paradoxical types of description that finally reveal a very abstract configuration. A similar but less extreme example has been analysed in chapter 5 of the present study. Thus, in Penna's *A Menina Morta*, we are often faced not only with a set of descriptions, but also with a number of narrative segments that, given the elliptical qualities of a linear plot, function very much as descriptions.

In sum, as narration (especially after the modernistic experience) becomes less logically linear, less 'grammatical,' and more and more fragmented – through a series of splintering achronologies and multiple focalizations – it becomes more like description. Moreover, as narration ceases to fit the *fabula/sjužet* distinction of Russian formalists (for example, in the case of the 'stream of consciousness'), its foregrounding qualities seem to recede into the background. Description – no longer an interruption, but a rather versatile text-type – can then be foregrounded or blended in to the extent that, in many more recent novels, one can no longer establish a distinction between description and narration. In fact, in a text such as Oliveira's *Finisterra*, the terms 'description' and 'narration' become a pair of abstract labels no longer relevant to specific textual traits.

We have seen how in nineteenth-century realistic prose fiction description is generally foregrounded through discrete effects of *mise en abyme*. Moreover, analyses by Jean Ricardou and Mieke Bal of Flaubert's *Madame Bovary* (discussed in chapter 1) bring forth this textual device as a means to emancipate description from its backgrounding function. Such characteristics are, effectively, due to the fact that *mise en abyme* always operates according to grounding distinctions, thereby foregrounding any text-type where it may occur, be it a dialogue, a description, or a mere epigraph. One can, therefore, state that, no matter the historical period or fictional genre, foregrounded descriptions can always be revealed wherever descriptive segments constitute *mises en abyme*.

In more recent texts, however, one is no longer dealing, exclusively, with discrete occurrences, but with the fact that description itself has assumed narrative powers. Yet, in the context of a diachronical overview, one should note that the changes I have mentioned, as far as description is concerned, relate mainly to its *functions*, and not to its *stylistic* and *discursive* characteristics. Concerning the latter, one could posit that descriptive segments have not changed significantly as far as their internal organization is concerned. It is this consistency that allows us to isolate a given descriptive segment in any fictional text. In Pérez Galdós' *La de Bringas*, we have found descriptive segments evocative of 'baroque metafiction,' while in Simon's *Histoire* (analysed in chapter 3 of the present work) the first postcard to be described behaves very much like a nineteenth-century *tableau*, in spite of its specific punctuation. Historical changes in description do not have an impact on the very nature of its discrete segments. In fact, although I noted, in the case of Simon, how in the depiction of a postcard entitled 'vue des grands boulevards,' the main theme (or main discursive frame) is split through a number of sub-themes in order to create a 'discohesive' effect, such a process is not uncommon in baroque fiction, from which Simon seems to have borrowed his taste for an endless proliferation of details.

3. FOREGROUNDED DESCRIPTION AND THE OTHER ARTS

Ever since Lessing's *Laocoön, or On the Limits of Painting and Poetry* (1766), parallels have continued to be established between literature and the visual arts.[9] In chapter 3 of the present study, when analysing the differences and similarities between the reading of representational paintings (or photographs), and literary description, I pointed out characteristics that cut across different media.

It is interesting, however, to recognize that in all the fictional examples we have examined, there exists a more or less direct relationship between literary description and other artistic disciplines. Thus, in Zola's *Une Page d'amour*, we are presented with five views of Paris, which are described as if they were impressionistic paintings. In Galdós' *La de Bringas*, we have seen that the entire first chapter of the novel consists of a description of a cenotaph, which proves to be a rather complex type of collage. As for the twentieth-century fictional works, some descriptions in Penna's *A Menina Morta* evoke a cinematic-like effect. Moreover, it should be noted that this long novel was generated after a naïve painting that the author used to contemplate while imagining its fictional potential. In more recent novels we have seen the many artistic visual referents described in Simon's *Histoire* (particularly the turn-of-the-century postcards), as well as the parallels established in Oliveira's *Finisterra* between literary description and painting, photography, children's art, film, and sculpture.

Is it that foregrounded description in prose fiction always points to some connection or relationship with other media, especially with the visual arts, which by their very nature are mainly descriptive? The characteristics of the five novels we have examined should not necessarily imply that *all* cases of foregrounded description have necessarily to reveal a cross-disciplinary focus. Nevertheless, we are left with the impression that there is a difference between simply creating descriptive segments and describing (as if through a highly personalized form of reading) aesthetic objects (Simon and Oliveira), or merely imitating such an effect (Zola, Galdós, and Penna). Indeed, description is always foregrounded by concerns pertaining to its own creation, as if the descriptor were caught up in the effect of 'distanciation,' which such *interfering* intertexts (to use Mary Ann Caws' terminology) would provoke.[10]

In fact, by focusing on the characteristics of other descriptive arts, the descriptor and the descriptee become very alert both to the possibilities and to the limits of literary description. That is, such positive and deliberate 'interference' creates a state of metafictional or metadescriptive awareness sufficient to bring to the fore what in other contexts might have remained backgrounded.

Similar characteristics, nevertheless, take place in any descriptive segment that can be viewed as constituting a *mise en abyme*. Indeed, with its power to condense semantically, through mirroring effects, a large amount of intra- and/or extratextual information, *mises en abyme* always contain – in terms of their reception – an explicit or implicit metatextual quality, which, in the particular case of description, leads us to reflect on the versatile possibilities of this text-type.

More research, however, needs to be done in the area of foregrounded description in prose fiction, not only concerning possible parallels with other media, but also with other text-types such as commentary and lyrical poetry. A larger variety of literatures and historical periods must, of necessity, be taken into account, especially since it could well be argued that this particular text-type is not merely characteristic of the western prose fiction written during the past two centuries. Curiously, many of the descriptions we have analysed have, to a certain extent, a range of features similar to the ones found in lyrical poems. The latter, no matter the historical period or culture, tend to consist of descriptions that can, at times, be read as implied narrations. This can be verified, for example, in many classical Chinese poems by Li Po or Tu Fu (even in their English translations), as well as in a large number of poems and lyrical ballads belonging to oral and traditional literatures. Nevertheless, even though lyrical poetry has always enjoyed wide critical attention, description in prose fiction has often been ignored, probably because literary critics have until very recently been most concerned with plot mechanisms. This may explain why prose fiction texts that do not rely mainly on the developments of a main plot have been frequently ignored or misinterpreted. However, especially in an age during which the frontiers between description and narration, between prose fiction and poetry have crumbled, foregrounded description, and its related topics, will remain a relevant area of inquiry, as well as a pervasive text-type.

Notes

INTRODUCTION

1 Some positive approaches to literary description are the critical works of
Genette (1966), Mieke Bal (1981, 1982), Riffaterre (1987), as well as the first
three chapters of Seymour Chatman's *Coming to Terms: The Rhetoric of Narrative in Fiction and Film*. Also useful are the critical works of such authors as
Émile Zola (1880), Robbe-Grillet (1963), and Claude Simon (1970, 1980, 1985).

2 According to Fleischman (1990), '[a] prevailing view in discourse literature is
that the foreground of narrative consists of the ordered set of events,
reported by PFV [perfective] action verbs (accomplishments and achievements), that constitute the main plot line, while background consists of
descriptive, collateral material, typically packaged as IPFV [imperfective]
stative and activity predicates' (169–70).

3 According to Havránek (1942) the notion of foregrounding [*aktualisace*] is
defined as follows: 'By *foregrounding* ... we mean the use of the devices of the
language in such a way that this use itself attracts attention and is perceived
as uncommon, as deprived of automatization, as deautomatized, such as a
live poetic metaphor (as opposed to a lexical one, which is automatized)'
(10). Mukamovský (1948) also proposes a similar definition of foregrounding: 'The function of poetic language consists in the maximum of foregrounding of the utterance. Foregrounding is the opposite of automatization,
that is, the deautomatization of an act; the more an act is automatized, the
less it is consciously executed; the more it is foregrounded, the more completely conscious does it become' (19).

CHAPTER ONE

1 'On the Diegetic Functions of the Descriptive,' 281.

2 This notion is shared by a number of twentieth-century critics. According to Boris Eikhenbaum in 'Sur la théorie de la prose' (1925): 'Le roman du XIXème siècle se caractérise par un large emploi des *descriptions*, des *portraits psychologiques* et des dialogues' (200, emphasis mine). Referring to the nineteenth-century realistic novel, Ian Watt states in *The Rise of the Novel*: 'two ... aspects suggest themselves as of especial importance in the novel – characterization, and presentation of background' (17). More recently, in *Introduction à l'analyse du descriptif*, Philippe Hamon remarks: 'Il semble que la description commence à acquérir un statut littéraire ''normal'' simplement à la fin du XVIIIe siècle et au début du XIXe siècle' (23).

3 Unlike the *nouveau roman*, which, as the name itself indicates, is a typical French phenomenon, post-modern fiction can nowadays be found in a variety of cultures and literatures.

4 See Alexander Gelley, *Narrative Crossings: Theory and Pragmatics of Prose Fiction*. One should note that Gelley opts, however, in his 'pragmatic' examples, for a Lacanian psychoanalytic mode of inquiry, thereby abandoning his initial phenomenological project.

5 Literary critics such as Philippe Hamon, in *Introduction à l'analyse du descriptif*, and Alexander Gelley, in *Narrative Crossings*, have already provided, in the first chapters of their respective books, comprehensive analyses of approaches to and attitudes towards description, from Aristotle's concept of 'mimesis' to the present. Furthermore, Hamon has published an anthology of texts on description, *La Description littéraire de l'antiquité à Roland Barthes*. None the less, a more detailed analysis of twentieth-century criticism could bring into focus the question of fictional description as it is discussed through a variety of critical tendencies more relevant for our present work.

6 In 'L'Effet de réel' Barthes comments on Flaubert's description of Rouen as follows: 'l'écrivain accomplit ici la définition que Platon donne de l'artiste, qui est un faiseur au troisième degré, puisqu'il imite ce qui est déjà la simulation d'une essence' (86).

7 Hamon bases his analyses of description in prose fiction mainly on nineteenth-century French authors whose texts reveal a realistic mode of representation (e.g., Balzac, Flaubert, Maupassant, Zola, and Verne). Only when analysing the descriptive qualities of certain poems does he focus on twentieth-century writers such as Queneau, Apollinaire, Aragon, Eluard, and Breton.

8 Concerning the notion of 'grounding' in discourse linguistics, see Paul J. Hopper's 'Aspect and Foregrounding in Discourse,' Helen Dry's 'The Movement of Narrative Time,' and Tanya Reinhardt's 'Principles of Gestalt Perception in the Temporal Organization of Narrative Texts.'

9 Gérard Genette, in 'Frontières du récit,' had already mentioned that 'l'étude des rapports entre le narratif et le descriptif se ramène donc, pour l'essentiel, à considérer les *fonctions diégétiques* de la description, c'est-à-dire le rôle joué par les passages ou les aspects descriptifs dans l'économie générale du récit' (157).

10 One of the best examples of this attitude is Jean Cohen's analysis of poetical language in *Structure du langage poétique*.

11 For Barthes' concept of text, see 'De l'oeuvre au texte' in his *Le Bruissement de la langue*, 69–77.

12 Some specific journal issues on the subject are *Littérature*, no. 38 (1980), *Poétique*, no. 43 (1980); *Cahiers roumains d'études littéraires*, no. 2 (1981); *Yale French Studies*, no. 61 (1981), and *Pratiques*, no. 55 (1987). In book form one should mention Hamon's *La Description littéraire de l'antiquité à Roland Barthes: Une anthologie* (1991); Philippe Bonnefis' et al, *La Description: Nodier, Sue, Flaubert, Hugo, Verne, Zola, Alexis, Fénéon* (1981); a collection of articles under the general title *L'Ordre du descriptif* (1988); a series of articles published by the Semiotic Research Centre at Neuchâtel, under the title *La Schématisation descriptive: Types textuels, formes et fonctions discursives* (1988); and J.-M. Adam and A. Petitjean's *Le Texte descriptif: Poétique historique et linguistique textuelle* (1989). However, since the various contributions take the form of articles, description is not given an extended treatment.

13 In Randolph Quirk et al, *A Grammar of Contemporary English*, verbs are classified according to two major groups: 'dynamic' and 'stative' (97–8). Under 'dynamic' are 'activity verbs,' 'process verbs,' 'verbs of bodily sensation,' 'transitional event verbs,' and 'momentary verbs' (e.g., hit, jump, knock, etc.); 'stative verbs' include 'verbs of inert perception and cognition' as well as 'relational verbs.'

14 In Dry's 'The Movement of Narrative Time,' verbs that mark 'accomplishment' and 'achievement' can mainly be characterized as narrative and, therefore, as triggering a perception of time movement. She defines 'accomplishment' as 'a situation of some duration, having a natural endpoint, outcome or result state' (27), and 'achievement' as a punctual occurrence without duration that also has a culminating point or outcome. It should be noted, however, that according to Dry, 'activity and [s]tative sentences may [also] move time if it is clear from the context that the situation represented in the sentence is the outcome of a change of state' (23). As linguists such as Émile Benveniste observed (*Problèmes de linguistique générale*, vol. 1), the narrative versus descriptive qualities of verbs should be determined by a larger context. Discussing the validity of some grammatical categories in a section entitled 'Fonctions syntaxiques' (151–222), Benveniste

states: 'Il apparaît donc que, pour caractériser en propre, et sans considéra-
tion de type linguistique, l'opposition du verbe et du nom, nous ne pouvons
utiliser ni des notions telles que object et procès, ni des catégories comme
celle du temps, ni des différences morphologiques. Le critère existe cependant, il est d'ordre syntaxique. Il tient à la fonction du verbe dans l'énoncé'
(154).

15 Under metaphor, one should consider both the literary and the conventional
metaphors used in the everyday oral/written discourses of a particular language.

16 In this framework, the term *discourse* is used with the meaning it acquired in
discourse linguistics. M.A.K. Halliday and Ruqaiya Hassan define 'discourse
structure' as follows: 'the term is used to refer to the structure of some postu-
lated unit higher than the sentence, for example the paragraph, or some larger
entity such as episode or topic unit' (*Cohesion in English*, 10). 'Cohesion' is
defined as '[the] part of the text-forming component in the linguistic system'
and as 'the means whereby elements that are structurally unrelated to one
another are linked together, through the dependence of one on the other for
its interpretation' (27). The notion of 'coherence' in discourse analysis is defined by Robert de Beaugrande and Wolfgang Dressler in *Introduction to Text
Linguistics* as follows: 'COHERENCE ... concerns the ways in which the components of the TEXTUAL WORLD, i.e. the configuration of CONCEPTS and RELATIONS
which *underlie* the surface text, are *mutually accessible* and *relevant*' (4).

17 Referring to the notion of 'frame' in cognitive psychology, Ian Reid defines it
in 'Destabilizing Frames for Story' as 'a mental schema or ideational format
used for organizing information' (299). However, in this context, 'frame'
should be viewed as a mode of conveying descriptive information in such a
way as to determine specific types of reception. Consequently, beyond Iser's
notions in 'Passive Synthesis in the Reading Process,' description is not
always an amount of information the reader is meant to store or keep on hold
in his/her mind. In fact, by de-automatizing through text conventional
modes of triggering descriptive reception, authors such as Robbe-Grillet and
Simon have put into question the very mode of conveying and processing
descriptive information.

18 This process is analysed in detail by Denis Apothéloz in 'Eléments pour une
logique de la description et du raisonnement spatial.'

19 Contrary to the term *describer* used by several Anglo-American critics, the
term *descriptor* seems to be more appropriate to designate a fictional entity.

20 Reasserting her definition of post-modern fiction in *A Poetics of
Postmodernism: History, Theory, Fiction*, Linda Hutcheon in *The Politics of Postmodernism* defines it basically as 'historiographic metafiction.' However, in

Postmodernistic Fiction Brian McHale defines post-modern fiction differently, according to the ontological status of a variety of texts. When mentioning Robbe-Grillet's work, McHale makes a distinction between the modernist *nouveau roman* and the post-modernist *nouveau nouveau roman*. Thus, according to McHale, Robbe-Grillet's literary creations until the publication of *La Maison de rendez-vous* (1965) can be classified as modernist, while his subsequent literary production can be considered as post-modernist (13–15). A similar distinction could apply to Claude Simon, who may be seen as having first a modernist period where a basic Faulknerian intertext may be found (i.e., all books published until *La Route des Flandres*, 1960) and then a post-modern period encompassing his subsequent production.

21 One should note, however, that the notion of *mise en abyme* extensively analysed by Lucien Dällenbach in *Le Récit spéculaire: Essai sur la mise en abyme* is more useful in texts that present a realistic mode of representation than in texts with constant and deliberate mirroring effects. In some cases of the French New Novel, for example, the notion of *mise en abyme* can become quite arbitrary.

22 In this context, 'significance' is used in the sense Wolfgang Iser attributes to it in *The Act of Reading*. He defines 'significance' and 'meaning' as follows: 'Meaning is the referential totality which is implied by the aspects contained in the text and which must be assembled in the course of reading. Significance is the reader's absorption of the meaning into his own existence' (151).

CHAPTER TWO

1 Letter addressed to Antony Valabrègue, dated 18 August 1864, in Zola, *Correspondence*, I, 375.

2 In *Les Rougons-Macquart* (1961), II, 801–1092. All subsequent references are to this edition.

3 For more information about impressionism and expressionism in the works of Zola, see Joy Newton, 'Émile Zola impressioniste'and 'Zola et l'expressionisme' and Philippe Hamon, 'A propos de l'impressionisme de Zola.'

4 *Le Roman expérimental* (Paris: Garnier-Flammarion, 1971), 231–5. All subsequent references are to this edition.

5 'Lettre de Flaubert à Émile Zola,' in Zola, *Une Page d'amour* (Paris: Garnier-Flammarion, 1973), 369.

6 For more information about the illustrated editions of *Une Page d'amour*, see Zola, *Oeuvres complètes*, III, 1217–18. The preface to the first illustrated edition can be found in the same volume, 1219–20. All subsequent references to this preface are to this edition.

7 This term condenses the notions of narrative and descriptive voices.

8 According to Dällenbach (1977), this *mise en abyme* is defined as being constituted by the following: '1) la "présentifiction" diégétique du producteur ou du récepteur du récit, 2) la mise en évidence de la production ou de la réception comme telles, 3) la manifestation du contexte qui conditionne (qui a conditionné) cette production-réception' (100).

9 The concept of 'weaved metaphor' as a metonymical isotopy of metaphors is discussed in Michael Riffaterre, 'La Métaphore filée dans la poésie surréaliste.'

10 Unlike many of his critics, Zola was aware that literature could never be an absolute direct copy of reality, as can be observed in the epigraph to the present chapter.

11 It should be mentioned, none the less, that of all the types of *mise en abyme* discussed by Dällenbach (1977), the identification of the *mise en abyme* of the code is probably the one that depends most on the particular interests or mode of inquiry a reader might bring into play when faced with a given text.

12 Referring to this type in *Le Récit spéculaire*, Dällenbach remarks: 'L'énoncé dont il s'agit n'étant provisoirement envisagé que sous son aspect référentiel d'*histoire racontée* (ou *fiction*), il apparaît possible de définir sa mise en abyme comme une citation de contenu ou un résumé *intertextuels*.' He adds: 'Admis le fait que cette dernière [mise en abyme de l'énoncé] peut s'effectuer par *analogie* ou *contraste plus ou moins nets*, l'on reconnaîtra qu'entre la reproduction quasi mimétique et la libre transposition existe tout un éventail de possibilités dont chacune emporte une manière différente de faire le jeu du récit' (77, 78).

CHAPTER THREE

1 Claude Simon, preface to *Orion aveugle*, n.p.

2 Simon, *Histoire (roman)* (Paris, Les Éditions de Minuit, 1967). All subsequent references are to this edition.

3 The postcards in *Histoire* are not mere products of the author's imagination. Jean Ricardou, in *Le Nouveau roman*, shows us some of the postcards as being the 'cartes postales à partir desquelles s'est écrit "Histoire,"' (183). L. Dällenbach, in *Claude Simon*, also shows us postcards described in *Histoire* (107). In C.-G. Bjurström's 'Dimensions du temps chez Claude Simon,' in *Entretiens: Claude Simon*, there is an illustration entitled *Vue de Barcelone (Aquatinte, fin du XIXe siècle)* (145), which is described in *Histoire*: 'une aquatinte dont le titre VUE GÉNÉRALE DE BARCELONE en caractères romantiques épais dessinés en

trompe-l'oeil de façon à imiter le relief pouvait se lire sur la marge inférieure' (169).

4 By other texts I mean not only the texts in the postcards (which are presented as being written by different people), but also intertextual references to James Joyce's *Ulysses* (e.g., chap./part 3), and 'intra-intertextual' references to other books by Simon, namely *La Route des Flandres* (1960) for passages centred around De Reixach and Corinne, and *Le Palace* (1962) for passages concerning the Spanish Civil War.

5 The pages that constitute the preface to *Orion aveugle*, in Simon's handwriting, are not numbered.

6 Claude Simon's statement in an interview with C. Sarraute entitled 'Avec *La Route des Flandres* Claude Simon affirme sa manière' in *Le Monde* could also apply to a novel such as *Histoire*: 'J'étais hanté par deux choses: la discontinuité, l'aspect fragmentaire des émotions que l'on éprouve et qui ne sont jamais reliées les unes aux autres, et en même temps leur contiguïté dans la conscience' (9). Cited by Alastair Duncan in 'Claude Simon: La crise de la représentation.'

7 An interest in referential visual material such as illustrations, photographs, and paintings, can be seen in almost all of Simon's prose fiction. The author himself has made available a photograph entitled *Personnages dans un jardin*, described in *L'Herbe*, and the *Portrait de l'ancêtre*, described in *La Route des Flandres*. These can be seen in Bjurström, *Entretiens: Claude Simon*, or in the covers of Simon's novels published in the 'Collection "double"' by Éditions de Minuit. Other images described in some of Simon's novels can be found in Dällenbach's *Claude Simon*. One of the best examples of the author's interest in paintings and other visual art objects is *Orion aveugle*, a novel where Simon incorporates a series of illustrations he describes in the book. *Orion aveugle* is also the title of a painting by Poussin.

8 Fitch, 'When the Fictive Referent Is Itself a Work of Art: Simon's *Histoire*,' *Reflections in the Mind's Eye*, 153–79.

9 In the case of Simon's fictional production, as I later explain, it is very difficult to make a clear-cut distinction between 'narrative' and 'descriptive' voice. The term 'enunciative voice' is suggested in an attempt to encompass both categories.

10 The images on the postcards are black-and-white or hand-coloured photographs, collages of different media, and representational paintings. The following quotations from *Histoire* refer to the types of media used in the postcards: 'avec cette différence qu'on n'y voyait ni palmiers ni le fameux ciel bleu, car elles n'était pas en couleur' (104), 'c'était une photo en blanc et noir dont on s'était contenté de colorer le fond après coup) surmontant le fastueux

costume de poupée fait d'un morceau de soie bleu ciel cousu et brodé sur la carte postale' (116), and 'une brume délicate raffinée et barbare que le pinceau accumule en noirs' (132).

11 Although some of the postcards may present dated clichés evocative of Victorian *tableaux vivants*, the nature of the poses and the choice of settings presuppose a certain amount of artistic effort. In this respect, even though some of them may strike the narrator/descriptor as pictographic kitsch, they were nevertheless conceived as aesthetic objects.

12 In Latin, the verb *describere* is synonymous with *transcribere*. However, the etymological meaning of the verb 'to transcribe' is not only 'to copy,' but also 'to transpose.' In the case of *Histoire*, to transpose into a different medium and into a different context, thus creating, to a certain extent, particular types of intertextual relations.

13 This information is taken from Claude DuVerlie's 'Pictures for Writing: Premises for a Graphopictology,' in Randi Birn and Karen Gould, *Orion Blinded: Essays on Claude Simon.*

14 I use the term *pictographic reading* when referring to the reading of a painting or a photograph.

15 Since the object of this discussion is the use of postcards in Claude Simon's *Histoire*, I only mention the case of representational paintings and photographs, as well as description in prose fiction.

16 Some representational paintings or illustrations seem to defy this notion, either by presenting us with a large number of minute details that can only be perceived as we focus on specific pictographic segments, or by opting for an enormous pictographic surface. The latter is the case in certain murals that, by extending themselves through many metres, solicit a reading that can only be done (as in the case of written texts) in sequential terms.

17 Jean-Louis Schefer in *Scénographie d'un tableau* defines the pictorial lexia as 'unité de lecture macroscopique qui a pour but de déterminer tous les niveaux référés du texte' (171), and he adds: 'la lexie permet de définir un système par ses entrées (une structure par le nombre et le type de lectures que l'on *peut* en faire' (174).

18 Some of the pictogrammatic poems in Guillaume Apollinaire's *Calligrammes*, as well as concrete poems in general, present us with an attempt to escape the linearity of written language. In prose fiction, however, such explorations of the graphic potential are not at all common.

19 Louis Marin mentions in *Études sémiologiques: Écritures, peintures* that 'dans la peinture réprésentative fondée sur un système analogique comportant notamment une organisation illusioniste de l'espace plastique, le degré de contrainte qui en découle pour le regard est particulièrement fort' (22).

20 The description of the postcards is generally presented as a textual block. However, some descriptions are fragmented into two different segments, e.g., the postcard of Lourdes is described on 28 but its conclusion is to be found on 226. In the same way, the description of the postcard entitled 'Musique de Moïs' (385–6) is only concluded on 391. The fact that these descriptions are presented as two sets of segments does not imply a fragmentation of descriptive elements, since once joined, both segments form a unity.

21 According to Simon, relations of this type give descriptions their own dynamism: 'c'est le prodigieux dynamisme de la description qui, littéralement, projette autour d'elle, comme une pieuvre, des tentacules dans toutes les directions, sélectionne et convoque des matérieux, les assemble, les organise.' In Simon, 'Roman, description et action' in *The Feeling for Nature and the Landscape of Man*.

22 A recent edition of Lessing's work can be found in H.B. Nisbet, ed., *German Aesthetic and Literary Criticism*.

23 Although this depicting strategy generally refers to medieval or classical painting, namely to the depiction in Christian churches of the fourteen steps of the cross, it has been largely used by Italian futurist painters. A good example is Giacommo Balla's paintings *Dog on a Leash, Rhythm of a Violinist*, and *Girl Running on a Balcony* (all dated 1912). The aim of these painters was precisely to capture action as a sequence of motionless instants in time. In a similar manner, the art of sculpture, which may seem to us as producing the most static of objects, has resorted in the 20th century to the inclusion of a series of mobile elements in order to challenge or sabotage its immobile nature.

24 In this case we can only mention the occurrence of synesthesias after having assumed that the descriptor is reading a visual image that, given its nature, cannot include sounds or smell. The term 'effect of synesthesia' seems therefore to be more appropriate in this case.

25 In *Histoire*, a narrator mentions at least once the use of the present participle: 'la respiration pressée haletante de la phrase les participes présents se succédant, se pressant, s'accumulant' (108). However, in another passage, some visual associations are made concerning what we could consider as one of the stylistic effects of this verbal form: 'une confuse, une inextricable superposition d'images, mordant les unes sur les autres comme ces illustrations dans le dictionnaire ou certaines méthodes de culture physique homme courant ou homme sautant photos prises sur une plaque fixe à l'aide d'un appareil dont l'obturateur s'ouvre et se ferme à des intervalles très rapprochés ...' (286).

26 This type of reading also applies to other photographs in the novel, particularly the one described in great detail in chapter/part 9 of the novel.

27 The concept of 'weaved metaphor,' referring to a metonymical chain of meta-phors that are semantically related, is presented in Michael Riffaterre's 'La Métaphore filée dans la poésie surréaliste,' in Riffaterre, *La Production du texte*.

28 I have not mentioned Jurij Lotman's concept of 'frame,' presented in *The Structure of the Artistic Text*, because we are dealing with 'frame' at a discur-sive level. Lotman's concept (209–17), which pertains to a form of contextual-ization, becomes important only in so far as we may explore how given textual segments acquire a new meaning when placed in an overall context.

29 According to Jean Rousset in '"Histoire" de Claude Simon, *Le Jeu des cartes postales*,' almost all the postcard descriptions have a narrative function he names as 'fonction fabulatrice.'

30 When Brian T. Fitch, in 'Participe présent et procédés narratifs chez Claude Simon,' analyses the nature of the present participle in the narrative seg-ments of Simon's prose fiction, he states: 'les participes n'évoquent que l'image du geste lui-même [...] On dirait que le temps s'est arrêté, figeant l'action en pleine évolution sous forme d'image – d'où précisément le pou-voir évocateur du participe présent' (201). In fact, in Simon's fiction, the present participle functions as a tense whose main purpose is to abolish any attempts at viewing or opposing description and narration as two different (if not antithetic) categories.

31 The description of the sea leads us to infer the describer is reading and describing a sepia photograph: 'la mer d'une de ces teintes indéfinissables aux reflets roses amande saumon comme une plaque faiblement luisante' (36).

32 The text written on the postcards sent by Henri is extremely brief. It is basi-cally a series of dated salutations, as if the pictorial images could, by them-selves, stand for a lack of written news or personal impressions.

CHAPTER FOUR

1 'La de Bringas,' in *Técnicas de Galdós*, 125.

2 According to Galdós in his 'Prólogo' to Leopoldo Alas Clarín, *La Regenta* (1900), v–xix, naturalism was a typically Spanish tendency that, once exported to the rest of Europe, was reintroduced in Spain at a later date. He states: 'Francia, con su poder incontrastable, nos imponía una reforma de nuestra propia obra, sin saber que era nuestra; aceptámosla nosotros restau-rando el Naturalismo y devolviéndole lo que le habían quitado, el humor-ismo, y empleando éste en las formas narrativa y descriptiva conforme a la tradición cervantesca.' [France, with its insuperable power, was imposing on

us a reform of our own tendency without knowing that naturalism was ours all along. We accepted it none the less, and we restored to naturalism that which they had taken away: humour. The latter has been used, in both its descriptive and narrative forms, according to the tradition of Cervantes] (xi).

3 For a detailed study of humour in Galdós' novels, see Michael Nimetz, *Humour in Galdós: A Study of the 'Novelas contemporáneas,'* particularly the first chapter, 'Realism and Humour' (3–38).

4 In the present study I use the edition of *La de Bringas* annotated by Alda Blanco and Carlos Blanco Aguinaga. All subsequent references are to this edition.

5 Jon Juaristi, in 'Ironía, picaresca y parodia en *La de Bringas,*' makes a comparison between *La de Bringas* and the Spanish picaresque novel *La vida de Lazarillo de Tormes y de sus fortunas y adversidades.*

6 The notion of Menippean parody (from the philosopher Menippus of Gandara) as a sort of textual Carnival is discussed by Julia Kristeva in *Séméiotiké: Recherches pour une sémanalyse (Extraits).* According to Kristeva, 'La ménippée est à la fois comique et tragique, elle est plutôt *sérieuse,* au sens où le carnaval l'est et, par le statut de ses mots, elle est politiquement et socialement dérangeante' (104). The concept of 'Menippean satire' is also discussed by Northrop Frye in *Anatomy of Criticism,* 309–12.

7 Benito Pérez Galdós, *The Spendthrifts,* ed. Gerald Brenan, trans. Gamel Woollsley.

8 All Spanish and Portuguese quotations in this book are translated by me. However, at times, when translating shorter segments, I opt for a more literal translation to facilitate my analysis.

9 As William H. Shoemaker has indicated in *The Novelistic Art of Galdós,* there are practically no new characters in this novel. On 223, note 2, Shoemaker lists about eighteen characters from previous fictional works by Galdós.

10 A good example of zeugma at a stylistic level would be a sentence such as: 'She was dressed in rags and diamonds.' Notice that both rags and diamonds belong to the same metonymy – things one may wear – however, there is a sharp contrast between the two terms.

11 It is interesting to notice how the adjectives 'ondulante' [undulating] and 'quebradizo' [discontinued/breakable] seem to point to the very zeugmatic characteristics of the descriptive segment where they occur.

12 In the present study I take into account Linda Hutcheon's notions of 'satire' and 'parody' as they are developed in *A Theory of Parody: The Teachings of Twentieth-Century Art Forms.* This critic defines parody as a 'repetition with [a] critical distance, which marks difference rather than similarity' (6),

while satire, as opposed to parody, is 'both moral and social in its focus and ameliorative in its intention' (16). It should be noted that Hutcheon is referring mainly to the characteristics of the post-modern novel. However, as we shall later verify, in the case of Galdós' *La de Bringas* it is almost impossible to separate satire from parody, since the former is, in this specific case, always embedded in the latter. Let us note, none the less, that, unlike satire, parody does not always create a humorous effect. Indeed, in many twentieth-century fictional works parody is not directly identified with humour and sarcasm.

13 Like Gamel Woollsley in her English translation of *La de Bringas*, Peter Bly in *Pérez Galdós' La de Bringas* uses the term 'hair-picture' to refer to Francisco's cenotaph.

14 Such a process, which occurs at times in baroque fiction, would no doubt go against nineteenth-century notions of 'originality' and 'plagiarism.'

15 The notion of *mise en abyme* has been developed and analysed in great detail by Lucien Dällenbach in *Le Récit spéculaire*.

16 According to Robert H. Russell in 'La voz narrativa en *La de Bringas*,' the narrative voice 'se burla de todo, incluso de sí misma' [makes fun of everything, even of itself] (139).

17 According to Peter Bly, 'the hair-picture does succinctly sum up many, perhaps all, aspects of the novel: it is a "microcosmos"' (21). The idea of the first chapter of the novel as a *mise en abyme* is also succinctly discussed by Arthur Ramirez in 'The Heraldic Emblematic Image in Galdós' *La de Bringas*.'

18 Ricardo Gullón's analysis of *La de Bringas* focuses especially on parallels between the novel and the social characteristics of its time. Such an approach can also be found in Emilie Bergmann, ' "Los sauces llorando a moco y baba": Ekphrasis in Galdós' *La de Bringas*.' According to this critic, Francisco's cenotaph is 'symbolic of the nation's obliviousness to impending catastrophe, and its dedication to worthless but subtly destructive pursuits' (75).

19 In chap. 16 of *La de Bringas*, the descriptor/narrator refers to 'la época de Fernando VII, que si en política fue brutalidad, en artes fue tontería pura' [the epoch of Fernando VII, which, if in politics was an age of brutality, in the arts was one of pure silliness] (125).

20 Character caricaturization in Galdós is extensively analysed by Mariano Baquero Goyanes in 'Las caricaturas literarias de Galdós' in his *Perspectivismo y contraste: de Cadalso a Pérez de Ayala* (43–81). In this comparative study, Goyanes establishes parallels between caricatures in Galdós and in Dickens.

21 It is interesting to notice that Galdós planned, at a later date, to adapt *La de Bringas* into a play. His brief manuscript, together with some critical notes, can be read in Stephen Miller's 'A Fragment of "La de Bringas" for the Stage.'

22 Ironically, when referring to his temporary blindness, Francisco de Bringas mentions his 'pícara retina enferma' [picaresque and sick retina] (160).

23 Torquemada is the main character in three later novels by Galdós, which belong to the series *Novelas españolas contemporáneas: Torquemada en la cruz* (1893), *Torquemada en el Purgatorio* (1894), and *Torquemada y San Pedro* (1895).

24 The idea of a cenotaph, or something similar, is never abandoned by Francisco. In fact, when his doctor tells him that carpentry would be good for him (174), he immediately imagines the construction of a huge wardrobe from various scraps stored in the attics of the palace. Turning to his wife Rosalía, he tells her: 'Te haré un armario de mármol ... digo, un *panteón* para la ropa ...' [I shall make you a marble wardrobe ... I mean, a *pantheon* for your clothes ...] (175, emphasis mine).

CHAPTER FIVE

1 'Sob as Trevas da Melancolia: O Patriarcado em *A Menina Morta*,' 239.

2 In Cornélio Penna, *Romances Completos* (Rio de Janeiro: Aguilar, 1958). All subsequent references are to this edition.

3 For a definition of post-modern literature as 'historiographic metafiction,' see Linda Hutcheon, *A Poetics of Postmodernism: History, Theory, Fiction* and/or *The Politics of Postmodernism*.

4 In the English-speaking world, only Cornélio Penna's first novel, *Fronteira*, published for the first time in 1935, has been translated under the title *Threshold*.

5 Besides the edition in the volume of complete works that I am using, the novel was also published separately: Cornélio Penna, *A Menina Morta* (Rio de Janeiro: Livraria José Olympio, 1970). Both editions are now out of print.

6 Luiz Costa Lima has studied this novel extensively in *A Perversão do Trapesista: O Romance em Cornélio Penna*. I recommend, in particular, chapters 5 and 6, 97–193. More recently, in *A Aguarrás do Tempo: Estudos sobre a Narrativa*, he devotes an entire chapter, entitled 'Sob as Trevas da Melancolia: O Patriarcado em *A Menina Morta*' (239–85), to this novel.

7 'Menina,' in this context, means both 'young girl' and 'daughter of the master'; thus, in the present work, I have used, at times, the Portuguese word. Furthermore, this character is never given a name and is always referred to as the 'menina.'

8 Cornélio Penna's paintings and illustrations have been reproduced in *Pintura e Desenhos*, in Cornélio Penna, *Romances Completos*, 1325–51.

9 The portrait of the dead young girl is mentioned and reproduced in the 'Introdução Geral' by Adonias Filho, in Penna's *Romances Completos*, xxxvii. In this same edition is an interview with Penna in which, referring to the

painting, he states: 'A menina morta tomou conta de todo o meu pensamento e surgiu cercada por outros personagens que ocurreram de tôda a parte, trazendo já seus capítulos delineados. Sua presença se tornou quase real ao meu lado, e ouvi que murmura [sic] muita coisas em meus sonhos. Não eram recordações de fatos já ocorridos, mas apenas a criação de tudo em tôrno dela, na fantasmagoria de existências, de episódios, de detalhes.' [The dead young girl took hold of all my thoughts and appeared surrounded by other characters that came from everywhere, already bringing their delineated chapters. Her presence by my side became almost real, and I heard her murmuring many things in my dreams. They were not memories of something that had occurred, but the creation of everything around her in the phantasmagoria of existences, of episodes, of details] (xiii). In the same edition is a short article by Augusto Frederico Schmidt, 'O Anjo entre os Escravos' (723–5) published for the first time in *Correio da Manhã*, Rio de Janeiro, (27–02–1955), where he states: 'o que levou a escrever o seu livro, a sua história, foi um certo quadro que ele recebeu por herança de uns parentes seus' [what led him to write his book, his story, was a certain painting he received as an inheritance from some of his relatives] (723). Besides the above references, the painting is also mentioned in several passages of the novel.

10 Costa Lima, 'Sob as Trevas da Melancolia,' 249.

11 Ibid, 246.

12 The word *grotão* in Portuguese evokes 'gruta' [grotto]; the augmentative '-ão' gives us the impression that *grotão* could mean a 'huge grotto.'

13 Acording to Costa Lima, 'Mariana não tem interior; como também sucede com o marido e a filha morta, é vista ou descrita pelos comentários de terceiros.' [Mariana has no internal make-up; the same also applies to her husband and to her dead daughter, since they are all seen or described by others] (1976, 131).

14 In a sub-chapter entitled 'O Tempo Real,' in *A Perversão do Trapesista*, 97–9, Costa Lima establishes the accuracy of all the historical data contained in the novel.

15 An example is the psychoanalytic case studies in Serge Leclaire's *Démasquer le réel: Un essai sur l'objet en psychanalyse*, which can also be read as well-crafted literary texts.

16 Quimbundo is a native language spoken in the central and northern parts of Angola, where many of the black slaves brought to Brazil were captured.

17 A description containing many figures of speech cannot readily be visualized. The same applies to a description containing many sub-topics.

18 For a definition of the 'fantastic' as a mode, see Rosemary Jackson, *Fantasy: The Literature of Subversion*, 35.

19 'Braúna' is a black dye extracted from the 'baraúna' tree, a tropical variety for which I could find no English translation.

20 Concerning the stylistic characteristics of this novel, Costa Lima states: 'A tinta negra da escrita, a sintaxe compacta das suas frases dão uma imagem ilusória de um todo sem fraturas. Na verdade, analiticamente o percebemos, imensos borrões se interpõem entre frase e frase, mesmo entre palavra e palavra.' [The black ink of writing, the compact syntax of its sentences transmit the illusory image of an unfragmented totality. In fact, we understand it analytically, there are huge ink-stains that came in between phrases, even in between words] (1989, 261).

21 In 'Demônios e Vampiros' in Luiz Costa Lima (1976), the 'menina' is compared to a vampire (chap. 7, 163–93).

CHAPTER SIX

1 *Carlos de Oliveira et le roman*, 607.

2 Neo-realism in Portuguese and Italian literatures can be seen as a form of social-realism.

3 For a more detailed comparison of the first and subsequent editions of De Oliveira's *Uma Abelha na Chuva*, see João Camilo dos Santos' 'Deux versions de "Uma Abelha na Chuva" (1953 et 1971)' in his *Carlos de Oliveira et le roman*, 512–42, in particular, the section entitled 'Donner à voir plutôt que raconter et expliquer,' (524–7).

4 Carlos de Oliveira, *Finisterra*, 2nd ed., (Lisbon: Sá da Costa, 1979). All references to this novel are to this edition.

5 See Diogo Pires Aurélio, 'Teoria da representação em "Finisterra"'; Eduarda Dionísio, '"Finisterra": Cálculos, sonhos, tentativas'; and Maria de Lurdes Ferraz, 'Aproximação a "Finisterra,"' 8. According to these critics, *Finisterra* cannot be read as a traditional novel.

6 The main character–'enunciative voice' often refers to a variety of familiar documents, to a series of photographs, and to a detailed blueprint executed prior to the construction of the house.

7 As examples of alliteration one could mention: 'pasta de espessura sem fulhas,' and 'curvatura só insinuada, crinas erguidas ao céu' (emphasis added).

8 For a detailed analysis of the referent as a reader-writer construction, see Paul Ricoeur, 'La triple *mimésis*' in *Temps et récit*, and Brian T. Fitch, 'Fictional Referentiality' in *Reflections in the Mind's Eye*, 3–26.

9 Zima, 'Ideology and Theory: The Relationship between Ideological and Theoretical Discourses,' 151.

10 Ricoeur, 117–24.

11 For a comparison between some of the descriptive segments in *Finisterra* and in *O Aprendiz de Feiticeiro*, see J. Camilo dos Santos, '"Finisterra": roman du regard et de la mémoire' in his *Carlos de Oliveira et le roman*, 597–622, in particular 599–600.

CONCLUSION

1 *Le Discours de Stockholm*, 19-20.
2 Robbe-Grillet, 'La Chambre secrète,' in *Instantanés*.
3 In 'Description in the Cinema' in *Coming to Terms: The Rhetoric of Narrative in Fiction and Film*, Seymour Chatman uses the term 'text-type' to refer to fictional forms such as description and narration.
4 The notion of reader as a textual entitity can be found even in the titles of critical anthologies, such as Susan R. Suleiman and Inge Crosman, ed., *The Reader in the Text: Essays on Audience and Interpretation*.
5 In *Les Figures du discours*, Pierre Fontanier (1821–30) defines description as a non-trope with a series of subgenres (420–33).
6 This occurs at a time when science, in the fields of physiology and psychology, was presenting many of its findings in a narrative form (for example, many of Freud's 'case studies').
7 'Historical Changes of the Function of Spatial Description in Literary Texts.'
8 'Description Is No Textual Handmaiden,' *Coming to Terms*, 35–7.
9 A good example of recent works in this area can be found in Mary Ann Caws (1981, 1989), and in Wendy Steiner (1988).
10 *The Art of Interference: Stressed Readings in Verbal and Visual Texts.*

Bibliography

A) LITERARY TEXTS

Apollinaire, Guillaume. *Calligrammes*. Paris: Gallimard, 1966.
Balzac, Honoré de [1833]. *Eugénie Grandet*. Paris: Garnier frères, 1965.
Biely, Andrey [1911]. *St. Petersburg*. Trans. John Cournos. New York: Grove, 1959.
Faulkner, William [1931]. *The Sound and the Fury*. London: Penguin, 1975.
Huysmans, J.-K. [1884]. *A Rebours*. Paris: Garnier-Flammarion, 1975.
Joyce, James [1922]. *Ulysses*. London: Penguin, 1978.
Mendes Pinto, Fernão [1614]. *Peregrinação*. 2 vols. Lisbon: Edições Afrodite, 1971.
Oliveira, Carlos de. *Alcateia*. Coimbra: Coimbra Editora, 1944.
– *Casa na Duna*. Lisbon: Sá da Costa, 1977.
– *Finisterra: Paisagem e Povoamento*. 2nd ed. Lisbon: Sá da Costa, 1979.
– *Micropaisagem*. Lisbon: Publicações D. Quixote, 1968.
– *Pequenos Burgueses*. Lisbon: Sá da Costa, 1978.
– *O Aprendiz de Feiticeiro*. Lisbon: Sá da Costa, 1982.
– *Trabalho Poético*. 2 vols. Lisbon: Sá da Costa, 1982.
– *Uma Abelha na Chuva*. 1st ed. Coimbra: Coimbra Editora, 1953.
– *Uma Abelha na Chuva*. [final ed.]. Lisbon: Sá da Costa, 1976.
Penna, Cornélio [1954]. *A Menina Morta*. In *Romances Completos*. Rio de Janeiro: Editora José Aguilar, 1958, 729–1296.
– [1935]. *Fronteira*. In *Romances Completos*. Rio de Janeiro: Editora José Aguilar, 1958, 9–165.
– *Threshold*. Trans. Tona and Edward A. Riggio. Philadelphia: Franklin, 1975.
Pérez Galdós, Benito [1882]. *El amigo Manso*. Buenos Aires: Espasa-Calpe Argentina, 1955.
– [1884]. *La de Bringas*. Madrid: Cátedra, 1983.
– [1881]. *La desheredada*. Madrid: Librería y Casa Editorial Hernando, 1983.

– *The Spendthrifts*. Ed. Gerald Brenan; trans. Gamel Woollsley. London: Weiden-
    feld & Nicolson, 1952.
– [1884]. *Tormento*. Madrid: Alianza Editorial, 1968.
– [1894]. *Torquemada en el Purgatorio*. Madrid: Hernando, 1920.
– [1893]. *Torquemada en la cruz*. Madrid: Hernando, 1916.
– [1895]. *Torquemada y San Pedro*. Madrid: Hernando, 1921.
Pinget, Robert. *L'Inquisitoire*. Paris: Éditions de Minuit, 1962.
Puig, Manuel. *Maldición eterna a quién lea estas páginas*. Barcelona, Caracas, Méx-
    ico: Seix Barral, 1980.
Robbe-Grillet, Alain. 'La Chambre secrète.' In *Instantanés*. Paris: Éditions du
    Seuil, 1962, 97–109.
– *La Jalousie*. Paris: Éditions de Minuit, 1957.
– *La Maison de rendez-vous*. Paris: Éditions de Minuit, 1965.
– *Topologie d'une cité fantôme*. Paris: Éditions de Minuit, 1976.
– *Le Voyeur*. Paris: Éditions de Minuit, 1955.
Simon, Claude. *L'Herbe*. Paris: Éditions de Minuit, 1958.
– *Histoire*. Paris: Éditions de Minuit, 1967.
– *Leçon de choses*. Paris: Éditions de Minuit, 1975.
– *Orion aveugle*. Geneva: Skira, 1970.
– *Le Palace*. Paris: Éditions de Minuit, 1962.
– *La Route des Flandres*. Paris: Éditions de Minuit, 1960.
La vida de Lazarillo de Tormes y de sus fortunas y adversidades. Madrid: Cátedra,
    1983.
Woolf, Virginia [1931]. *The Waves*. London: Penguin, 1976.
Zola, Émile [1877]. *L'Assommoir*. Paris: Fasquelle, 1960.
– [1890]. *La Bête humaine*. Paris: Garnier-Flammarion, 1970.
– [1885]. *Germinal*. Paris: Garnier frères, 1979.
– [1878]. *Une Page d'amour*. In *Les Rougon-Macquart: Histoire naturelle et social
    d'une famille sous le Second Empire*. Paris: Bibliothèque de la Pléiade, 1961. II,
    801–1092.
– [1867]. *Thérèse Raquin*. Paris: Garnier-Flammarion, 1970.

B) SECONDARY SOURCES CITED

Adam, Jean-Michel. 'Approche linguistique de la séquence descriptive.' *Pra-
    tiques*, no. 55 (1987), 3–27.
Adam, Jean-Michel, and André Petitjean. 'Les Enjeux textuels de la description.'
    Pratiques, no. 34 (1982), 93–117.
– 'Introduction au type descriptif.' *Pratiques*, no. 34 (1982), 77–91.
– *Le Texte descriptif: Poétique historique et linguistique textuelle*. Paris: Nathan, 1989.

Apothéloz, Denis. 'Eléments pour une logique de la description et du raisonnement spatial.' *Degrés*, no. 35–6 (1983), 3–19.

Aurélio, Diogo Pires. 'Teoria da Representação em "Finisterra." *Expresso* (Lisbon: 07-12-78), 10.

Bal, Mieke. 'Descriptions.' In *Narratologie*. Utrecht: HES Publishers, 1981. 89–109.

– 'Mise en abyme et iconicité.' *Littérature*, no. 29 (1971), 1–14.

– 'On Meanings and Descriptions.' *Studies in Twentieth Century Literature*, (Fall 1981, Spring 1982), 100–47.

Baquero Goyanes, Mariano. 'Las caricaturas literarias de Galdós.' In *Perspectivismo y contraste: de Cadalso a Pérez de Ayala*. Madrid: Gredos, 1963.

Barthes, Roland. 'De l'oeuvre au texte.' In *Le Bruissement de la langue*. Paris: Seuil, 1984. 69–77.

– 'L'Effet de réel.' *Communications*, no. 11 (1968), 84–9.

– 'Introduction à l'analyse structurale des récits.' *Communications*, no. 8 (1966), 1–27.

– *Sade, Fourrier, Loyola*. Paris: Seuil, 1971.

– *S/Z*. Paris: Seuil, 1970.

Benveniste, Émile. '"Être" et "avoir" dans leurs fonctions linguistiques.' In *Problèmes de linguistique générale*. Paris: Gallimard, 1966, I, 187–207.

– 'Fonctions syntaxiques.' In *Problèmes de linguistique générale*, Paris: Gallimard, 1966, I, 151–222.

Bergmann, Emilie. '"Los sauces llorando a moco y baba": Ekphrasis in Galdós' *La de Bringas*.' *Anales Galdosianos* (1985), 75–82.

Bjurström, C.-G. 'Dimensions du temps chez Claude Simon.' In *Entretiens: Claude Simon*, no. 31 (1972), 141–58.

Bland, D.S. 'Endangering the Reader's Neck: Background Description in the Novel.' In Philip Stevick, ed. *The Theory of the Novel*. New York: Free Press, 1947, 313–31.

Bly, Peter. *Pérez Galdós' 'La de Bringas.'* London: Grant and Cutler, 1981.

Bonnefis, Philippe. 'Le Descripteur mélancolique.' In Philippe Bonnefis, Pierre Reboul, et al. *La Description: Nodier, Sue, Flaubert, Hugo, Verne, Zola, Alexis, Fénéon*. Lille: Presses Universitaires de Lille, 1981, 103–51.

Booth, Wayne. *The Rhetoric of Fiction*. Chicago: University of Chicago Press, 1961, 62–3, and 154–5.

Bourneuf, Roland. 'L'Organisation de l'espace dans le roman.' *Études françaises*, III, no. 1 (1970), 77–94.

Cahiers roumains d'études littéraires: Description/Narration, no. 2 (1981).

Casey, Edward S. 'Phenomenological Method and Literary Description.' *Yale French Studies*, no. 61 (1981), 176–201.

Caws, Mary Ann. *The Art of Interference: Stressed Readings in Verbal and Visual Texts*. Princeton, NJ: Princeton University Press, 1989.
- *The Eye in the Text: Essays on Reception, Mannerism to Modern*. Princeton, NJ: Princeton University Press, 1981.
Chatman, Seymour. 'Description in the Cinema.' In *Coming to Terms: The Rhetoric of Narrative in Fiction and Film*. Ithaca: Cornell University Press, 1990, 38–55.
- 'Description Is No Textual Handmaiden.' In *Coming to Terms: The Rhetoric of Narrative in Fiction and Film*. Ithaca: Cornell University Press, 1990, 22–37.
- 'Narrative and Two Other Text-Types.' In *Coming to Terms: The Rhetoric of Narrative in Fiction and Film*. Ithaca: Cornell University Press, 1990, 6–21.
Cohen, Jean. *Structure du langage poétique*. Paris: Flammarion, 1966.
Costa Lima, Luiz. 'O Real e a Produção do simbólico.' In *A Perversão do Trapesista: O Romance em Cornélio Penna*. Rio de Janeiro: Imago Editora, 1976, 97–193.
- 'Sob as Trevas da Melancolia: O Patriarcado em *A Menina Morta*.' In *A Aguarrás do Tempo: Estudos sobre a Narrativa*. Rio de Janeiro: Rocco, 1989, 239–84.
Culler, Jonathan. *Flaubert: The Uses of Uncertainty*. Ithaca: Cornell University Press, 1974.
Dällenbach, Lucien. *Claude Simon*. Paris: Seuil, 1988.
- 'L'Oeuvre dans l'oeuvre chez Zola.' In Cogny, Pierre, ed. *Le Naturalisme*. Paris: 10/18 (1978). 125–39.
- *Le Récit spéculaire: Essai sur la mise en abyme*. Paris: Seuil, 1977.
- 'Reflexivity and Reading.' In *Mirrors and After: Five Essays on Literary Theory and Criticism*. New York: Graduate School, City University of New York, 1986, 9–23.
De Beaugrande, and Wolfgang Dressler. *Introduction to Text Linguistics*. London: Longman, 1972.
Debray-Genette, Raymonde. 'La Pierre descriptive.' *Poétique*, no. 43 (1980), 293–304.
- 'Traversées de l'espace descriptif.' *Poétique*, no. 51 (1982), 329–44; *Degrés: Approches de l'espace*, nos. 36–7 (1983).
Dionísio, Eduarda. '"Finisterra": cálculos, sonhos, tentativas.' *Jornal de Letras Artes e Ideias* (August 1981), 9–10.
Dos Santos, João Camilo. *Carlos de Oliveira et le roman*. Paris: Fondation Calouste Gulbenkian, Centre culturel portugais, 1987.
Dry, Helen. 'The Movement of Narrative Time.' *Journal of Literary Semantics*. XII, no. 2 (1983), 19–51.
Duncan, Alastair B. 'Claude Simon: La crise de la représentation.' *Critique*, no. 414 (1981), 1181–200.
- 'La Description chez Balzac, Flaubert et Zola.' *Littérature*, no. 38 (1980), 95–105.
DuVerlie, Claude. 'Pictures for Writing: Premises for a Graphopictology.' In

Randi Birn and Karen Gould, eds. *Orion Blinded: Essays on Claude Simon*. London and Toronto: Associated University Presses, 1981, 200–18.

Eikhenbaum, Boris [1925]. 'Sur la théorie de la prose.' In Tzvetan Todorov, ed. *Théorie de la littérature*. Paris: Seuil, 1965, 197–211.

Ferraz, Maria de Lurdes. 'Aproximação a "Finisterra."' *Jornal de Letras, Artes e Ideias*. (August 1981), 6–8.

Filho, Adonias. 'Introdução Geral.' In Cornélio Penna, *Romances Completos*. Rio de Janeiro: Editora José Aguilar, 1958. xii-lxvii.

Fitch, Brian T. 'Fictional Referentiality.' In *Reflections in the Mind's Eye: Reference and Its Problematization in Twentieth-Century French Fiction*. Toronto: University of Toronto Press, 1991, 3–26.

– 'Participe présent et procédés narratifs chez Claude Simon.' *Situations*, no. 3 (1983), 199–216.

– 'When the Fictive Referent Is Itself a Work of Art: Simon's *Histoire*.' In *Reflections in the Mind's Eye: Reference and Its Problematization in Twentieth-Century French Fiction*. Toronto: University of Toronto Press, 1991, 153–79.

Fleischman, Suzanne. 'Discourse Functions of Tense-Aspect Oppositions in Narrative: Toward a Theory of Grounding.' In *Linguistics*, no. 23 (1985), 851–82.

– *Tense and Narrativity: From Medieval Performance to Modern Fiction*. Austin: University of Texas Press, 1990.

Fontanier, Pierre [1821–30]. *Les Figures du discours*. Paris: Flammarion, 1977.

Frank, Joseph. 'Spatial Form in Modern Literature.' In *The Widening Gyre*. New Brunswick, NJ: Rutgers University Press, 1963, 3–62.

– 'Spatial Form: Thirty Years After.' In Jeffrey R. Smiten et al. *Spatial Form in Narrative*. Ithaca: Cornell University Press, 1981, 202–43.

Frye, Northrop [1957]. *Anatomy of Criticism: Four Essays*. Princeton, NJ: Princeton University Press, 1971.

Gelley, Alexander. *Narrative Crossings: Theory and Pragmatics of Prose Fiction*. Baltimore: Johns Hopkins University Press, 1987, 3–78, 139–71.

– 'The Represented World: Toward a Phenomenological Theory of Description in the Novel.' *Journal for Aesthetics and Art Criticism*, XXXVII, no. 4 (1979), 415–22.

Genette, Gérard. *Figures III*. Paris: Seuil, 1972.

– 'Frontières du récit.' *Communications*, no. 8 (1966), 152–72.

Gullón, Ricardo. 'La de Bringas.' In *Técnicas de Galdós*. Madrid: Taurus, 1970, 103–34.

– *Espacio y novela*. Barcelona: Antoni Bosch, 1980.

– 'On Space in the Novel.' *Critical Inquiry*, II, no. 1 (1975), 11–28.

Halliday, M.A.K., and Ruqaiya Hassan. *Cohesion in English*. London: Longman, 1976.

Hamon, Philippe. 'A propos de l'impressionisme de Zola.' *Les Cahiers naturalistes*, no. 34 (1967), 139–47.
– *La Description littéraire de l'Antiquité à Roland Barthes: Une anthologie*. Paris: Éditions Macula, 1991.
– *Introduction à l'analyse du descriptif*. Paris: Hachette, 1981.
– *Le personnel du roman: Le système des personnages dans les 'Rougon-Macquart' d'Émile Zola*. Geneva: Droz, 1983.
– 'Qu'est-ce qu'une description?' *Poétique*, no. 12 (1972), 465–85.
Havránek, Bohuslav [1942]. 'The Functional Differentiation of the Standard Language.' In Paul L. Garvin, ed. *A Prague School Reader on Esthetics, Literary Structure, and Style*. Washington, DC: Georgetown University Press, 1964, 17–30.
Hopper, Paul J. 'Aspect and Foregrounding in Discourse.' *Syntax and Semantics*, XII (1979), 213–41.
Hutcheon, Linda. *A Poetics of Postmodernism: History, Theory, Fiction*. New York and London: Routledge, 1988.
– *The Politics of Postmodernism*. New York and London: Routledge, 1989.
– *A Theory of Parody: The Teachings of Twentieth-Century Art Forms*. New York and London: Methuen, 1985.
Ibsch, Elrud. 'Historical Changes of the Function of Spatial Description in Literary Texts.' *Poetics Today*, III, no. 4 (1982), 97–113.
Iser, Wolfgang. 'Passive Synthesis in the Reading Process.' In *The Act of Reading: A Theory of Aesthetic Response*. Baltimore: Johns Hopkins University Press, 1978, 135–59.
Issacharoff, Michael. *L'Espace et la nouvelle*. Paris: José Corti, 1976, 1–37.
– 'Qu'est-ce que l'espace littéraire.' *L'Information littéraire*, no. 3 (1978), 117–22.
Jackson, Rosemary. *Fantasy: The Literature of Subversion*. London and New York: Methuen, 1981.
Jiménez-Fajardo, Salvador. *Claude Simon*. Boston: Twayne, 1971.
Juaristi, Jon. 'Ironía, picaresca y parodia en *La de Bringas*.' *Nueva revista de filología hispánica*, XXXVIII, no. 1 (1990), 277–96.
Klinkowitz, Jerome. 'The Novel as Artifact: Spatial Form in Contemporary Fiction.' In Jeffrey R. Smiten et al. *Spatial Form in Narrative*. Ithaca: Cornell University Press, 1981, 37–60.
Kristeva, Julia. *Sémeiotiké: Recherches pour une sémanalyse (Extraits)*. Paris: Éditions du Seuil, 1969.
Leclaire, Serge. *Démasquer le réel: Un essai sur l'objet en psychanalyse*. Paris: Seuil, 1971.
Lessing, Gotthold Ephraim [1766]. *Laocoon, or On the Limits of Painting and Poetry*. In H.B. Nisbet, ed. *German Aesthetic and Literary Criticism*. Cambridge: Cambridge University Press, 1985, 58–133.

Liddell, Robert. 'Background.' In *A Treatise on the Novel*. London: Cape, 1947, 110–28.

Littérature: Le Décrit, no. 38 (1980).

Lotman, Jurij. *The Structure of the Artistic Text*. Ann Arbor: University of Michigan Press, Dept. of Slavic Languages and Literatures, 1977.

Lukács, Georg [1936]. 'Raconter ou décrire.' In *Problèmes du réalisme*. Paris: L'Arche Éditeur, 1975, 130–75.

Marin, Louis. *Études sémiologiques: Écritures, peintures.* Paris: Klincksieck, 1971.

McHale, Brian. *Postmodernistic Fiction*. New York and London: Methuen, 1987.

Mickelsen, David. 'Types of Spatial Structure in Narrative.' In Jeffrey R. Smiten et al. *Spatial Form in Narrative*. Ithaca: Cornell University Press, 1981, 62–78.

Miller, Stephen. 'A Fragment of "La de Bringas" for the Stage.' *Romance Quarterly*, XXXIII, no. 1 (1986), 114–16.

Mitchell, W.J.T. 'Space, Ideology, and Literary Representation.' *Poetics Today*, X, no. 2 (1989), 91–102.

– 'Spatial Form in Literature: Toward a General Theory.' In *The Language of Images.* Chicago: University of Chicago Press, 1980, 271–99.

Mukařovský, Jan [1948]. 'Standard Language and Poetic Language.' In Garvin, Paul L., ed. *A Prague School Reader on Esthetics, Literary Structure, and Style*. Washington, DC: Georgetown University Press, 1964, 9–17.

Newton, Joy. 'Emile Zola impressioniste.' *Les Cahiers naturalistes*, no. 34 (1967), 124–37.

– 'Zola et l'expressionisme: Le point de vue hallucinatoire.' *Les Cahiers naturalistes*, no. 41 (1971), 1–14.

Nimetz, Michael. *Humour in Galdós: A Study of the 'Novelas contemporáneas.'* New Haven and London: Yale University Press, 1968.

Pérez Galdós, Benito. 'Prólogo.' In Leopoldo Alas Clarín. *La Regenta*. Madrid: Librería de Fernando Fé, 1900. v-xix.

Poétique: Sur la description, no. 43 (1980).

Pratiques: Raconter et décrire, no. 34 (1982).

Quirk, Randolph, Sidney Greenbaum, et al. *A Grammar of Contemporary English*. London: Longman, 1973.

Ramirez, Arthur. 'The Heraldic Emblematic Image in Galdós' *La de Bringas.' Revista de estudios hispánicos*, XIV, no. 1 (1980), 65–74.

Reformatsky, A.A. 'An Essay on the Analysis of the Composition of the Novella' (n.d.). In Stephen Barm and John Bolt, ed. *Russian Formalism: A Collection of Articles and Texts in Translation*. Edinburgh: Scottish Academic Press, 1973, 85–100.

Reid, Ian. 'Destabilizing Frames for Story.' In *Short Story Theory at a Crossroads*. Baton Rouge: Louisiana State University Press, 1989, 299–310.

Reinhardt, Tanya. 'Principles of Gestalt Perception in the Temporal Organization of Narrative Texts.' *Linguistics*, no. 22 (1984), 779–809.

Ricardou, Jean. *Le Nouveau roman*. Paris: Seuil, 1973.

– 'Problèmes de la description.' In *Problèmes du nouveau roman*. Paris: Seuil, 1967, 91–121.

– 'Le Texte en conflit (problèmes de la belligérance textuel à partir de *Madame Bovary*).' In *Nouveaux problèmes du roman*. Paris: Seuil, 1978, 24–52.

Ricoeur, Paul. 'La Triple *mimésis*.' In *Temps et récit*. Paris: Seuil, 1983, I, 85–129.

Riffaterre, Michael. 'La Métaphore filée dans la poésie surréaliste.' In *La Production du texte* Paris: Seuil, 1979, 217–34.

– 'On the Diegetic Functions of the Descriptive.' *Style*, XX, no. 3 (1987), 281–93.

Robbe-Grillet, Alain. 'Temps et description dans le roman d'aujourd'hui.' In *Pour un nouveau roman*. Paris: Gallimard/Idées, 1963, 155–69.

Rousset, Jean. '"Histoire" de Claude Simon, *Le Jeu des cartes postales*.' *Versants*, no. 1 (1981), 121–33.

Russell, Robert H. 'La voz narrativa en *La de Bringas*.' *Anales Galdosianos* (1986), 135–9.

Sarraute, C. 'Avec *La Route des Flandres* Claude Simon affirme sa manière.' *Le Monde* (08-09-60), 9.

Schefer, Jean-Louis. *Scénographie d'un tableau*. Paris: Seuil, 1969.

Schmidt, Augusto Frederico. 'O Anjo entre os Escravos: Nota Preleminar.' In Cornélio Penna, *Romances Completos*. Rio de Janeiro: Editora José Aguilar, 1958, 723–5.

Shklovsky, Viktor [1929]. 'La Construction de la nouvelle et du roman.' In Tzvetan Todorov, ed. *Théorie de la littérature*. Paris: Seuil, 1965, 170–96.

Shoemaker, William H. 'La de Bringas.' In *The Novelistic Art of Galdós*. Valencia: Albatrós Hispanófila, 1980, II, 222–33.

Simon, Claude. *Le Discours de Stockholm*. Paris: Éditions de Minuit, 1985.

– 'Roman, description et action.' In Paul Hallberg, ed. *The Feeling for Nature and the Landscape of Man: Proceedings of the 45th Nobel Symposium Held September 10-12, 1978 in Göteborg*. Göteborg: Royal Society of Arts and Sciences, 1980, 79–93.

Steiner, Wendy. *Pictures of Romance: Form against Context in Painting and Literature*. Chicago: University of Chicago Press, 1988.

Suleiman, Susan R., and Inge Crosman, ed. *The Reader in the Text: Essays on Audience and Interpretation*. Princeton, NJ: Princeton University Press, 1980.

Tinyanov, Yuri [1929]. 'On Literary Evolution.' In Ladislav Mateijka, ed. *Readings in Russian Poetics: Formalist and Structuralist Views*. Boston: MIT, 1971, 66–78.

Tomachevsky, B. [1925]. 'Thématique.' In Tzvetan Todorov, ed. *Théorie de la littérature*. Paris: Seuil, 1965, 263–307.

Valdés, Mario. 'A Method of Inquiry.' In *Shadows in the Cave: A Phenomenological*

Approach to Literary Criticism Based on Hispanic Texts. Toronto: University of Toronto Press, 1982, 119–40.

Watt, Ian. 'Realism and the Novel Form.' In *The Rise of the Novel*. Berkeley: University of California Press, 1957, 9–34.

Wellek, René, and Austin Warren. 'The Nature and Modes of Narrative Fiction.' In *Theory of Literature*. New York: Harcourt Brace, 1942, 212–25.

Yale French Studies: Towards a Theory of Description, no. 61 (1981).

Zima, Peter V. 'Ideology and Theory: The Relationship between Ideological and Theoretical Discourses.' *Semiotic Inquiry*, XI, nos. 2–3 (1991), 139–58.

Zola, Émile [1880]. 'De la description.' In *Le Roman expérimental*. Paris: Garnier-Flammarion, 1971, 231–5.

– [1864]. 'Lettre de Zola à Antony Valabrègue (18-08-1864).' In B.H. Baker, ed. *Correspondence*. (Paris and Montreal: Les Presses de l'Université de Montréal and Éditions du centre national de recherche scientifique, 1978), I, 375.

– 'Préface' [to the first illustrated edition of *Une Page d'amour*]. In *Oeuvres complètes*, ed. Cercle du livre précieux, Paris: Fasquelle, 1967, III, 1219–20.

Zoran, Gabriel. 'Towards a Theory of Space in Narrative.' *Poetics Today*, no. 5 (1984), 309–35.

C) CONSULTED WRITINGS ON LITERARY DESCRIPTION AND RELATED TOPICS

Adam, Jean-Michel. 'Textualité et séquentialité, l'exemple de la description.' *Langue française*, no. 74 (1987), 51–72.

Allerton, D.J. 'Grammar and Meaning.' In *Essentials of Grammatical Theory: A Consensus View of Syntax and Morphology*. London: Routledge and Kegan Paul, 1979, 236–39.

Aslanoff, Cyrille. 'L'adjectif dans la description claudélienne.' *Poétique*, no. 99 (1994), 369–79.

Auerbach, Erich [1946]. *Mimesis: The Representation of Reality in Western Literature*. Princeton, NJ: Princeton University Press, 1953.

Bachelard, Gaston. *La poétique de l'espace*. Paris: P.U.F., 1957.

Badescu, Irina. 'Quelques remarques sur la fonction du descriptif.' *Cahiers roumains d'études littéraires*, no. 2 (1981), 74–80.

Beaujour, Michel. 'Some paradoxes of description.' *Yale French Studies*, no. 61 (1981), 27–59.

Bessière, Jean. 'Description, éffet de visibilité et temps: H. James, G. Stein, M. Proust, I. Calvino.' In *L'Ordre du Descriptif*. Paris: P.U.F., 1988, 97–120.

Brown, Gillian, and George Yule. 'Coherence in the Interpretation of Discourse.' In *Discourse Analysis*. London and New York: Longman, 1983, 223–71.

Buescu, Helena Carvalhão. 'Natureza e Descrição.' In *Incidências do Olhar: Percepção e Representação*. Lisbon: Caminho, 1990, 181–285.

Buisine, Alain. 'Un Cas limite de la description: L'énumération. L'exemple de *Vingt mille lieues sous les mers*.' In Philippe Bonnefis, Pierre Reboul, et al. *La Description: Nodier, Sue, Flaubert, Hugo, Verne, Zola, Alexis, Fénéon*. Lille: Presses Universitaires de Lille, 1981, 81–101.

Butor, Michel. 'L'Espace du roman.' In *Essais sur le roman*. Paris: Gallimard/ Idées 1960, 48–58.

Chatman, Seymour. 'What Novels Can Do That Films Can't (and Vice Versa).' In W.J.T. Mitchell, ed. *On Narrative*. Chicago: University of Chicago Press, 1981, 117–36.

Clüver, Claus. 'On Intersemiotic Transposition.' *Poetics Today*, X, no. 1 (1989), 55–90.

Davis, Lennard J. '"Known Unknown" Locations: The Ideology of Place.' In *Resisting Novels (Ideology and Fiction)*. New York and London: Methuen, 1987, 52–101.

De Aguiar e Silva, Vítor M. 'A Descrição.' In *Teoria da Literatura*. Coimbra: Livraria Almedina, 1982, I. 708–13.

Didier, Béatrice. 'Senancour et la description romantique.' *Poétique*, no. 51 (1982), 315–28.

Dry, Helen. 'Sentence Aspect and Movement of Narrative Time.' *Text*, I, no. (1981), 233–40.

Duhamel, Brigitte, and Caroline Masseron. 'Trois machines romanesques.' *Pratiques*, no. 55 (1987), 100–27.

Duncan, Alastair B. 'La Description chez Balzac, Flaubert et Zola.' *Littérature*, no. 38 (1980), 95–105.

Gabbi, Gabriella. 'Per una semantica e una pragmatica del testo descrittivo.' *Lingua e stile*, no. 1 (1981), 61–81.

Galand-Hallyn, Perrine. 'Descriptions décadentes: L'"Inquiet plaisir" de Désiré Nisard.' *Poétique*, no. 99 (1994), 321–37.

Genette, Gérard. 'La Littérature et l'espace.' In *Figures II*. Paris: Éditions du Seuil, 1969, 43–48.

Goodman, Nelson. 'Twisted Tales; or Story, Study and Symphony.' In W.J.T. Mitchell, ed. *On Narrative*. Chicago: University of Chicago, 1981, 99–115.

Greimas, A.-J. 'Description et narrativité dans *La Ficelle* de Guy de Maupassant.' *Cahiers roumains d'études littéraires*, no. 2 (1981), 4–19.

Hirsch, Michèle. 'Madame Bovary "L'Éternel imparfait" et la description.' In Philippe Bonnefis, Pierre Reboul, et al. *La Description: Nodier, Sue, Flaubert, Hugo, Verne, Zola, Alexis, Fénéon*. Lille: Presses Universitaires de Lille, 1981, 43–59.

Howell, Robert. 'Fictional Objects: How They Are and How They Aren't.' *Poetics*, no. 8 (1979), 129–77.

Imbert, Patrick. 'Sémiostyle: La description chez Balzac, Flaubert, Zola.' *Littérature*, no. 38 (1980), 106–28.

– *Sémiotique de la description balzacienne*. Ottawa: Université d'Ottawa, 1978.

– 'La Structure de la description réaliste dans la littérature européene.' *Semiotica*, no. 44 (1983), 95–112.

Jorge, Carlos Figeiredo. 'La Description depuis le naturalisme: Un changement de dominante dans le discours du roman – *A Quinta das Virtudes* de Mário Cláudio.' *Dedalus: Revista Portuguesa de Literatura Comparada*, no. 1 (1991), 333–45.

Kaempfer, Jean. 'Robert Pinget: La description dans quelques états.' *Poétique*, no. 88 (1991), 379–98.

Kiltay, Jeffrey. 'Descriptive Limits.' *Yale French Studies*, no. 61 (1981), 225–43.

Lafon, Henri. 'Sur la description dans le roman du XVIIIe siècle.' *Poétique*, no. 51 (1982) 303–13.

Le Calvez, Éric. 'Structurer le topos et sa graphie (La Description dans *L'Éducation sentimentale*).' *Poétique*, No. 78 (1989), 151–71.

– 'La description modalisée: Un problème de poétique génétique (à propos de *L'Éducation sentimentale*).' *Poétique*, no. 99 (1994), 339–68.

Magureanu, Anca. 'Description/vs/narration: Une mise en question?' *Cahiers roumains d'études littéraires*, no. 2 (1981), 42–8.

Mavrakis, Annie. 'Décrire l'invisible: Sur *Dominique* de Fromentin.' *Poétique*, no. 100 (1994), 435–47.

Miéville, Denis. 'Description et représentation.' In *La Schématisation descriptive: Types textuels, formes et fonctions discursives*. Neuchâtel: Travaux du centre de recherches sémiologiques, no. 55 (1988).

Molino, Jean. 'Logiques de la description.' *Poétique*, no. 91 (1992), 363–82.

Mosher, Harold F., Jr. 'Toward a Poetics of "Descriptized" Narration.' *Poetics Today*, XII, no. 3 (1991), 425–45.

Perrone-Moisés, Leyla. 'Balzac et les fleurs de l'écritoire.' *Poétique*, no. 43 (1980), 305–23.

Petitjean, André. 'Fonctions et fonctionnements des descriptions dans l'écriture réaliste.' *Pratiques*, no. 55 (1987), 61–88.

Rabkin, Eric S. 'Spatial Form and Plot.' In Jeffrey R. Smiten et al. *Spatial Form in Narrative*. Ithaca: Cornell University Press, 1981, 79–99.

Reis, Carlos, and Ana Cristina Lopes. 'Descrição.' In *Dicionário de Narratologia*. Coimbra: Almedina, 1987, 87–91.

– 'Espaço.' In *Dicionário de Narratologia*. Coimbra: Almedina, 1987, 129–91.

Revaz, Françoise. 'Du descriptif au narratif et à l'injonction: Les prédicats fictionnels.' In *La Schématisation descriptive: Types textuels, formes et fonctions discursives*. Neuchâtel: Travaux du centre de recherches sémiologiques, no. 55 (1988), 89–115.

Ricard, François. 'Le Décor romanesque.' *Études françaises*, VIII, no. 4 (1972), 343–62.

Richard, Jean-Pierre. 'Variations d'un paysage.' *Poétique*, no. 51 (1982), 345–58.

Riffaterre, Michael. 'Système d'un genre descriptif.' *Poétique*, no. 9 (1972), 14–30.

Stern, Laurent. 'Narrative versus Description in Historiography.' *New Literary History*, XXI, no. 3 (1989), 555–77.

Sternberg, Meir. 'Ordering the Unordered: Time, Space, and Descriptive Coherence.' *Yale French Studies*, no. 61 (1981), 60–88.

Toma, Dolores. 'La Description: Nommer, dire.' *Cahiers roumains d'études littéraires*, no. 2, (1981), 67–73.

Van Buuren, Maarten. 'L'Essence des choses: Étude de la description dans l'oeuvre de Claude Simon.' *Poétique*, no. 43 (1980), 324–33.

Van Dijk, Teun A. 'Action, Action Description, and Narrative.' *New Literary History*, VI, no. 2 (1975), 273–94.

Vidan, Ivo. 'Time Sequence in Spatial Fiction.' In Jeffrey R. Smiten et al. *Spatial Form in Narrative*. Ithaca: Cornell University Press, 1981, 131–57.

Vouilloux, Bernard. 'Le Tableau: Description et peinture.' *Poétique*, no. 65 (1986), 3–18.

Yacobi, Tamar. 'Plots of Space: World and Story in Isak Dinesen.' *Poetics Today*, XII, no. 3 (1991), 447–93.

Zeraffa, Michel. 'Objet, chose, fiction.' *Revue d'esthétique: Pour l'objet*, nos. 3–4, Paris: 10/18 (1979), 321–35.

Index